Psychology's Identity

CREATED FOR PSYCHOLOGY 105
AT THE PENNSYLVANIA STATE UNIVERSITY

Dennis Coon | John O. Mitterer | Tara L. Kuther
B. R. Hergenhahn | Duane P. Schultz | Sydney Ellen Schultz

CENGAGE
Learning™

Australia • Brazil • Japan • Korea • Mexico • Singapore • Spain • United Kingdom • United States

CENGAGE
Learning™

Psychology's Identity:
Created for Psychology 105
at the Pennsylvania State University

Dennis Coon/John O. Mitterer/Tara L. Kuther/
B. R. Hergenhahn/Duane P. Schultz/
Sydney Ellen Schultz

Executive Editors:
Michele Baird

Maureen Staudt

Michael Stranz

Project Development Manager:
Linda deStefano

Senior Marketing Coordinators:
Sara Mercurio

Lindsay Shapiro

Production/Manufacturing Manager:
Donna M. Brown

PreMedia Services Supervisor:
Rebecca A. Walker

Rights & Permissions Specialist:
Kalina Hintz

Cover Image:
Getty Images*

For product information and technology assistance, contact us at
Cengage Learning Customer & Sales Support, 1-800-354-9706

For permission to use material from this text or product,
submit all requests online at **cengage.com/permissions**
Further permissions questions can be emailed to
permissionrequest@cengage.com

ISBN-13: 978-495-46455-6

ISBN-10: 0-495-46455-4

Cengage Learning
5191 Natorp Boulevard
Mason, Ohio 45040
USA

Cengage Learning is a leading provider of customized learning solutions with
office locations around the globe, including Singapore, the United Kingdom,
Australia, Mexico, Brazil, and Japan. Locate your local office at:
international.cengage.com/region

Cengage Learning products are represented in Canada by Nelson Education, Ltd.

For your lifelong learning solutions, visit **custom.cengage.com**

Visit our corporate website at **cengage.com**

Printed in the United States of America

CUSTOM CONTENTS

CHAPTER 1

Introduction

The definition of psychology has changed as the focus of psychology has changed. At various times in history, psychology has been defined as the study of the psyche or the mind, of the spirit, of consciousness, and more recently as the study of, or the science of, behavior. Perhaps, then, we can arrive at an acceptable definition of modern psychology by observing the activities of contemporary psychologists:

- Some seek the biological correlates of mental events such as sensation, perception, or ideation.

- Some concentrate on understanding the principles that govern learning and memory.

- Some seek to understand humans by studying nonhuman animals.

- Some study unconscious motivation.

- Some seek to improve industrial-organizational productivity, educational practices, or child-rearing practices by utilizing psychological principles.

- Some attempt to explain human behavior in terms of evolutionary theory.

- Some attempt to account for individual differences among people in such areas as personality, intelligence, and creativity.

- Some are primarily interested in perfecting therapeutic tools that can be used to help individuals with mental disturbances.

- Some focus on the strategies that people use in adjusting to the environment or in problem solving.

- Some study how language develops and how, once developed, it relates to a variety of cultural activities.

- Some explore computer programs as models for understanding human thought processes.

- Still others study how humans change over the course of their lives as a function of maturation and experience.

These are just a few of the activities that engage contemporary psychologists.

Clearly, no single definition of psychology can take into consideration the wide variety of activities engaged in by the more than 150,000 members and affiliates of the American Psychological Association, not to mention the many other psychologists around the world. It seems best to say simply that psychology is defined by the professional activities of psychologists. These activities are characterized by a rich diversity of methods, topics of interest, and assumptions about human nature. A primary purpose of this book is to examine the origins of modern psychology and to show that most of the concerns of today's psychologists are manifestations of themes that have been part of psychology for hundreds or, in some cases, thousands of years.

Problems in Writing a History of Psychology

Historiography is the study of the proper way to write history. The topic is complex, and there are no final answers to many of the questions it raises. In this section, we offer our answers to a few basic questions that must be answered in writing a history.

Where to Start

Literally, *psychology* means the study of the psyche, or mind, and this study is as old as the human species. The ancients, for example, attempted to account for dreams, mental illness, emotions, and fantasies. Was this psychology? Or did psychology commence when explanations of human cognitive experience, such as those proposed by the early Greeks, became more systematic? Plato and Aristotle, for example, created elaborate theories that attempted to account for such processes as memory, perception, and learning. Is this the point at which psychology started? Or did psychology come into existence when it became a separate science in the 19th century? It is common these days to begin a history of psychology at the point where psychology became a separate science. This latter approach is unsatisfactory for two reasons: (1) It ignores the vast philosophical heritage that molded psychology into the type of science that it eventually became; and (2) it omits important aspects of psychology that are outside the realm of science. Although it is true that since the mid-19th century, psychology has, to a large extent, embraced the scientific method, many highly influential psychologists did not feel compelled to follow the dictates of the scientific method. Their work cannot be ignored.

This book's coverage of the history of psychology will not go back to the conceptions of the ancients. I believe that such conceptions are within the domain of psychology, but space does not permit such a comprehensive history. Rather, this book starts with the major Greek philosophers whose explanations of human behavior and thought processes are the ones that philosophers and psychologists have been reacting to ever since.

What to Include

Typically, in determining what to include in a history of anything, one traces those people, ideas, and events that led to what is important now. This book, too, takes this approach by looking at the way psychology is today and then attempting to show how it became that way. There is at least one major danger in using the present state of psychology as a guide in writing its history, however. Stocking (1965) calls such an approach to history **presentism,** as contrasted with what he calls **historicism**—the study of the past for its own sake without attempting to show the relationship between the past and present. Copleston (2001) describes historicism as it applies to philosophy:

> If one wishes to understand the philosophy of a given epoch, one has to make the attempt to understand the mentality and presuppositions of the men who lived in that epoch, irrespective of whether one shares that mentality and those presuppositions or not. (p. 11)

On the other hand, presentism attempts to understand the past in terms of contemporary knowledge and standards. Presentism implies that the present state of a discipline represents its highest state of development and that earlier events led directly to this state. In this view, the latest is the best. Although I use present psychology as a guide to what to include in psychology's history, I do not believe that current psychology is necessarily the best psychology. The field is simply too diverse to make such a judgment. At present, psychology is exploring many topics, methods, and assumptions. Which of these explorations will survive for inclusion in future history books is impossible to say. Using psychology's present as a frame of reference therefore does not necessarily assume that psychology's past evolved into its present or that current psychology represents the best psychology. In general, then, I assume historicism provides a better framework for understanding psychology's history than presentism.

Although contemporary psychology provides a guide for deciding what individuals, ideas, and events to include in a history of psychology, there remains the question of how much detail to include. If, for example, we attempted to trace all causes of an idea, we would be engaged in an almost unending search. In fact, after attempting to trace the origins of an idea or a concept in psychology, we are left with the impression that nothing is ever entirely new. Seldom, if ever, is a single individual solely responsible for an idea or a concept. Rather, individuals are influenced by other individuals, who in turn were influenced by other individuals, and so on. A history of almost anything, then, can be viewed as an unending stream of interrelated events. The "great" individuals are typically those who synthesize existing nebulous ideas into a clear, forceful viewpoint. Attempting to fully document the origins of an important idea or concept in a history book would involve so many details that the book would become too long and boring. The usual solution is to omit large amounts of information, thus making the history selective. Typically, only those individuals who did the most to develop or popularize an idea are covered. For example, Charles Darwin is generally associated with evolutionary theory when, in fact, evolutionary theory existed in one form or another for thousands of years. Darwin documented and reported evidence supporting evolutionary theory in a way that made the theory's validity hard to ignore. Thus, although Darwin was not the first to formulate evolutionary theory, he did much to substantiate and popularize it, and we therefore associate it with his name. The same is true for Freud and the notion of unconscious motivation.

This book focuses on those individuals who either did the *most* to develop an idea or, for whatever reason, have become closely associated with an idea. Regrettably, this approach does not do justice to many important individuals who could be mentioned or to other individuals who are lost to antiquity or were not loud or lucid enough to demand historical recognition.

Choice of Approach

Once the material to be included in a history of psychology has been chosen, the choice of approach remains. One approach is to emphasize the influence of such nonpsychological factors as developments in other sciences, political climate, technological advancement, and economic conditions. Together, these and other factors create a **Zeitgeist,** or a spirit of the times, which many historians consider vital to the understanding of any historical development. An alternative is to take the **great-person approach** by emphasizing the works of individuals such as Plato, Aristotle, Descartes, Darwin, or Freud. Ralph Waldo Emerson (1841/1981) embraced the great-person approach to history, saying that history "resolves itself very easily into the biography of a few stout and earnest persons" (p. 138). Another approach is the **historical develop-**

ment approach, showing how various individuals or events contributed to changes in an idea or concept through the years. For example, one could focus on how the idea of mental illness has changed throughout history.

In his approach to the history of psychology, E. G. Boring (1886–1968) stressed the importance of the Zeitgeist in determining whether, or to what extent, an idea or viewpoint will be accepted. Clearly, ideas do not occur in a vacuum. A new idea, to be accepted or even considered, must be compatible with existing ideas. In other words, a new idea will be tolerated only if it arises within an environment that can assimilate it. An idea or viewpoint that arises before people are prepared for it will not be understood well enough to be critically evaluated. The important point here is that validity is not the only criterion by which ideas are judged; psychological and sociological factors are at least as important. New ideas are always judged within the context of existing ideas. If new ideas are close enough to existing ideas, they will at least be understood; whether they are accepted, rejected, or ignored is another matter.

The approach taken in this book is to combine the Zeitgeist, the great-person, and the historical development approaches to writing history. This book will attempt to show that sometimes the spirit of the times seems to produce great individuals and sometimes great individuals influence the spirit of the times. I will also show how both great individuals and the general climate of the times can change the meaning of an idea or a concept. In other words, I take an **eclectic approach,** which entails using whatever approach seems best able to illuminate an aspect of the history of psychology.

Why Study the History of Psychology?

Perspective

As we have seen, ideas are seldom, if ever, born fully developed. Rather, they typically develop over a long period of time. Seeing ideas in their historical perspective allows the student to more fully appreciate the subject matter of modern psychology. However, viewing the problems and questions currently dealt with in psychology as manifestations of centuries-old problems and questions is humbling and sometimes frustrating. After all, if psychology's problems have been worked on for centuries, should they not be solved by now? Conversely, knowing that our current studies have been shared and contributed to by some of the greatest minds in human history is exciting.

Deeper Understanding

With greater perspective comes deeper understanding. Having a knowledge of history, the student need not take on faith the importance of the subject matter of modern psychology. A student with a historical awareness knows where psychology's subject matter came from and why it is considered important. Just as we gain a greater understanding of a person's current behavior by learning more about that person's past experiences, so do we gain a greater understanding of current psychology by studying its historical origins. Boring (1950) made this point in relation to experimental psychologists:

> The experimental psychologist . . . needs historical sophistication within his own sphere of expertness. Without such knowledge he sees the present in distorted perspective, he mistakes old facts and old views for new, and he remains unable to evaluate the significance of new movements and methods. In this matter I can hardly state my faith too strongly. A psychological sophistication that contains no component of historical orientation seems to me to be no sophistication at all. (p. ix)

Recognition of Fads and Fashions

While studying the history of psychology, one is often struck by the realization that a viewpoint does not always fade away because it is incorrect; rather, some viewpoints disappear simply because they become unpopular. What is popular in psychology varies with the Zeitgeist. For example, when psychology first emerged as a science, the emphasis was on "pure" science—that is, on the gaining of knowledge without any concern for its usefulness. Later,

when Darwin's theory became popular, psychology shifted its attention to human processes that were related to survival or that allowed humans to live more effective lives. Today, one major emphasis in psychology is on cognitive processes, and that emphasis is due, in part, to recent advances in computer technology.

The illustrious personality theorist Gordon W. Allport (1897–1967) spoke of fashions in psychology:

> Our profession progresses in fits and starts, largely under the spur of fashion. . . . We never seem to solve our problems or exhaust our concepts; we only grow tired of them. . . .
>
> Fashions have their amusing and their serious sides. We can smile at the way bearded problems receive tonsorial transformation. Having tired of "suggestibility," we adopt the new hairdo known as "persuasibility." Modern ethnology excites us, and we are not troubled by the recollection that a century ago John Stuart Mill staked down the term to designate the new science of human character. . . . Reinforcement appeals to us but not the age-long debate over hedonism. The problem of freedom we brush aside in favor of "choice points." We avoid the body-mind problem but are in fashion when we talk about "brain models." Old wine, we find, tastes better from new bottles.
>
> The serious side of the matter enters when we and our students forget that the wine is indeed old. Picking up a recent number of the *Journal of Abnormal and Social Psychology*, I discover that the twenty-one articles written by American psychologists confine 90 per cent of their references to publications of the past ten years, although most of the problems they investigate have gray beards. . . . Is it any wonder that our graduate students reading our journals conclude that literature more than a decade old has no merit and can be safely disregarded? At a recent doctoral examination the candidate was asked what his thesis on physiological and psychological conditions of stress had to do with the body-mind problem. He confessed that he had never heard of the problem. An undergraduate said that all he knew about Thomas Hobbes was that he sank with the *Leviathan* when it hit an iceberg in 1912. (Allport, 1964, pp. 149–151)

With such examples of how research topics move in and out of vogue in science, we see again that "factuality" is not the only variable determining whether an idea is accepted. By studying the emotional and societal factors related to the accumulation of knowledge, the student can place currently accepted knowledge into a more realistic perspective. Such a perspective allows the student to realize that what body of knowledge is accepted as important or as "true" is at least partially subjective and arbitrary. As Zeitgeists change, so does what is considered fashionable in science, and psychology has not been immune to this process.

Avoiding Repetition of Mistakes

George Santayana said, "Those who cannot remember the past are condemned to repeat it." Such repetition would be bad enough if it involved only successes, because so much time and energy would be wasted. It is especially unfortunate, however, if mistakes are repeated. As we will see in this text, psychology has had its share of mistakes and dead ends. One mistake was the embracing of *phrenology*, the belief that personality characteristics could be understood by analyzing the bumps and depressions on a person's skull (see Chapter 8). One dead end may have been the entire school of structuralism, whose members attempted to study the elements of thought by using the introspective method (see Chapter 9). It is generally thought that the efforts of the structuralists, although extremely popular at the time, were sterile and unproductive. Yet it was important for psychology that such an effort was made, for we learned that such an approach led to little that was useful. This and other important lessons would be lost if the errors of the past were repeated because of a lack of historical information.

A Source of Valuable Ideas

By studying history, we may discover ideas that were developed at an earlier time but, for whatever reason, remained dormant. The history of science offers several examples of an idea taking hold only after being rediscovered long after it had originally been proposed. This fact fits nicely into the Zeitgeist interpretation of history, suggesting that some conditions are better suited for the acceptance of an idea than others. The notions of evolution, unconscious motivation, and conditioned responses had been proposed and reproposed several times before they were offered in an atmosphere that allowed their critical evaluation. Even Copernicus's "revolutionary" heliocentric theory had been entertained by the Greeks many centuries before he proposed it. A final example is that of lateralization of brain function. Many believe that the idea that the two cerebral hemispheres function in radically different ways is a new one. However, more than 100 years ago, Brown-Séquard's article "Have We Two Brains or One?" (1890) was one of many written on the topic. No doubt, many potentially fruitful ideas in psychology's history are still waiting to be tried again under new, perhaps more receptive, circumstances.

Curiosity

Instead of asking the question, Why study the history of psychology? it might make more sense to ask, Why not? Many people study U.S. history because they are interested in the United States, and younger members of a family often delight in hearing stories about the early days of the family's elder members. In other words, wanting to know as much as possible about a topic or person of interest, including a topic's or a person's history, is natural. Psychology is not an exception.

What Is Science?

At various times in history, influential individuals (such as Galileo and Kant) have claimed that psychology could never be a **science** because of its concern with subjective experience. Many natural scientists still believe this, and some psychologists would not argue with them. How a history of psychology is written will be influenced by whether psychology can be considered a science. To answer the question of whether psychology is a science, however, we must first attempt to define science. Science came into existence as a way of answering questions about nature by examining nature directly, rather than by depending on church dogma, past authorities, superstition, or abstract thought processes alone. From science's inception, its ultimate authority has been **empirical observation** (that is, the direct observation of nature), but there is more to science than simply observing nature. To be useful, observations must be organized or categorized in some way, and the ways in which they are similar to or different from other observations must be noted. After noting similarities and differences among observations, many scientists take the additional step of attempting to explain what they have observed. Science, then, is often characterized as having two major components: (1) empirical observation and (2) theory. According to Hull (1943), these two aspects of science can be seen in the earliest efforts of humans to understand their world:

> Men are ever engaged in the dual activity of making observations and then seeking explanations of the resulting revelations. All normal men in all times have observed the rising and setting of the sun and the several phases of the moon. The more thoughtful among them have then proceeded to ask the question, "Why? Why does the moon wax and wane? Why does the sun rise and set, and where does it go when it sets?" Here we have the two essential elements of modern science: The making of observations constitutes the empirical or factual component, and the systematic attempt to explain these facts constitutes the theoretical component. As science has developed, specialization, or division of labor, has occurred; some men have devoted their time mainly to the making of observations, while a smaller number have occupied themselves with the problems of explanation. (p. 1)

A Combination of Rationalism and Empiricism

What makes science such a powerful tool is that it combines two ancient methods of attaining knowledge: **rationalism** and **empiricism**. The rationalist believes that mental operations or principles must be employed before knowledge can be attained. For example, the rationalist says that the validity or invalidity of certain propositions can be determined by carefully applying the rules of logic. The empiricist maintains that the source of all knowledge is sensory observation. True knowledge therefore can be derived from or validated only by sensory experience. After centuries of inquiry, it was discovered that by themselves rationalism and empiricism had limited usefulness. Science combined the two positions, and knowledge has been accumulating at an exponential rate ever since.

The rational aspect of science prevents it from simply collecting an endless array of disconnected empirical facts. Because the scientist must somehow make sense out of what he or she observes, theories are formulated. A **scientific theory** has two main functions: (1) It organizes empirical observations, and (2) it acts as a guide for future observations. The latter function of a scientific theory generates **confirmable propositions.** In other words, a theory suggests propositions that are tested experimentally. If the propositions generated by a theory are confirmed through experimentation, the theory gains strength; if the propositions are not confirmed by experimentation, the theory loses strength. If the theory generates too many erroneous propositions, it must be either revised or abandoned. Thus, scientific theories must be testable. That is, they must generate hypotheses that can be validated or invalidated empirically. In science, then, the direct observation of nature is important, but such observation is often guided by theory.

The Search for Laws

Another feature of science is that it seeks to discover lawful relationships. A **scientific law** can be defined as a consistently observed relationship between two or more classes of empirical events. For example, when X occurs, Y also tends to occur. By stressing lawfulness, science is proclaiming an interest in the general case rather than the particular case. Traditionally, science is not interested in private or unique events but in general laws that can be publicly observed and verified. That is, a scientific law is general and, because it describes a relationship between empirical events, it is amenable to **public**

observation. The concept of public observation is an important aspect of science. All scientific claims must be verifiable by any interested person. In science, there is no secret knowledge available only to qualified authorities.

There are two general classes of scientific laws. One class is **correlational laws,** which describe how classes of events vary together in some systematic way. For example, scores on intelligence tests tend to correlate positively with scores on creativity tests. With such information, only prediction is possible. That is, if we knew a person's score on an intelligence test, we could predict his or her score on a creativity test, and vice versa. A more powerful class of laws is **causal laws,** which specify how events are causally related. For example, if we knew the causes of a disease, we could predict *and* control that disease—preventing the causes of a disease from occurring prevents the disease from occurring. Thus, correlational laws allow prediction, but causal laws allow prediction and control. For this reason, causal laws are more powerful than correlational laws and thus are generally considered more desirable.

A major goal of science is to discover the causes of natural phenomena. Specifying the causes of natural events, however, is highly complex and usually requires substantial experimental research. It cannot be assumed, for example, that contiguity proves causation. If rain follows a rain dance, it cannot be assumed that the dance necessarily caused the rain. Also complicating matters is the fact that events seldom, if ever, have a single cause; rather, they have multiple causes. Questions such as, What caused the Second World War? and What causes schizophrenia? are still far from answered. Even simpler questions such as, Why did John quit his job? or Why did Jane marry John? are, in reality, enormously complex. In the history of philosophy and science, the concept of causation has been one of the most perplexing (see, for example, Clatterbaugh, 1999).

The Assumption of Determinism

Because a main goal of science is to discover lawful relationships, science assumes that what is being investigated is lawful. For example, the chemist assumes that chemical reactions are lawful, and the physicist assumes that the physical world is lawful. The assumption that what is being studied can be understood in terms of causal laws is called **determinism.** Taylor (1967) defined determinism as the philosophical doctrine that "states that for everything that ever happens there are conditions such that, given them, nothing else could happen" (p. 359). The determinist, then, assumes that everything that occurs is a function of a finite number of causes and that, if these causes were known, an event could be predicted with complete accuracy. However, knowing *all* causes of an event is not necessary; the determinist simply assumes that they exist and that as more causes are known, predictions become more accurate. For example, almost everyone would agree that the weather is a function of a finite number of variables such as sunspots, high-altitude jet streams, and barometric pressure; yet weather forecasts are always probabilistic because many of these variables change constantly and others are simply unknown. The *assumption* underlying weather prediction, however, is determinism. *All sciences assume determinism.*

Revisions in the Traditional View of Science

The traditional view is that science involves empirical observation, theory formulation, theory testing, theory revision, prediction, control, the search for lawful relationships, and the assumption of determinism. Some prominent philosophers of science, however, take issue with at least some aspects of the traditional view of science. Among them are Karl Popper and Thomas Kuhn.

Karl Popper

Karl Popper (1902–1994) disagreed with the traditional description of science in two fundamental ways. First, he disagreed that scientific activity starts with empirical observation. According to Popper, the older view of science implies that scientists wander around making observations and then attempt

Karl Popper

PERMISSION BY ESTATE OF SIR KARL POPPER

to explain what they have observed. Popper (1963/ 2002a) showed the problem with such a view:

> Twenty-five years ago I tried to bring home [this] point to a group of physics students in Vienna by beginning a lecture with the following instructions: "Take pencil and paper: carefully observe, and write down what you have observed!" They asked, of course, *what* I wanted them to observe. Clearly the instruction, "observe!" is absurd . . . observation is always selective. It needs a chosen object, a definite task, an interest, a point of view, a problem. (p. 61)

So for Popper, scientific activity starts with a problem, and the problem determines what observations scientists will make. The next step is to propose solutions to the problem (conjectures) and then attempt to find fault with the proposed solutions (refutations). Popper saw scientific method as involving three stages: problems, theories (proposed solutions), and criticism.

Principle of falsifiability. According to Popper, the demarcation criterion that distinguishes a scientific

theory from a nonscientific theory is the **principle of falsifiability.** A scientific theory must be refutable. Contrary to what many believe, if any conceivable observation agrees with a theory, the theory is weak, not strong. Popper spent a great deal of time criticizing the theories of Freud and Adler for this reason. Without exception, everything a person does can be seen as supportive of either of these theories. This is because those theories are so vague that no matter what happens their verification can be claimed. According to Popper, it is also vagueness that prevents a meaningful test of the horoscopes created by astrologers (1963/2002a, p. 49). Popper contrasted such theories with those of Einstein, which predict precisely what should or should not happen if they are correct. Thus, Einstein's theories, unlike the theories of Freud and Adler, and astrological predictions, were refutable and therefore scientific.

Thus, for Popper, for a theory to be scientific, it must make **risky predictions**—predictions that run a real risk of being incorrect. Theories that do not make risky predictions or that explain phenomena *after* they have already occurred are, according to Popper, not scientific. In addition to vagueness, another major problem with many psychological theories (such as Freud's and Adler's) is that they engage more in **postdiction** (explaining phenomena after they have already occurred) than in prediction. Whether due to vagueness or the emphasis on postdiction, these theories make no *risky* predictions and are in no danger of being falsified. They are, therefore, unscientific.

According to Popper, it is a theory's incorrect predictions, rather than its correct ones, that cause scientific progress. This idea is nicely captured by Marx and Goodson (1976):

> In real scientific life theories typically contribute not by being right but by *being wrong*. In other words, scientific advance in theory as well as experiments tends to be built upon the successive corrections of many errors, both small and large. Thus the popular notion that a theory must be right to be useful is incorrect. (p. 249)

In Popper's view, *all* scientific theories will eventually be found to be false and will be replaced by more adequate theories; it is always just a matter of time. For this reason, the highest status that a scientific theory can attain, according to Popper, is *not yet disconfirmed*. Popperian science is an unending search for better and better solutions to problems or explanations of phenomena. Brett (1912–1921/1965) nicely captured this point:

> We tend to think of science as a "body of knowledge" which began to be accumulated when men hit upon "scientific method." This is a superstition. It is more in keeping with the history of thought to describe science as the myths about the world which have not yet been found to be wrong. (p. 37)

Does this mean Popper believed that nonscientific theories are useless? Absolutely not! He said,

> Historically speaking all—or very nearly all—scientific theories originate from myths, and . . . a myth may contain important anticipations of scientific theories. . . . I thus [believe] that if a theory is found to be non-scientific, or "metaphysical" . . . it is not thereby found to be unimportant, or insignificant, or "meaningless," or "nonsensical." (1963/2002a, p. 50)

Popper used falsification as a demarcation between a scientific and a nonscientific theory but not between a useful and useless theory. Many theories in psychology fail Popper's test of falsifiability either because they are stated in such general terms that they are confirmed by almost any observation or because they engage in postdiction rather than prediction. Such theories lack scientific rigor but are often still found to be useful. Freud's and Adler's theories are examples.

Thomas Kuhn

Until recently, it was widely believed that the scientific method guaranteed objectivity and that science produced information in a steady, progressive way. It was assumed that the world consists of knowable "truths" and that following scientific procedures allowed science to systematically approximate those truths. In other words, scientific activity was guided by the **correspondence theory of truth,** "the notion that the goal, when evaluating scientific laws or the-

Thomas S. Kuhn

ories, is to determine whether or not they correspond to an external, mind-independent world" (Kuhn, 2000a, p. 95). Thomas Kuhn (1922–1996) changed that conception of science by showing science to be a highly subjective enterprise.

Paradigms and normal science. According to Kuhn, in the physical sciences one viewpoint is commonly shared by most members of a science. In physics or chemistry, for example, most researchers share a common set of assumptions or beliefs about their subject matter. Kuhn refers to such a widely accepted viewpoint as a **paradigm.** Although Kuhn used the term *paradigm* in several ways, most typically he defined it as "the entire constellation of beliefs, values, techniques, and so on shared by the members of a given [scientific] community" (1996, p. 175). For those scientists accepting a paradigm, it becomes *the* way of looking at and analyzing the subject matter of their science. Once a paradigm is accepted, the activities of those accepting it become a matter of exploring the implications of that paradigm. Kuhn referred to such activities as **normal science.** Normal science provides what Kuhn called a "mopping-up" operation for a paradigm. While following a paradigm, scientists explore in depth the problems defined by the paradigm and utilize the techniques suggested by the paradigm while exploring those problems. Kuhn likened normal science to **puzzle solving.** Like puzzles, the problems of normal science have an assured solution, and there are "rules that limit both the nature of acceptable solutions and the steps by which they are to be obtained" (Kuhn, 1996, p. 38). Kuhn saw neither normal science nor puzzle solving as involving much creativity: "Perhaps the most striking feature of . . . normal research problems . . . is how little they aim to produce major novelties, conceptual or phenomenal" (1996, p. 35). Although a paradigm restricts the range of phenomena scientists examine, it does guarantee that certain phenomena are studied thoroughly.

> By focusing attention upon a small range of relatively esoteric problems, the paradigm forces scientists to investigate some part of nature in a detail and depth that would otherwise be unimaginable. . . . During the period when the paradigm is successful, the profession will have solved problems that its members could scarcely have imagined and would never have undertaken without commitment to the paradigm. And at least part of that achievement always proves to be permanent. (Kuhn, 1996, pp. 24–25)

That is the positive side of having research guided by a paradigm, but there is also a negative side. Although normal science allows for the thorough analysis of the phenomena on which a paradigm focuses, it blinds scientists to other phenomena and perhaps better explanations for what they are studying.

> Mopping-up operations are what engage most scientists throughout their careers. They constitute what I am here calling normal science. Closely examined, whether historically or in the contemporary laboratory, that enterprise seems an attempt to force nature into the preformed and relatively inflexible box that the paradigm supplied. No part of the aim of normal science is to call forth new sorts of phenomena; indeed, those that will not fit the box are often not seen at all. Nor do scientists normally aim to invent new theories, and they are often intolerant of those invented by others. Instead, normal-scientific research is directed to the articulation of those phenomena and theories that the paradigm already supplies. (Kuhn, 1996, p. 24)

A paradigm, then, determines what constitutes a research problem *and* how the solution to that problem is sought. In other words, a paradigm guides all of the researcher's activities. More important, however, is that researchers become emotionally involved in their paradigm; it becomes part of their lives and is therefore very difficult to give up.

How sciences change. How do scientific paradigms change? According to Kuhn, not very easily. First, there must be persistent observations that a currently accepted paradigm cannot explain; these are called **anomalies.** Usually, a single scientist or a small group of scientists will propose an alternative viewpoint, one that will account for most of the phenomena that the prevailing paradigm accounts for and will also explain the anomalies. Kuhn indicated that there is typically great resistance to the new paradigm and that converts to it are won over very slowly. Eventually, however, the new paradigm wins out and displaces the old one. According to Kuhn, this describes what happened when Einstein challenged the Newtonian conception of the universe. Now the Einsteinian paradigm is generating its own normal science and will continue to do so until it is overthrown by another paradigm.

Kuhn portrayed science as a method of inquiry that combines the objective scientific method and the emotional makeup of the scientist. Science progresses, according to Kuhn, because scientists are forced to change their *belief systems;* and belief systems are very difficult to change, whether for a group of scientists or for anyone else.

The stages of scientific development. According to Kuhn, the development of a paradigm that comes to dominate a science occurs over a long period of time. Prior to the development of a paradigm, a science typically goes through a **preparadigmatic stage,** during which a number of competing viewpoints exist. During this period, which Kuhn referred to as *prescientific,* a discipline is characterized by a number of rival camps or schools, a situation contrary to unification and that results in essentially random fact gathering. Such circumstances continue to exist until one school succeeds in defeating its competitors and becomes a paradigm. At this point, the discipline becomes a science, and a period of normal science begins. The normal science generated by the paradigm continues until the paradigm is displaced by a new one, which in turn will generate its own normal science. Kuhn saw sciences as passing through three distinct stages: the preparadigmatic stage during which rival camps or schools compete for dominance of the field, the **paradigmatic stage** during which the puzzle-solving activity called normal science occurs, and the **revolutionary stage** during which an existing paradigm is displaced by another paradigm.

Paradigms and Psychology

What has all of this to do with psychology? Psychology has been described as a preparadigmatic discipline (Staats, 1981) because it does not have one widely accepted paradigm but instead several competing schools or camps that exist simultaneously. For example, in psychology today we see camps that can be labeled behavioristic, functionalistic, cognitive, neurophysiological, psychoanalytic, evolutionary, and humanistic. Some see this preparadigmatic situation as negative and insist that psychology is ready to synthesize all of its diverse elements into one unified paradigm (for example, Staats, 1981, 1989, 1991). Other psychologists do not agree that psychology is a preparadigmatic discipline but claim that psychology is a discipline that has, and perhaps has always had, several coexisting paradigms (or at least themes or research traditions). For these psychologists, there has never been, nor has there been a need for, a Kuhnian-type revolution (for example, Koch, 1981, 1993; Leahey, 1992; Royce, 1975; Rychlak, 1975). The latter psychologists view the coexistence of several paradigms in psychology as healthy and productive and perhaps inevitable because psychology studies humans.

Mayr (1994) notes that Kuhn was a physicist and perhaps his analysis of scientific change applied to that science but not others. For example, Mayr observes that several paradigms have always existed simultaneously in biology, and there was a kind of Darwinian competition for the acceptance of ideas among them. Successful ideas, no matter what their source, survived, and unsuccessful ideas did not. This natural selection among ideas is called *evolutionary epistemology* and it conflicts with Kuhn's concept of paradigm shifts. The question remains whether psychology is more like biology or like physics in this regard. In this text it is assumed that psychology is a multiparadigmatic discipline rather than a discipline at the preparadigmatic stage of development.

Since Kuhn first published *The Structure of Scientific Revolutions* in 1962 (a second edition was published in 1970 and a third in 1996) psychologists have generally embraced Kuhnian concepts and terminology in describing the status and history of their discipline. Driver-Linn (2003) discusses the possible reasons for Kuhn's widespread usage among psychologists and some of the ambiguities and disagreements resulting from that usage.

Popper Versus Kuhn

A major source of disagreement between Kuhn and Popper concerns Kuhn's concept of normal science. As we have seen, Kuhn says that once a paradigm has been accepted, most scientists busy themselves with research projects dictated by the paradigm—that is, doing normal science.

For Popper, what Kuhn called normal science is not science at all. Scientific problems are not like puzzles because there are no restrictions either on what counts as a solution or on what procedures can be followed in solving a problem. According to Popper, scientific problem solving is a highly imaginative, creative activity, nothing like the puzzle solving described by Kuhn. Furthermore, for Kuhn, science cannot be understood without considering psychological and sociological factors. For him, there is no such thing as a neutral scientific observation. Observations are always made through the lens of a paradigm. In Popperian science, such factors are foreign; problems exist, and proposed solutions either pass the rigorous attempts to refute them or they do not. Thus, Kuhn's analysis of science stresses convention and subjective factors, and Popper's analysis stresses logic and creativity. D. N. Robinson (1986) suggests that the views of both Kuhn and Popper may be correct: "In a conciliatory spirit, we might suggest that the major disagreement between Kuhn and Popper vanishes when we picture Kuhn as describing what science has been historically, and Popper asserting what it ought to be" (p. 24). However, it should be noted that there is a basic difference between Popper's and Kuhn's philosophies of science. Popper believed that there are truths about the physical world that science can approximate. In other words, Popper accepted the correspondence theory of truth. Kuhn, on the other hand, rejected this theory saying instead that the paradigm accepted by a group of scientists creates the "reality" they explore. For this reason, Kuhn "was led to the radical view that truth itself is relative to a paradigm" (Okasha, 2002, p. 88).

Other philosophers of science claim that any attempt to characterize science is misleading. For them, there is no one scientific method or principle, and any description of science must focus on the creativity and determination of individual scientists. In this spirit, the illustrious physicist Percy W. Bridgman (1955) said that scientists do not follow "any prescribed course of action. . . . Science is what scientists do and there are as many scientific methods as there are individual scientists" (p. 83). In his book *Against Method: Outline of an Anarchistic Theory of Knowledge* (1975), Paul Feyerabend (1924–1994) aligned himself with those philosophers of science who claim that scientists follow no prescribed set of rules. In fact, he said that whatever rules do exist must be broken in order for scientific progress to occur. Feyerabend (1975) summarized this position as follows:

> My thesis is that anarchism helps to achieve progress in any one of the senses one cares to choose. Even a law-and-order science will succeed only if anarchistic moves are occasionally allowed to take place (p. 27).

> For nobody can say in abstract terms, without paying attention to idiosyncrasies of person and circumstances, what precisely it was that led to progress in the past, and nobody can say what moves will succeed in the future (p. 19).

Even with the revisions suggested by Popper, Kuhn, and Feyerabend, many traditional aspects of science remain. Empirical observation is still considered the ultimate authority, lawful relationships are still sought, theories are still formulated and tested, and determinism is still assumed.

Is Psychology a Science?

Is psychology a science? The scientific method has been used with great success in psychology. Experimental psychologists have demonstrated lawful relationships between classes of environmental events (stimuli) and classes of behavior, and they have devised rigorous, refutable theories to account for those relationships. The theories of Hull and Tolman are examples, and there are many others. Other psychologists work hand in hand with chemists and neurologists who are attempting to determine the biochemical correlates of memory and other cognitive processes. Still other psychologists are working with evolutionary biologists and geneticists in an effort to understand the evolutionary origins of human social behavior. In fact, we can safely say that scientifically oriented psychologists have provided a great deal of useful information in every major area of psychology—for example, learning, perception, memory, personality, intelligence, motivation, and psychotherapy. However, although some psychologists are clearly scientists, many, if not most, are not. We will see the reasons for this shortly.

Determinism, Indeterminism, and Nondeterminism

Determinism. Scientifically oriented psychologists are willing to assume determinism while studying humans. Although all determinists believe that all behavior is caused, there are different types of determinism. **Biological determinism** emphasizes the importance of physiological conditions or genetic predispositions in the explanation of behavior. For example, evolutionary psychologists claim that much human behavior, as well as that of nonhuman animals, reflects dispositions inherited from our long evolutionary past. **Environmental determinism** stresses the importance of environmental stimuli as determinants of behavior. The following illustrates the type of determinism that places the cause of human behavior in the environment:

> Behavior theory emphasizes that environmental events play the key role in determining human behavior. The source of action lies not inside the person, but in the environment. By developing a full understanding of how environmental events influence behavior, we will arrive at a complete understanding of behavior. It is this feature of behavior theory—its emphasis on environmental events as the determinants of human action—which most clearly sets it apart from other approaches to human nature. . . . If behavior theory succeeds, our customary inclination to hold people responsible for their actions, and look inside them to their wishes, desires, goals, intentions, and so on, for explanations of their actions, will be replaced by an entirely different orientation . . . one in which responsibility for action is sought in environmental events. (Schwartz & Lacey, 1982, p. 13)

Sociocultural determinism is a form of environmental determinism, but rather than emphasizing the physical stimuli that cause behavior, it emphasizes the cultural or societal rules, regulations, customs, and beliefs that govern human behavior. For example, Erikson (1977) referred to culture as "a version of human existence" (p. 79). To a large extent, what is considered desirable, undesirable, normal, and abnormal are culturally determined; thus, culture acts as a powerful determinant of behavior.

Other determinists claim that behavior is caused by the interaction of biological, environmental, and sociocultural influences. In any case, determinists believe that behavior is caused by antecedent events and set as their job the discovery of those events. It is assumed that, as more causes are discovered, human behavior will become more predictable and controllable. In fact, the prediction and control of behavior is usually recognized as an acceptable criterion for demonstrating that the causes of behavior have been discovered.

Although determinists assume that behavior is caused, they generally agree that it is virtually impossible to know *all* causes of behavior. There are at least two reasons for this limitation. First, behavior typically has many causes. As Freud said, much behavior is *overdetermined*; that is, behavior is seldom, if ever, caused by a single event or even a few events. Rather, a multitude of interacting events typically causes behavior. Second, some causes of behavior may be fortuitous. For example, a reluctant decision to attend a social event may result in meeting one's future spouse. About such meetings Bandura (1982) says, "Chance encounters play a prominent role in shaping the course of human lives," and he gives the following example:

> It is not uncommon for college students to decide to sample a given subject matter only to leave enrollment in a particular course to the vagaries of time allocation and course scheduling. Through this semifortuitous process some meet inspiring teachers who have a decisive influence on their choice of careers. (p. 748)

Fortuitous circumstances do not violate a deterministic analysis of behavior; they simply make it more complicated. By definition, fortuitous circumstances are not predictable relative to one's life, but when they occur they are causally related to one's behavior.

Fortuity is but one of the factors contributing to the complexity of the causation of human behavior. Determinists maintain that it is the complexity of the causation of human behavior that explains why predictions concerning human behavior must be probabilistic. Still, determinists believe that as our knowledge of the causes of behavior increases, so will the accuracy of our predictions concerning that behavior.

What biological, environmental, and sociocultural determinism all have in common is that the determinants of behavior they emphasize are directly measurable. Genes, environmental stimuli, and cultural customs are all accessible and quantifiable and thus represent forms of **physical determinism.**

However, some scientific psychologists emphasize the importance of cognitive and emotional experience in their explanation of human behavior. For them, the most important determinants of human behavior are subjective and include a person's beliefs, emotions, sensations, perceptions, ideas, values, and goals. These psychologists emphasize **psychical determinism** rather than physical determinism. Among the psychologists assuming psychical determinism are those who stress the importance of mental events of which we are conscious and those, like Freud, who stress the importance of mental events of which we are not conscious.

Besides accepting some type of determinism, scientific psychologists also seek general laws, develop theories, and use empirical observation as their ultimate authority in judging the validity of those theories. Psychology, as it is practiced by these psychologists, is definitely scientific, but not all psychologists agree with their assumptions and methods.

Indeterminism. First, some psychologists believe that human behavior is determined but that the causes of behavior cannot be accurately measured. This belief reflects an acceptance of Heisenberg's **uncertainty principle.** The German physicist Werner Karl Heisenberg (1901–1976) found that the very act of observing an electron influences its activity and casts doubt on the validity of the observation. Heisenberg concluded that nothing can ever be known with certainty in science. Translated into psychology, this principle says that, although human behavior is indeed determined, we can never learn at least some causes of behavior because in attempting to observe them we change them. In this way, the experimental setting itself may act as a confounding variable in the search for the causes of human behavior. Psychologists who accept this viewpoint believe that there are specific causes of behavior but that they cannot be accurately known. Such a position is called **indeterminism.** Another example of indeterminacy is Immanuel Kant's (1724–1804) conclusion that a science of psychology is impossible because the mind could not be objectively employed to study itself. MacLeod (1975) summarized Kant's position as follows:

Kant challenged the very basis of a science of psychology. If psychology is the study of "the mind," and if every observation and every deduction is an operation of a mind which silently imposes its own categories on that which is being observed, then how can a mind turn in upon itself and observe its own operations when it is forced by its very nature to observe in terms of its own categories? *Is there any sense in turning up the light to see what the darkness looks like* [emphasis added]? (p. 146)

Nondeterminism. Some psychologists completely reject science as a way of studying humans. These psychologists, usually working within either a humanistic or an existential paradigm, believe that the most important causes of behavior are self-generated. For this group, behavior is freely chosen and thus independent of physical or psychical causes. This belief in **free will** is contrary to the assumption of determinism, and therefore the endeavors of these psychologists are nonscientific. Such a position is known as **nondeterminism.** For the nondeterminists, because the individual freely chooses courses of action, he or she alone is responsible for them.

Determinism and responsibility. Although a belief in free will leads naturally to a belief in personal responsibility, one version of psychical determinism also holds humans responsible for their actions. William James (1884/1956) distinguished between *hard determinism* and *soft determinism*. With hard determinism, he said, the causes of human behavior are thought to function in an automatic, mechanistic manner and thus render the notion of personal responsibility meaningless. With soft determinism, however, cognitive processes such as intentions, motives, beliefs, and values intervene between experience and behavior. The soft determinist sees human behavior as resulting from thoughtful deliberation of the options available in a given situation. Because rational processes manifest themselves prior to actions, the person bears responsibility for those actions. Although soft determinism is still determinism, it is a version that allows uniquely human cognitive processes into the configuration of the causes of human behavior. Soft determinism, then, offers a compromise between hard determinism and free will—a compromise that allows for human responsibility. (For examples of contemporary psychologists who accept soft determinism, see Bandura, 1989; D. N. Robinson, 1985; Sperry, 1993.)

Whether we consider psychology a science depends on which aspect of psychology we focus on. One highly respected psychologist and philosopher of science answers the question, Is psychology a science? in a way that stresses psychology's nonscientific nature:

> Psychology is misconceived when seen as a coherent science or as any kind of coherent discipline devoted to the empirical study of human beings. Psychology, in my view, is not a single discipline but a collection of studies of varied cast, some few of which may qualify as science, whereas most do not. (Koch, 1993, p. 902)

Sigmund Koch (1917–1996) argued that psychology should embrace both science and the humanities in its effort to understand humans. Koch's more comprehensive view of psychology has been highly influential, and most of the May 2001 issue of *American Psychologist* explores its implications.

Psychology should not be judged too harshly because some of its aspects are not scientific or even antiscientific. Science as we now know it is relatively new, whereas the subject matter of most, if not all, sciences is very old. What is now studied scientifically was once studied philosophically or theologically, as Popper noted. First came the nebulous categories that were debated for centuries in a nonscientific way. This debate readied various categories of inquiry for the "fine-tuning" that science provides.

In psychology today, there is inquiry on all levels. Some concepts have a long philosophical heritage and are ready to be treated scientifically; other concepts are still in their early stages of development and are not ready for scientific treatment; and still other concepts, by their very nature, may never be amenable to scientific inquiry. All these levels and types of inquiry appear necessary for the growth of psychology, and all sustain each other.

Persistent Questions in Psychology

The questions that psychology is now attempting to answer are often the same questions it has been trying to answer from its inception. In many cases, only the methods for dealing with these persistent questions have changed. We have already encountered one of psychology's persistent questions: Is human behavior freely chosen or is it determined? In the following section, we will review additional persistent questions and, in so doing, preview much of what will be covered in the remainder of this text.

What Is the Nature of Human Nature?

A theory of human nature attempts to specify what is universally true about humans. That is, it attempts to specify what all humans are equipped with at birth. One question of interest here is, How much of our animal heritage remains in human nature? For example, are we inherently aggressive? Yes, say the Freudians. Is human nature basically good and nonviolent? Yes, say members of the humanistic camp, such as Rogers and Maslow. Or is our nature neither good nor bad but neutral, as the behaviorists such as Watson and Skinner claim? The behaviorists maintain that experience makes a person good or bad or whatever the person is. Do humans possess a free will? Yes, say the existential psychologists; no, say the scientifically oriented psychologists. Associated with each of psychology's paradigms is an assumption about the nature of human nature, and each assumption has a long history. Throughout this text, we will sample these conceptions about human nature and the methodologies they generate.

How Are the Mind and the Body Related?

The question of whether there is a mind and, if so, how it is related to the body is as old as psychology itself. Every psychologist must address this question either explicitly or implicitly. Through the years, almost every conceivable position has been taken on the mind-body relationship. Some psychologists attempt to explain everything in physical terms; for them, even so-called mental events are ultimately explained by the laws of physics or chemistry. These individuals are called **materialists** because they believe that matter is the only reality, and therefore everything in the universe, including the behavior of organisms, must be explained in terms of matter. They are also called **monists** because they attempt to explain everything in terms of one type of reality—matter. Other psychologists take the opposite extreme, saying that even the so-called physical world consists of ideas. These individuals are called **idealists,** and they, too, are monists because they attempt to explain everything in terms of consciousness. Many psychologists, however, accept the existence of both physical and mental events and assume that the two are governed by different principles. Such a position is called dualism. The **dualist** believes that there are physical events and mental events. Once it is assumed that both a physical and a mental realm exist, the question becomes how the two are related. For the monist, of course, there is no mind-body problem.

Types of dualisms. One form of dualism, called **interactionism,** claims that the mind and body interact. That is, the mind influences the body, and the body influences the mind. According to this interactionistic conception, the mind is capable of initiating behavior. This was the position taken by Descartes and is the one taken by most members of the humanistic-existential camp. The psychoanalysts, from Freud to the present, are also interactionists. For them, many bodily ailments are *psychogenic,* caused by mental events such as conflict, anxiety, or frustration. A currently popular way of explaining mind-body relationships is through **emergentism,** which claims that mental states emerge from brain states. One kind of emergentism claims that once mental events emerge from brain activity, they (mental events) can influence subsequent brain activity and thus behavior. Because of the postulated reciprocal influence between brain activity (body) and mental events (mind), this kind of emergentism represents interactionism. Sperry (1993), for example, accepted this kind of emergentism.

Another form of emergentism that is not interactionist is **epiphenomenalism.** According to the epiphenomenalist, the brain causes mental events but mental events cannot cause behavior. In this view, mental events are simply behaviorally irrelevant by-products (epiphenomena) of brain processes.

Another dualist position is that an environmental experience causes both mental events and bodily responses *simultaneously* and that the two are totally independent of each other. This position is referred to as **psychophysical parallelism.**

According to another dualist position, called **double aspectism,** a person cannot be divided into a mind and a body but is a unity that simultaneously experiences events physiologically and mentally. Just as "heads" and "tails" are two aspects of a coin, mental events and physiological events are two aspects of a person. Mind and body do not interact, nor can they ever be separated. They are simply two aspects of each experience we have as humans. Other dualists maintain that there is a **preestablished harmony** between bodily and mental events. That is, the two types of events are different and separate but are coordinated by some external agent—for example, God. Finally, in the 17th century, Nicolas de Malebranche (1638–1715) suggested that when a desire occurs in the mind, God causes the body to act. Similarly, when something happens to the body, God causes the corresponding mental experience. Malebranche's position on the mind-body relationship is called **occasionalism.**

All the preceding positions on the mind-body problem are represented in psychology's history, and we will therefore encounter them throughout this text. Figure 1.1 shows Chisholm's whimsical summary of the proposed mind-body relationships.

Nativism Versus Empiricism

To what extent are human attributes such as intelligence inherited, and to what extent are they determined by experience? The **nativist** emphasizes the role of inheritance in his or her explanation of the origins of various human attributes, whereas the empiricist emphasizes the role of experience. Those who consider some aspect of human behavior

Figure 1.1
Chisholm's depictions of various mind-body relationships. The bird drawn with the broken line represents the mind, and the bird drawn with the unbroken line represents the body. (Redrawn from Taylor, 1963, p. 130.) Used by permission of Roderick M. Chisholm.

instinctive or who take a stand on human nature as being good, bad, gregarious, and so on are also nativists. Empiricists, on the other hand, claim that humans are the way they are largely because of their experiences. Obviously, this question is still unresolved. The nativism-empiricism controversy is closely related to the question concerning the nature of human nature. For example, those who claim that humans are aggressive by nature are saying that humans are innately predisposed to be aggressive.

Most, if not all, psychologists now concede that human behavior is influenced by both experience and inheritance; what differentiates nativists from empiricists is the emphasis they place on one or the other.

Mechanism Versus Vitalism

Another persistent question in psychology's history is whether human behavior is completely explicable in terms of mechanical laws. According to **mechanism,** the behavior of all organisms, including humans, can be explained in the same way that the behavior of any machine can be explained—in terms of its parts and the laws governing those parts. To the mechanist, explaining human behavior is like explaining the behavior of a clock, except that humans are more complex. In contrast, according to **vitalism,** life can never be completely reduced to material things and mechanical laws. Living things contain a vital force that does not exist in inanimate objects. In ancient times, this force was referred to as soul, spirit, or breath of life, and it was its departure from the body that caused death.

The mechanism-vitalism debate has been prominently featured in psychology's history, and we will encounter it in various forms throughout this text.

Rationalism Versus Irrationalism

Rationalistic explanations of human behavior usually emphasize the importance of logical, systematic, and intelligent thought processes. Perhaps for this reason, most of the great contributions to mathematics have been made by philosophers in the rationalistic tradition, such as Descartes and Leibniz. Rationalists tend to search for the abstract universal principles that govern events in the empirical world. Most of the early Greek philosophers were rationalists, and some went so far as to equate wisdom with virtue. When one knows the truth, said Socrates, one acts in accordance with it. Thus, wise humans are good humans. The greatest passion, to the Greeks, was the passion to know. There are other passions, of course, but they should be rationally controlled. Western philosophy and psychology has, to a large extent, perpetuated the glorification of the intellect at the expense of emotional experience.

It was not always agreed, however, that the intellect is the best guide for human thought and behavior. At various times in history, human emotionality has been appreciated more than the human intellect. This was the case during the early Christian era, during the Renaissance, and at various other times under the influence of existential-humanistic philosophy and psychology. All these viewpoints stress human feeling over human rationality and are therefore referred to as *irrational*.

Any explanation of human behavior that stresses unconscious determinants is also irrational. The psychoanalytic theories of Freud and Jung, for example, exemplify **irrationalism** because they claim that the true causes of behavior are unconscious and as such cannot be pondered rationally.

The tension between conceptions of humans that stress intellect (reason) and those that stress the emotions or the unconscious mind (spirit) has appeared throughout psychology's history and still manifests itself in contemporary psychology.

How Are Humans Related to Nonhuman Animals?

The major question here is whether humans are qualitatively or quantitatively different from other animals. If the difference is quantitative (one of degree), then at least something can be learned about humans by studying other animals. The school of behaviorism relied heavily on animal research and maintained that the same principles governed the behavior of both nonhumans and humans. Therefore, the results of animal research could be readily generalized to the human level. Representing the other extreme are the humanists and the existentialists who believe that humans are qualitatively different from other animals, and therefore nothing important about humans can be learned by studying nonhuman animals. Humans, they say, are the only animals that freely choose their courses of action and are therefore morally responsible for that action. It thus makes sense to judge human behavior as "good" or "bad." Similar judgments of animal behavior are meaningless. Without the ability to reason and to choose, there can be no guilt. Most psychologists can be placed somewhere between the two extremes, saying that some things can be learned about humans by studying other animals and some things cannot.

What Is the Origin of Human Knowledge?

The study of knowledge is called **epistemology** (from the Greek *episteme*, meaning to know or understand). The epistemologist asks such questions as, What can we know, What are the limits of knowledge, and How is knowledge attained? Psychology has always been involved in epistemology because one of its major concerns has been determining how humans gain information about themselves and their world. The radical empiricist insists that all knowledge is derived from sensory experience, which is somehow registered and stored in the brain. The rationalist agrees that sensory information is often, if not always, an important first step in attaining knowledge but argues that the mind must then actively transform this information in some way before knowledge is attained. Some nativists would say that some knowledge is innate. Plato and Descartes, for example, believed that many ideas were a natural part of the mind.

In answering epistemological questions, the empiricists postulate a **passive mind** that represents physical experiences as mental images, recollections, and associations. In other words, the passive mind is seen as reflecting cognitively what is occurring, or what has occurred, in the physical world. Physical experiences that occur consistently in some particular pattern will be represented cognitively in that pattern and will tend to be recalled in that pattern. The rationalists, however, postulate an **active mind** that *transforms* the data from experience in some important way. Whereas a passive mind is seen as representing physical reality, the active mind is seen as a mechanism by which physical reality is organized, pondered, understood, or valued. For the rationalist, the mind adds something to our mental experience that is not found in our physical experience.

For the empiricist then, knowledge consists of the accurate description of physical reality as it is revealed by sensory experience and recorded in the mind. For the rationalist, knowledge consists of concepts and principles that can be attained only by a pondering, active mind. For some nativists, at least some knowledge is inherited as a natural component of the mind. The empiricist, rationalist, and nativist positions, and various combinations of them, have always been part of psychology; in one form or another, they are still with us today. In this text, we will see how these three major philosophical positions have manifested themselves in various ways throughout psychology's history.

Objective Versus Subjective Reality

The difference between what is "really" present physically (physical or objective reality) and what we actually experience mentally (subjective or phenomenal reality) has been an issue at least since the early Greeks. Some accept **naive realism,** saying that what we experience mentally is exactly the same as what is present physically. Many others, however, say that at least something is lost or gained in the translation from physical to phenomenal experience. A discrepancy between the two types of

experience can exist if the sense receptors can respond only partially to what is physically present—for example, to only certain sounds or colors. A discrepancy can also exist if information is lost or distorted as it is being transmitted from the sense receptors to the brain. Also, the brain itself can transform sensory information, thus creating a discrepancy between physical and phenomenal reality. The important question here is, Given the fact that there is a physical world and a psychological world, how are the two related? A related question is, Given the fact that all we can ever experience directly is our own subjective reality, how can we come to know anything about the physical world? We are confronted here with the problem of **reification,** or the tendency to believe that because something has a name it also has an independent existence. J. S. Mill (1843/1874) described this fallacy:

> The fallacy may be enunciated in this general form—Whatever can be thought of apart exists apart: and its most remarkable manifestation consists in the personification of abstractions. Mankind in all ages have had a strong propensity to conclude that wherever there is a name, there must be a distinguishable separate entity corresponding to the name; and every complex idea which the mind has formed for itself by operating upon its conceptions of individual things, was considered to have an outward objective reality answering to it. (p. 527)

Throughout human history, entities such as souls, minds, gods, demons, spirits, and selves have been imagined and then assumed to exist. Of course, in more recent times, procedures have been available to determine whether imagined entities have referents in the empirical world. As we have seen, scientific theory attempts to correlate words and symbols with empirical observations. In the case of reification, however, the relationship between the imagined and the real is simply assumed to exist. The tendency toward reification is a powerful and persistent one, and we will encounter it often.

The Problem of the Self

Our physical experiences are highly diverse, and yet we experience unity among them. Also, we grow older, gain and lose weight, change locations, exist in different times; yet with all of this and more, our life's experiences have continuity. We perceive ourselves as the same person from moment to moment, from day to day, and from year to year even though little about us remains the same. The question is, What accounts for the unity and continuity of our experience? Through the centuries, entities such as a soul or a mind have been proposed. More recently, the self has been the most popular proposed organizer of experience.

The self has often been viewed as having a separate existence of its own, as is implied by the statement "I said to myself." Besides organizing one's experiences and providing a sense of continuity over time, the self has often been endowed with other attributes, such as being the instigator and evaluator of action. Other experiences that contribute to the belief in an autonomous self include the feeling of intentionality or purpose in one's thoughts and behavior, the awareness of being aware, the ability to selectively direct one's attention, and moments of highly emotional, insightful experiences. As we will see, to postulate a self with autonomous powers creates a number of problems that psychology has struggled with through the years and still does. Clearly, whether an autonomous self or mind is proposed as the organizer of experience or as the instigator of behavior, one is confronted with the mind-body problem.

Universalism Versus Relativism

Throughout the histories of philosophy, science, and psychology there have been individuals who sought, or claimed to have discovered, universal truths about the world in general or about people in particular. The goal of such universalists is to describe the general laws, principles, or essences that govern the world and our perception of it. Likewise, there have been individuals who claim that such universal truths either do not exist or, if they do, that they cannot be known. These relativists say that humans always influence what they observe and, therefore, the search for universals that exist independently of human existence must be in vain. Instead, they say all "truth" must be relative to individual or group perspectives. For them, there is no Truth, only truths. This debate concerning **universalism** versus **relativism** was articulated by the early Greek philosophers (see Chapter 2) and, as we will see, has been an ongoing theme in the history of philosophy and psychology. We have already seen one example of this debate when we reviewed Popper's and Kuhn's philosophies of science. Although Popper believed scientific knowledge must always be tentative, he assumed the existence of a physical world and that knowledge of that world can be approximated by engaging in the kind of science he described. Popper, then, was a universalist. On the other hand, Kuhn believed that scientific activity is always guided by a paradigm and any conclusions reached about the world tend to be in accordance with the dictates of that paradigm. In other words, according to Kuhn, conceptions of the world change as paradigms change, and therefore it makes no sense to talk about a world that exists independently of human observers. Kuhn was a relativist.

In Chapter 21 we will see that the tension between modernism and postmodernism in contemporary philosophy and psychology is the most current manifestation of the ancient tension between universalism and relativism.

As we will see throughout this text, the positions psychologists have taken on the preceding issues have represented a wide variety of assumptions, interests, and methodologies, and this continues to be the case in contemporary psychology.

Summary

Psychology is best defined in terms of the activities of psychologists, and those activities have changed through the centuries. Although psychology goes back at least to the dawn of civilization, our version of the history of psychology begins with the early Greeks. The approach to writing this text exemplifies presentism because current psychology is used as a guide in determining what to cover historically. However, in general, historicism is considered the more valid approach to understanding psychology's history. In presenting the history of psychology, this text combines coverage of great individuals, persistent ideas, the spirit of the times, and contributions from other fields. Such a combined approach is referred to as eclectic. By studying the history of psychology, a student gains perspective and a deeper understanding of modern psychology. Also, he or she will learn that sometimes sociocultural conditions determine what is emphasized in psychology. Finally, by studying the history of psychology, previous mistakes can be avoided, potentially important ideas can be discovered, and the natural curiosity about something thought to be important can be satisfied.

Traditionally, science was viewed as starting with empirical observation and then proceeding to the development of theory. Theories were then evaluated in terms of their ability to generate predictions that either were or were not supported by experimental outcome. Theories that generated predictions that were confirmed became stronger, and those making erroneous predictions were revised or abandoned. By linking empirical observation and theory, science combined the philosophical schools of empiricism and rationalism. Science assumes determinism and seeks general laws. Popper disagreed with the traditional view of science, saying that scientific activity does not start with empirical observation but with a problem of some type that guides the scientist's empirical observations. Furthermore, Popper maintained that if a scientific theory is consistently confirmed, it is more likely a bad theory than a good one. A good theory must make risky predictions that, if not confirmed, refute the theory. To be classified as scientific, a theory must specify in advance the observations that if made would refute it. What distinguishes a scientific theory from a nonscientific theory is the principle of falsifiability. A scientific theory must run the risk of being incorrect, and it must specify the conditions under which it would be. In psychology, theories such as those of Freud and Adler are too vague to

allow precise testing and they emphasize postdiction rather than prediction. For both reasons they violate the principle of falsifiability. Kuhn also disagreed with the traditional view of science. Kuhn's analysis of science stresses sociological and psychological factors. At any given time, scientists accept a general framework within which they perform their research, a framework Kuhn called a paradigm. A paradigm determines what constitutes research problems and how those problems are solved. For Popper, scientific activity is guided by problems, whereas for Kuhn, scientific activity is guided by a paradigm that scientists believe to be true. For Popper, science involves creative problem solving; for Kuhn, it involves puzzle solving. According to Kuhn, scientific progress occurs in three stages: the preparadigmatic, the paradigmatic, and the revolutionary. A fundamental distinction between Popper's and Kuhn's conceptions of science is reflected in the fact that Popper accepted the correspondence theory of truth and Kuhn did not. Other philosophers of science, such as Feyerabend, claim that it is misleading to characterize science or scientific method in any particular way. For them, science is what scientists do, and any existing rules and regulations must be violated for scientific progress to occur.

Some aspects of psychology are scientific and some are not. Psychologists who are willing to assume physical or psychical determinism while studying humans are more likely to have a scientific orientation than are those who are unwilling to make that assumption. Nondeterminists assume that human behavior is freely chosen and therefore not amenable to traditional scientific analysis. The indeterminist believes that human behavior is determined but that the determinants of behavior cannot always be known with certainty. Psychology need not apologize for its nonscientific aspects because those aspects have often made significant contributions to the understanding of humans. Also, in some cases, the concepts developed by nonscientific psychologists are later fine-tuned by psychologists using the scientific method.

Many questions that have persisted throughout psychology's history were summarized, including the following: To what extent are humans free, and to what extent is their behavior determined by knowable causes? What is the nature of human nature? How are the mind and body related? To what extent are human attributes determined by heredity (nativism) as opposed to experience (empiricism)? Can human behavior be completely understood in terms of mechanistic principles, or must some additional vitalistic principle be postulated? To what extent is human behavior rational as opposed to irrational? How are humans related to nonhuman animals? What is the origin of human knowledge? What is the difference between what exists physically and what is experienced mentally, and how is this difference to be known and accounted for? How has the concept of self been used throughout psychology's history to account for one's continuity of experience over time, and what are the problems associated with the concept of self? Are there knowable universal truths about the world in general or about people in particular, or must truth always be relative to individual or group perspectives?

Discussion Questions

1. Discuss the choices that must be made before writing a history of psychology. Include in your answer a distinction between presentism and historicism.
2. What is gained by studying the history of psychology?
3. Summarize the major characteristics of science.
4. Discuss why psychology can be described both as a science and as a nonscience. Include in your answer the characteristics of science that some psychologists are unwilling to accept while studying humans.
5. In what ways did Popper's view of science differ from the traditional view?
6. According to Popper, what are the two primary reasons that theories such as those of Freud and Adler are unscientific?
7. Summarize Kuhn's views on how sciences change. Include in your answer the definitions of the terms *preparadigmatic discipline, paradigm, normal science,* and *scientific revolution.*
8. Within the realm of science, what is the correspondence theory of truth? Explain why it can be said that Popper accepted this theory and Kuhn did not.

9. Summarize Feyerabend's view of science.
10. Should psychology aspire to become a single-paradigm discipline? Defend your answer.
11. Is psychology a science? Defend your answer.
12. Define the terms *physical determinism, psychical determinism, indeterminism,* and *nondeterminism.*
13. Distinguish between *hard determinism* and *soft determinism.*
14. What does a theory of human nature attempt to accomplish?
15. Summarize the various proposed answers to the mind-body problem. Include in your answer definitions of the terms *monism, dualism, materialism, idealism, emergentism, interactionism, psychophysical parallelism, epiphenomenalism, preestablished harmony, double aspectism,* and *occasionalism.*
16. Discuss the nativist and empiricist explanations of the origin of human attributes.
17. First describe the positions of mechanism and vitalism and then indicate which of the two positions you accept and why.
18. Discuss rationalism and irrationalism as they apply to explanations of human behavior.
19. Describe how each of the following would explain how we gain knowledge: the empiricist, the rationalist, and the nativist.
20. Discuss the problems involved in discovering and explaining discrepancies that may exist between what is physically before us and what we experience subjectively. Define and give an example of reification.
21. For what reasons has a concept of self been employed by psychologists? What problems does this concept solve, and what problems does it create?
22. Summarize the debate between universalism and relativism concerning the nature of truth.

InfoTrac College Edition

 Explore InfoTrac College Edition, your online library. Go to *http://infotrac.cengage.com/*

Search terms:
Popper's philosophy of science
Determinism
Human nature
Mind and body
Knowledge, theory of

Suggestions for Further Reading

Churchland, P. M. (1998). *Matter and consciousness: A contemporary introduction to the philosophy of mind* (rev. ed.). Cambridge, MA: MIT Press.

Conant, J., & Haugeland, J. (Eds.) (2000). *Thomas S. Kuhn: The road since* Structure. Chicago: University of Chicago Press.

Honderich, T. (1993). *How free are you? The determinism problem.* New York: Oxford University Press.

Klemke, E. D., Hollinger, R., & Kline, A. D. (Eds.). (1988). *Introductory readings in the philosophy of science.* Buffalo, NY: Prometheus Books.

Kuhn, T. S. (1996). *The structure of scientific revolutions* (3rd ed.). Chicago: University of Chicago Press.

Notturno, M. A. (Ed.) (1996). *Karl R. Popper: Knowledge and the body-mind problem.* New York: Routledge.

Okasha, S. (2002). *Philosophy of science: A very short introduction.* New York: Oxford University Press.

Popper, K. (1982). *Unended quest: An intellectual autobiography.* La Salle, IL: Open Court.

Popper, K. (2002). *Conjectures and refutations: The growth of scientific knowledge.* New York: Routledge. (Original work published 1963).

Raphael, F. (1999). *Popper.* New York: Routledge.

Robinson, D. N. (1982). *Toward a science of human nature: Essays on the psychologies of Mill, Hegel, Wundt, and James.* New York: Columbia University Press.

Robinson, D. N. (1985). *Philosophy of psychology.* New York: Columbia University Press.

Stevenson, L., & Haberman, D. L. (1998). *Ten theories of human nature* (3rd ed.). New York: Oxford University Press.

Glossary

Active mind A mind that transforms, interprets, understands, or values physical experience. The rationalists assume an active mind.

Anomalies Persistent observations that cannot be explained by an existing paradigm. Anomalies eventually cause one paradigm to displace another.

Biological determinism The type of determinism that stresses the biochemical, genetic, physiological, or anatomical causes of behavior.

Causal laws Laws describing causal relationships. Such laws specify the conditions that are necessary and sufficient to produce a certain event. Knowledge of causal laws allows both the prediction and control of events.

Confirmable propositions Within science, propositions capable of validation through empirical tests.

Correlational laws Laws that specify the systematic relationships among classes of empirical events. Unlike causal laws, the events described by correlational laws do not need to be causally related. One can note, for example, that as average daily temperature rises, so does the crime rate without knowing (or even caring) if the two events are causally related.

Correspondence theory of truth The belief that scientific laws and theories are correct insofar as they accurately mirror events in the physical world.

Determinism The belief that everything that occurs does so because of known or knowable causes, and that if these causes were known in advance, an event could be predicted with complete accuracy. Also, if the causes of an event were known, the event could be prevented by preventing its causes. Thus, the knowledge of an event's causes allows the prediction and control of the event.

Double aspectism The belief that bodily and mental events are inseparable. They are two aspects of every experience.

Dualist Anyone who believes that there are two aspects to humans, one physical and one mental.

Eclectic approach Taking the best from a variety of viewpoints. The approach to the history of psychology taken in this text is eclectic because it combines coverage of great individuals, the development of ideas and concepts, the spirit of the times, and contributions from other disciplines.

Emergentism The contention that mental processes emerge from brain processes. The interactionist form of emergentism claims that once mental states emerge, they can influence subsequent brain activity and thus behavior. The epiphenomenalist form claims that emergent mental states are behaviorally irrelevant.

Empirical observation The direct observation of that which is being studied in order to understand it.

Empiricism The belief that the basis of all knowledge is experience.

Environmental determinism The type of determinism that stresses causes of behavior that are external to the organism.

Epiphenomenalism The form of emergentism that states that mental events emerge from brain activity but that mental events are subsequently behaviorally irrelevant.

Epistemology The study of the nature of knowledge.

Free will *See* **Nondeterminism.**

Great-person approach The approach to history that concentrates on the most prominent contributors to the topic or field under consideration.

Historical development approach The approach to history that concentrates on an element of a field or discipline and describes how the understanding of or approach to studying that element has changed over time. An example is a description of how mental illness has been defined and studied throughout history.

Historicism The study of the past for its own sake, without attempting to interpret and evaluate it in terms of current knowledge and standards, as is the case with presentism.

Historiography The study of the proper way to write history.

Idealists Those who believe that ultimate reality consists of ideas or perceptions and is therefore not physical.

Indeterminism The contention that even though determinism is true, attempting to measure the causes of something influences those causes, making it impossible to know them with certainty. This contention is also called Heisenberg's uncertainty principle.

Interactionism A proposed answer to the mind-body problem maintaining that bodily experiences influence the mind and that the mind influences the body.

Irrationalism Any explanation of human behavior stressing determinants that are not under rational control—for example, explanations that emphasize the importance of emotions or unconscious mechanisms.

Materialists Those who believe that everything in the universe is material (physical), including those things that others refer to as mental.

Mechanism The belief that the behavior of organisms, including humans, can be explained entirely in terms of mechanical laws.

Monists Those who believe that there is only one reality. Materialists are monists because they believe that only matter exists. Idealists are also monists because they believe that everything, including the "material" world, is the result of human consciousness and is therefore mental.

Naive realism The belief that what one experiences mentally is the same as what is present physically.

Nativist Anyone who believes that important human attributes such as intelligence are largely inherited.

Nondeterminism The belief that human thought or behavior is freely chosen by the individual and is therefore not caused by antecedent physical or mental events.

Normal science According to Kuhn, the research activities performed by scientists as they explore the implications of a paradigm.

Occasionalism The belief that the relationship between the mind and body is mediated by God.

Paradigm A viewpoint shared by many scientists while exploring the subject matter of their science. A paradigm determines what constitutes legitimate problems and the methodology used in solving those problems.

Paradigmatic stage According to Kuhn, the stage in the development of a science during which scientific activity is guided by a paradigm. That is, it is during this stage that normal science occurs. (*See also* **Normal science.**)

Passive mind A mind that simply reflects cognitively one's experiences with the physical world. The empiricists assume a passive mind.

Physical determinism The type of determinism that stresses material causes of behavior.

Postdiction An attempt to account for something after it has occurred. Postdiction is contrasted with prediction, which attempts to specify the conditions under which an event that has not yet occurred will occur.

Preestablished harmony The belief that bodily events and mental events are separate but correlated because both were designed to run identical courses.

Preparadigmatic stage According to Kuhn, the first stage in the development of a science. This stage is characterized by warring factions vying to define the subject matter and methodology of a discipline.

Presentism Interpreting and evaluating historical events in terms of contemporary knowledge and standards.

Principle of falsifiability Popper's contention that for a theory to be considered scientific it must specify the observations that if made would refute the theory. To be considered scientific, a theory must make risky predictions. (*See also* **Risky predictions.**)

Psychical determinism The type of determinism that stresses mental causes of behavior.

Psychophysical parallelism The contention that experiencing something in the physical world causes bodily and mental activity simultaneously and that the two types of activities are independent of each other.

Public observation The stipulation that scientific laws must be available for any interested person to observe. Science is interested in general, empirical relationships that are publicly verifiable.

Puzzle solving According to Kuhn, normal science is like puzzle solving in that the problems worked on are specified by a paradigm, the problems have guaranteed solutions, and certain rules must be followed in arriving at those solutions.

Rationalism The philosophical belief that knowledge can be attained only by engaging in some type of systematic mental activity.

Reification The belief that abstractions for which we have names have an existence independent of their names.

Relativism The belief that because all experience must be filtered through individual and group perspectives the search for universal truths that exist independently of human experience must be in vain. For the relativist, there is no Truth, only truths.

Revolutionary stage According to Kuhn, the stage of scientific development during which an existing paradigm is displaced by a new one. Once the displacement is complete, the new paradigm generates normal science and continues doing so until it too is eventually displaced by a new paradigm.

Risky predictions According to Popper, predictions derived from a scientific theory that run a real chance of showing the theory to be false. For example, if a meteorological theory predicts that it will rain at a specific place at a specific time, then it must do so or the theory will be shown to be incorrect.

Science Traditionally, the systematic attempt to rationally categorize or explain empirical observations. Popper described science as a way of rigorously testing proposed solutions to problems, and Kuhn emphasized the importance of paradigms that guide the research activities of scientists. Feyerabend believed it is impossible to give a generalized conception of science or scientific method.

Scientific law A consistently observed relationship between classes of empirical events.

Scientific theory Traditionally, a proposed explanation of a number of empirical observations; according to Popper, a proposed solution to a problem.

Sociocultural determinism The type of environmental determinism that stresses cultural or societal rules, customs, regulations, or expectations as the causes of behavior.

Uncertainty principle *See* **Indeterminism.**

Universalism The belief that there are universal truths about ourselves and about the physical world in general that can be discovered by anyone using the proper methods of inquiry.

Vitalism The belief that life cannot be explained in terms of inanimate processes. For the vitalist, life requires a force that is more than the material objects or inanimate processes in which it manifests itself. For there to be life, there must be a vital force present.

Zeitgeist The spirit of the times.

CHAPTER 2

The Early Greek Philosophers

The World of Precivilized Humans

Imagine living about 15,000 years ago. What would your life be like? It seems safe to say that in your lifetime you would experience most of the following: lightning, thunder, rainbows, the phases of the moon, death, birth, illness, dreams (including nightmares), meteorites, eclipses of the sun or moon, and perhaps one or more earthquakes, tornadoes, floods, droughts, or volcanic eruptions. Because these events would touch your life directly, it seems natural that you would want to account for them in some way, but how? Many of these events—for example, lightning—cannot be explained by the average citizen even today. But we have faith that scientists can explain such events, and we are comforted and less fearful. However, as an early human, you would have no such scientific knowledge available. As mentioned in the previous Chapter, thoughtful humans have always made empirical observations and then attempted to explain those observations. Although observation and explanation became key components of science, the explanations early humans offered were anything but scientific.

Animism and Anthropomorphism

Humans' earliest attempts to explain natural events involved projecting human attributes onto nature. For example, the sky or earth could become angry or could be tranquil, just as a human could. Looking at all of nature as though it were alive is called **animism,** and the projection of human attributes onto nature is called **anthropomorphism;** both were involved in early attempts to make sense out of life (Cornford, 1957; Murray, 1955). Early humans made no distinctions between animate (living) and inanimate objects or between material and immaterial things.

Another approach used to explain the world assumed that a ghost or spirit dwelt in everything, including humans, and that these spirits were as real as anything else. The events in both nature and human conduct were explained as the whims of the spirits that resided in everything. The word *spirit* is derived from the Latin word for "breath" (Hulin, 1934, p. 7). Breath (later spirit, soul, psyche, or ghost) is what gives things life, and when it leaves a thing, death results. This vital spirit can sometimes leave the body and return, as was assumed to be the case in dreaming. Also, because one can dream of or think of a person after his or her biological death, it was assumed that the person must still exist, for it was believed that if something could be thought of, it must exist (reification). With this logic, anything the mind could conjure up was assumed to be real; therefore, imagination and dreams provided an array of demons, spirits, monsters, and (later) gods, who lurked behind all natural events.

Magic

Because an array of spirits with human qualities was believed to exist, attempting to communicate with the spirits and otherwise influence them seemed a natural impulse. If, for example, a spirit was providing too much or too little rain, humans made attempts to persuade the spirit to modify its influence. Similarly, a sick person was thought to be possessed by an evil spirit, which had to be coaxed to leave the body or driven out. Elaborate methods, called **magic,** evolved that were designed to influence the spirits. People believed that appropriate words, objects, ceremonies, or human actions could influence the spirits. As rudimentary as these beliefs were, they at least gave early humans the feeling that they had some control over their fate.

Humans have always needed to understand, predict, and control nature. Animism, anthropomorphism, magic, religion, philosophy, and science can all be seen as efforts to satisfy those needs. Waterfield (2000) elaborates this point:

> All systems of belief evolve to elucidate the order of things and to make sense of the world. In this sense, science is just as much a myth as anything else; it is a framework or model designed to explain and form reality for those people who accept it—that is, for those people who voluntarily become members of that society—and for only as long as there are enough people to accept it. If this is so, then so far from banishing gods, science has merely been the matrix for a new generation of scientific gods, children of the old gods. (p. xxxii)

Early Greek Religion

In the fifth and sixth centuries B.C., the Greeks' explanations of things were still predominately religious in nature. There were two major theologies to choose from: the Olympian and the Dionysiac-Orphic. **Olympian religion** consisted of a belief in the Olympian gods as described in the Homeric poems. The gods depicted typically showed little concern with the anxieties of ordinary humans. Instead, they tended to be irascible, amoral, and little concerned with the immortality of humans. Within Olympian religion, it was believed that the "breath-soul" did survive death, but did so without any of the memories or personality traits of the person whose body it had occupied. Such a belief concerning life after death encouraged living one's life in the fullest, most enjoyable way. Typically, the ideal life was seen as involving the pursuit of glory through the performance of noble deeds: "In the thought of glory most Greeks found a consolation for the shadowy doom which awaited them in the grave" (Bowra, 1957, p. 51). The Olympian gods also personified orderliness and rationality and valued intelligence. In short, the Olympian gods tended to have the same characteristics and beliefs

as the members of the Greek upper class; it hardly seems surprising that the Greek nobility favored the Olympian religion.

The major alternative to Olympian religion was **Dionysiac-Orphic religion.** The wealthy Greek upper class was made possible, to a large extent, by a large class of peasants, laborers, and slaves whose lives were characterized by economic and political uncertainty. To these relatively poor, uneducated individuals, the Dionysiac-Orphic religion was most appealing. The Dionysiac-Orphic religion was based on the legend of Dionysus, the god of wine and frenzy, and his disciple Orpheus. Central to Dionysiac-Orphic religion was the belief in the **transmigration of the soul.** One version of this belief was that during its divine existence, at which time it dwelled among the gods, the soul had committed a sin; as punishment, the soul was locked into a physical body, which acted as its prison. Until the soul was redeemed, it continued a "circle of births," whereby it might find itself first inhabiting a plant, then an animal, then a human, then a plant again, and so on. What the soul longed for was its liberation from this transmigration and a return to its divine, pure, transcendent life among the gods. The rites that were practiced in hopes of freeing the soul from its prison (the body) included fasting, special diets, dramatic ceremonies, and various taboos.

Later in history, the Orphic idea that the soul seeks to escape its contaminated, earthly existence and enter into a more heavenly state following death gained enormous popularity and indeed became an integral part of the Judeo-Christian heritage.

In their efforts to make sense out of themselves and their world, the early Greeks had the Olympian and Dionysiac-Orphic religions from which to choose. Then, as now, which type of explanations individuals found congenial was as much a matter of temperament and circumstances as it was a matter of rational deliberation.

As we will see next, many of the first Greek philosophers leaned toward the relative rationality of Olympian religion. A few highly influential philosophers, however, embraced the mysticism of Dionysiac-Orphic religion; Pythagoras and Plato are two prominent examples.

The First Philosophers

Magic, superstition, and mysticism, in one form or another, dominated attempts to understand nature for most of early history. It was therefore a monumental step in human thought when *natural* explanations were offered instead of supernatural ones. Such explanations, although understandably simple, were first offered by the early Greeks. Philosophy (literally, the love of knowledge or wisdom) began when natural explanations (*logos*) replaced supernatural ones (*mythos*). Waterfield (2000) uses Kuhnian terminology to describe the importance of this development: "The presocratic revolution was a genuine revolution—a paradigm shift of the first importance" (p. xxiii). The first philosophers were called *cosmologists* because they sought to explain the origin, the structure, and the processes governing the cosmos (universe). However, the Greek word *kosmos* not only referred to the totality of things but also suggested an elegant, ordered universe. The aesthetic aspect of the meaning of the term *kosmos* is reflected in the English word *cosmetic*. Thus, to the early Greek cosmologists, the universe was ordered and pleasant to contemplate. The assumption of orderliness was extremely important because an orderly universe is, at least in principle, an explicable universe.

Thales

As noted in Chapter 1, seldom, if ever, is an idea born fully developed by a single individual. **Thales** (ca. 625–547 B.C.), often referred to as the first philosopher, had a rich, intellectual heritage. He traveled to Egypt and Babylonia, both of which enjoyed advanced civilizations that no doubt influenced him. For example, the Egyptians had possessed for centuries the knowledge of geometry that Thales demonstrated. In Egypt and Babylonia, however, knowledge was either practical (geometry was used to lay out the fields for farming) or was used primarily in a religious context (anatomy and physiology were used to prepare the dead for their journey into the next world). Thales was important because he emphasized natural explanations and minimized

supernatural ones. That is, in his **cosmology,** Thales said that things in the universe consist of natural substances and are governed by natural principles; they do not reflect the whims of the gods. The universe is therefore knowable and within the realm of human understanding.

Thales searched for that one substance or element from which everything else is derived. The Greeks called such a primary element or substance a **physis,** and those who sought it were **physicists.** Physicists to this day are searching for the "stuff" from which everything is made. Thales concluded that the physis was water because many things seem to be a form of water. Life depends on water, water exists in many forms (such as ice, steam, hail, snow, clouds, fog, and dew), and some water is found in everything. This conclusion that water is the primary substance had considerable merit.

> The most important of Thales' views is his statement that the world is made of water. This is neither so far fetched as at first glance it might appear, nor yet a pure figment of imagination cut off from observation. Hydrogen, the stuff that generates water, has been held in our time to be the chemical element from which all other elements can be synthesized. The view that all matter is one is quite a reputable scientific hypothesis. As for observation, the proximity of the sea makes it more than plausible that one should notice that the sun evaporates water, that mists rise from the surface to form clouds, which dissolve again in the form of rain. The earth in this view is a form of concentrated water. The details might thus be fanciful enough, but it is still a handsome feat to have discovered that a substance remains the same in different states of aggregation. (Russell, 1959, pp. 16–17)

Besides this achievement, Thales also predicted eclipses, developed methods of navigation based on the stars and planets, and applied geometric principles to the measurement of such things as the heights of buildings. He is even said to have cornered the market on olive oil by predicting weather patterns. Such practical accomplishments brought great fame to Thales and respectability to philosophy. Thales showed that a knowledge of nature, which minimized supernaturalism, could provide power over the environment, something humans had been seeking since the dawn of history.

Perhaps the most important thing about Thales, however, was the fact that he offered his ideas as speculations and he welcomed criticism. With his invitation for others to criticize and improve on his teachings, Thales started the *critical tradition* that was to characterize early Greek philosophy: "I like to think that Thales was the first teacher who said to his students: 'This is how I see things—how I believe that things are. Try to improve upon my teaching'"(Popper, 1958, p. 29). We will come back to the importance of this critical tradition later in this chapter.

Anaximander

Anaximander (ca. 610–547 B.C.), who studied with Thales, argued that even water was a compound of more basic material. (Notice that Anaximander took the advice of his teacher and criticized him.) According to Anaximander, the physis was something that had the capability of becoming anything. This something he called the "boundless" or the "indefinite." Anaximander also proposed a rudimentary theory of evolution. From a mixture of hot water and earth, there arose fish. Because human infants cannot survive without a long period of protection, the first human infants grew inside these fish until puberty, at which time the carrier fish burst and humans who were developed enough to survive on their own emerged. Anaximander urged us not to eat fish because they are, in a sense, our mothers and fathers. We can see how the physical environment can influence one's philosophizing. Both Thales and Anaximander lived near the shores of the Mediterranean sea, and its influence on their philosophies is obvious.

Heraclitus

Impressed by the fact that everything in nature seemed to be in a constant state of flux, or change, **Heraclitus** (ca. 540–480 B.C.) assumed fire to be the physis because in the presence of fire everything is transformed into something else. To Heraclitus, the overwhelming fact about the world was that nothing ever "is"; rather, everything is "**becoming.**" Nothing is either hot or cold but is becoming hotter or colder; nothing is fast or slow but is becoming faster or slower. Heraclitus' position is summarized in his famous statement: "It is impossible to step twice into the same river" (Waterfield, 2000, p. 41). Heraclitus meant that the river becomes something other than what it was when it was first stepped into.

Heraclitus believed that all things existed somewhere between polar opposites—for example, night-day, life-death, winter-summer, up-down, heat-cold, sleeping-waking. For him, one end of the pole defined the other, and the two poles were inseparable. For example, only through injustice can justice be known, and only through health can illness be known.

Heraclitus raised an epistemological question that has persisted to this day: How can something be known if it is constantly changing? If something is different at two points in time, and therefore not really the same object, how can it be known with certainty? Does not knowledge require permanence? It was at this point in history that the senses became a questionable means of acquiring knowledge because they could provide information only about a constantly changing world. In answer to the question, What can be known with certainty? empirical events could not be included because they were in a constant state of flux. Those seeking something unchangeable, and thus knowable, had two choices. They could choose something that was real but undetectable by the senses, as the atomists and the Pythagorean mathematicians did (discussed later), or they could choose something mental (ideas or the soul), as the Platonists and the Christians did. Both groups believed that anything experienced through the senses was too unreliable to be known. Even today, the goal of science is to discover general laws that are abstractions *derived* from sensory experience. Scientific laws as abstractions are thought to be flawless; when manifested in the empirical world, however, they are only probabilistic.

Heraclitus' philosophy clearly described the major problem inherent in various brands of empiricism. That is, the physical world is in a constant state of flux, and even if our sense receptors could accurately detect physical objects and events, we would be aware only of objects and events that change from moment to moment. It is for this reason that empiricists are said to be concerned with the process of becoming rather than with being. **Being** implies permanence and thus at least the possibility of certain knowledge, whereas a knowledge of empirical events (because they are becoming) can be only probabilistic at best. Throughout psychology's history, those claiming that there are certain permanent and therefore knowable things about the universe or about humans have tended to be rationalists. Those saying that everything in the universe, including humans, is constantly changing and thus incapable of being known with certainty have tended to be empiricists.

Parmenides

Taking a view exactly the opposite of Heraclitus', **Parmenides** (born ca. 515 B.C.) believed that all change was an illusion. There is only one reality; it is finite, uniform, motionless, and fixed and can be understood only through reason. Thus, for Parmenides, knowledge is attained only through rational thought because sensory experience provides only illusion. Parmenides supported his position with logic. Like the earliest humans, he believed that being able to speak or think of something implied its existence because we cannot think of something that does not exist (reification). The following is a summary of Parmenides' argument:

> When you think, you think of something; when you use a name, it must be of something. Therefore both thought and language require objects outside themselves, and since you can think of a thing or speak of it at one time as well as another, whatever can be thought or spoken of must exist at all times. Consequently there can be no change, since change consists in things coming into being and ceasing to be. (Russell, 1945, p. 49)

Zeno of Elea (ca. 495–430 B.C.), a disciple of Parmenides, used logical arguments to show that motion was an illusion. He said that for an object to go from point A to point B, it must first go half the distance between A and B. Then it must go half the remaining distance, then half of that distance, and so on. Because there is an infinite number of points between any two points, the process can never stop. Also, the object must pass through an infinite number of points in a finite amount of time, and this is impossible. Therefore, it is logically impossible for the object ever to reach point B. The fact that it seems to do so is a weakness of the senses. This reasoning, usually known as **Zeno's paradox,** is often expressed in the following form: If one runner in a race is allowed to leave slightly before a second runner, the second runner can never overtake the first runner, no matter how slow the first runner or how swift the second.

We have in Parmenides and Zeno examples of how far unabated reason can take a person. They concluded that either logic, mathematics, and reason were correct or the information provided by the senses was; and they opted for logic, mathematics, and reason. The same mistake has been made many times in history. Other misconceptions can result from relying exclusively on sensory data. It was not until science emerged in the 16th century that rationalism and empiricism were wed, and sensory information provided that which was reasoned about. Science therefore minimized the extremes of both rationalism and empiricism.

Pythagoras

Largely through his influence on Plato, **Pythagoras** (ca. 580–500 B.C.) has had a significant influence on Western thought. It is said that Pythagoras was the first to employ the term *philosophy* and to refer to himself as a *philosopher* (Guthrie, 1987, p. 19). Pythagoras postulated that the basic explanation for everything in the universe was found in numbers and in numerical relationships. He noted that the square of the hypotenuse of a right-angle triangle is exactly equal to the sum of the squares of its other two sides. Although this came to be called the Pythagorean theorem, it had probably been known to the Babylonians. Pythagoras also observed that a harmonious blending of tone results when one string on a lyre is exactly twice as long as another. This observation that strings of a lyre must bear certain relationships with one another to produce pleasant, harmonious sounds was, perhaps, psychology's first psychophysical law. Indeed, physical events (relationships between strings on musical instruments) were demonstrated to be systematically related to psychological events (perceived pleasantness of sounds). In fact, the Pythagoreans expressed this psychophysical relationship in mathematical terms.

Just as pleasant music results from the harmonious blending of certain tones, so too does health depend on the harmonious blending of bodily elements. The Pythagoreans thought illness resulted from a disruption of the body's equilibrium, and medical treatment consisted of attempts to restore that equilibrium. (We will see later that the Pythagorean approach to medicine became extremely influential.) Pythagoras took these and several other observations and created a school of thought that glorified mathematics. He and his followers applied mathematical principles to almost every aspect of human existence, creating "a great muddle of religious mysticism, music, mathematics, medicine, and cosmology" (Esper, 1964, p. 52).

According to the Pythagoreans, numbers and numerical relationships, although abstract, were nonetheless real and exerted an influence on the empirical world. The world of numbers existed independently of the empirical world and could be known in its pure form only through reason. When conceptualized, the Pythagorean theorem is exactly correct and applies to all right-angle triangles that ever were or ever will be. As long as the theorem is applied rationally to imagined triangles, it is flawless; when applied to actual triangles, however, the results are not absolutely correct because there are no perfect triangles in the empirical world. In fact, according to the Pythagoreans, *nothing* is perfect in the empirical world. Perfection is found only in the abstract mathematical world that lies beyond the senses and therefore can be embraced only by reason.

The Pythagoreans assumed a dualistic universe: one part abstract, permanent, and intellectually knowable (like that proposed by Parmenides) and the other empirical, changing, and known through the senses (like that proposed by Heraclitus). Sen-

sory experience, then, cannot provide knowledge. In fact, such experience interferes with the attainment of knowledge and should be avoided. This viewpoint grew into outright contempt for sensory experiences and for bodily pleasures, and the Pythagoreans launched a crusade against vice, lawlessness, and bodily excess of any type. Members of this school imposed on themselves long periods of silence to enhance clear, rational thought. Moreover, they attempted to cleanse their minds by imposing certain taboos and by hard physical and mental exercise. The taboos included eating flesh and eating beans. Among other things, beans cause excessive flatulence, a condition contrary to the tranquillity of mind necessary for seeking the truth. In a sense, the Pythagoreans introduced an early version of the belief "You are what you eat"; they believed that "each kind of food that is introduced into the human body becomes the cause of a certain peculiar disposition" (Guthrie, 1987, p. 107).

The Pythagoreans believed that the universe was characterized by a mathematical harmony and that everything in nature was interrelated. Following this viewpoint, they encouraged women to join their organization (it was *very* unusual for Greeks to look upon women as equal to men in any area), argued for the humane treatment of slaves, and, as mentioned, developed medical practices based on the assumption that health resulted from the harmonious workings of the body and illness resulted from some type of imbalance or discord.

The belief that experiences of the flesh are inferior to those of the mind—a belief that plays such an important role in Plato's theory and is even more important in early Christian theology—can be traced directly to the Pythagoreans. Eventually, Plato became a member of their organization. He based his Academy on Pythagorean concepts, and a sign above the entrance read, "Let no one without an understanding of mathematics enter here."

Pythagoras postulated two worlds, one physical and one abstract, the two interacting with one another. Of the two, the abstract was considered the better. Pythagoras also postulated a dualism in humans, claiming that, in addition to the flesh of the body, we have reasoning powers that allow us to attain an understanding of the abstract world. Furthermore, reasoning is a function of the soul, which the Pythagoreans believed to be immortal. Pythagoras' philosophy provides one of the first clear-cut mind-body dualisms in the history of Western thought.

We see many elements in common between Dionysiac-Orphic religion and Pythagorean philosophy. Both viewed the body as a prison from which the soul should escape; or, at the very least, the soul should minimize the lusts of the vile body that houses it by engaging in the rational contemplation of unchanging truths. Both accepted the notion of the transmigration of souls, and both believed that only purification could stop the "circle of births." The notion of transmigration fostered in the Pythagoreans a spirit of kinship with all living things. It is for this reason that they accepted women into their organizations, argued for the humane treatment of slaves, and were opposed to the maltreatment of animals. It is said of Pythagoras that "when he passed a puppy that was being whipped ... he took pity on it and made this remark: 'Stop, do not beat it; for it is the soul of a dear friend'" (Barnes, 2001, p. 29). It was for the same reason that the Pythagoreans were vegetarians. The origin of other Pythagorean taboos is more difficult to determine. For example, "do not urinate towards the sun" (Guthrie, 1987, p. 146).

We will see later in this chapter that Plato borrowed much from the Pythagoreans. It was through Platonic philosophy that elements of the Dionysiac-Orphic religion became part of the heritage of Western civilization.

Empedocles

Empedocles (ca. 490–430 B.C.) was a physician and a disciple of Pythagoras. He claimed his soul had been migrating for quite a while: "For already have I become a boy and a girl and a bush and a bird and a silent fish in the sea" (Barnes, 2001, p.157). Instead of one physis, Empedocles suggested four elements from which everything in the world is made: earth, fire, air, and water. Humans, too, he thought, consist of these four elements, with earth forming the solid

part of the body, water accounting for the liquids in the body, air providing the breath of life, and fire providing our reasoning ability.

Besides the four elements, Empedocles postulated two causal powers of the universe: love and strife. Love is a force that attracts and mixes the elements, and strife is a force that separates the elements. Operating together, these two forces create an unending cosmic cycle consisting of four recurring phases. In phase one, love dominates and there is a perfect mixture of the four elements ("one-from-many"). In phase two, strife disrupts the perfect mixture by progressively separating them. In phase three, strife has managed to completely separate the elements ("many-from-one"). In phase four, love again becomes increasingly dominant, and the elements are gradually recombined. As this cycle recurs, new worlds come into existence and then are destroyed. A world consisting of things we would recognize could exist only during the second and fourth phases of the cycle, when a mixture of the elements can exist. Along with the four elements, humans also possess the forces of love and strife, and these forces wax and wane within us just as they do in other material bodies. When love dominates, we have an urge to establish a union with the world and with other people; when strife dominates, we seek separation. Clearly, the ingredients are here for the types of intrapersonal and extrapersonal conflicts described by Freud and others much later in human history.

For Empedocles, the four elements and the forces of love and strife had always existed. In fact, all that can ever be must be a mixture of the elements and the two forces. Nothing beyond these mixtures is possible. He said, "From what does not exist nothing can come into being, and for what exists to be destroyed is impossible and unaccomplishable" (Barnes, 2001, p. 131). This is similar to the modern law of conservation of energy, which states that energy can take different forms but cannot be created or destroyed.

Empedocles also offered a theory of evolution that was more complex than the one previously suggested by Anaximander. In the phase when there is a mixture of love and strife, all types of things are created, some of them very bizarre. Animals did not form all at once but part by part, and the same was true of humans: "Many neckless heads sprang up. . . . Naked arms wandered, devoid of shoulders, and eyes strayed alone, begging for foreheads" (Barnes, 2001, p.142). As these various body parts roamed around, they were combined in a random fashion: "Many grew double-headed, double-chested—man-faced oxen arose, and again ox-headed men—creatures mixed partly from male partly from female nature" (Barnes, 2001, p. 143). Elsewhere, Empedocles described what happens when the four elements are acted on by love and strife: "As they mingled, innumerable types of mortal things poured forth, fitted with every sort of shape, a wonder to see" (Barnes, 2001, p. 128). Most random pairings resulted in creatures incapable of surviving, and they eventually perished. Some chance unions produced viable creatures, however, and they survived—humans among them. What we have here is an early version of natural selection by the survival of the fittest (Esper, 1964, p. 97).

Empedocles was also the first philosopher to offer a theory of perception. He assumed that each of the four elements was found in the blood. Objects in the outside environment throw off tiny copies of themselves called "emanations," or **eidola** (singular *eidolon*), which enter the blood through the pores of the body. Because like attracts like, the eidola will combine with elements that are like them. The fusion of external elements with internal elements results in perception. Empedocles believed that the matching of eidola with their corresponding internal elements occurred in the heart.

Because Empedocles was the first to attempt to describe how we form images of the world through a process similar to sensory perception, he is sometimes referred to as the first empirical philosopher. His view was that we perceive objects by internalizing copies of them.

To the Pythagorean notion that health reflected a bodily equilibrium, Empedocles added the four elements. Health occurs when the four elements of the body are in proper balance; illness results when they are not. Shortly we will see that the medical theories of Pythagoras and Empedocles were to be highly influential on later thinkers.

Anaxagoras

Anaxagoras (ca. 500–428 B.C.), a close friend and mentor of Pericles, taught that all things in the world as we know it were originally mixed together. Furthermore, everything in our world, including humans, continues to be an aggregate of that primordial mixture. Like Empedocles, Anaxagoras believed nothing can come from nothing. However, whereas Empedocles postulated four elements from which everything is derived, Anaxagoras postulated an infinite number of elements that he referred to as "seeds." As examples of these elements or seeds Anaxagoras listed water, fire, hair, bread, meat, air, wet, dry, hot, cold, thin, thick, wood, metal, and stone. However, these elements do not exist in isolation. Every element contains all the other elements. How then do objects become differentiated? Waterfield (2000) explains, "Everything is present in every seed and in every item of the universe, but in different proportions" (p. 118). It is the difference in the proportion of the seeds present that give objects their characteristics: "Things appear to be that of which they contain the most. Thus, for example, everything contains fire, but we only call it fire if that element predominates" (Russell, 1945, p. 62).

There was a single exception to Anaxagoras' claim that everything contains everything. Mind, he said, is pure in the sense that it contains no other elements. Also, mind is not necessarily present in other elements. Where it is present, life exists. For example, mind is present in humans and other living things but not in such things as stones or rivers. Anaxagoras was, therefore, a vitalist.

There was no "Providence" in Anaxagoras' philosophy, and he said little about ethics and religion. He was accused of atheism by his contemporaries and according to Russell (1945, p. 63) this accusation was probably true.

Democritus

Democritus (ca. 460–370 B.C.) was the last of the early Greek cosmologists; later philosophers were more concerned with human nature than with the nature of the physical universe. Democritus said that all things are made of tiny, indivisible parts called atoms (from the Greek *atomos,* meaning indivisible). The differences among things are explained by the shape, size, number, location, and arrangement of atoms. Atoms themselves were believed to be unalterable, but they could have different arrangements; so although the actual atoms do not change, the objects of which they are made can change. Humans, too, are bundles of atoms, and the soul or mind is made up of smooth, highly mobile fire atoms that provide our mental experiences. For Democritus, therefore, animate, inanimate, and cognitive events were reduced to atoms and atomic activity. Because the behavior of atoms was thought to be lawful, Democritus' view was deterministic. It also exemplified physical monism (materialism) because everything was explained in terms of the arrangement of atoms and there was no separate life force; that is, he denied vitalism. Democritus' view also incorporated **elementism,** because no matter how complex something was, Democritus believed it could be explained in terms of atoms and their activity. Finally, Democritus' philosophy exemplified **reductionism,** because he attempted to explain objects and events on one level (observable phenomena) in terms of events on another level (atoms and their activity). Reductionism is contrasted with elementism in that the former involves two different domains of explanation, whereas the latter attempts to understand a complex phenomenon by separating it into its simpler, component parts. Attempting to explain human behavior in terms of biochemical processes would exemplify reductionism, as would attempting to explain biochemical processes in terms of physics. Attempting to understand human thought processes by isolating and studying one process at a time or attempting to understand complex human behavior by isolating specific habits or stimulus-response associations would exemplify elementism. Democritus was both a reductionist and an elementist.

The explanations of sensation and perception offered by Empedocles and Democritus both emphasized the importance of eidola (emanations). However, for Democritus, sensations and perceptions arise when atoms (not tiny replicas) emanate from the surfaces of objects and enter the body through one of the five sensory systems (not bodily pores) and are transmitted to the brain (not the heart).

Upon entering the brain, the emanations sent by an object cause the highly mobile fire atoms to form a copy of them. This match between eidola and atoms in the brain causes perception. Democritus stressed that eidola are not the object itself and that the match between the eidola and the atoms in the brain may not be exact. Therefore, there may be differences between the physical object and the perception of it. As noted in Chapter 1, one of the most persistent problems in psychology has been determining what is gained or lost as objects in the environment are experienced through the senses. Democritus was well aware of this problem (Waterfield, 2000, pp. 176–177).

Democritus placed thinking in the brain, emotion in the heart, and appetite in the liver. He discussed five senses—vision, hearing, smell, touch, and taste—and suggested four primary colors— black, red, white, and green—from which all colors were derived. Because he believed that all bodily atoms scattered at death, he also believed that there was no life after death. His was the first completely naturalistic view of the universe, devoid of any supernatural considerations. Although his view contained no gods or spirits to guide human action, Democritus did not condone a life of hedonism (pleasure seeking). He preached moderation, as did his disciple Epicurus, 100 years later.

Early Greek Medicine

In the *Odyssey,* Homer described medical practitioners as roaming around selling their services to anyone needing them. The successful practitioners gained a reputation that preceded them; a few became viewed as godlike, and after their deaths, temples were erected in their honor. Other temples were named in honor of Asclepius, the Greek god of medicine. Asclepius was believed to be the son of Apollo and the father of Hygeia, the goddess of health. An ancient statue of Asclepius shows him with a snake wrapped around a rod. The snake symbolized mystery, power, and knowledge and was employed in several healing rituals. The rod and snake continue to symbolize the medical profession. At these temples, priests practiced medicine in accordance with the teachings of the famous deceased practitioners. The priests kept such teachings secret and carefully guarded. This **temple medicine** became very popular, and many wonderful cures were claimed. In fact, insofar as the ailments treated were psychosomatic, it is entirely possible that temple medicine was often effective because such medicine was typically accompanied by an abundance of ritual and ceremony. For example, patients would need to wait before being seen by a priest, drink "sacred" water, wear special robes, and sleep in a sanctuary. During the period of sleep—a high point in treatment—the patient (it was claimed) often had a dream in which a priest or god would directly cure the patient or tell him or her what to do in order to be cured. Thus, any healing that took place was essentially faith healing, and medical practices were magical.

Alcmaeon

Among the first to move away from temple medicine and toward more rational, naturalistic medicine was **Alcmaeon** (fl. ca. 500 B.C.). Alcmaeon (perhaps a Pythagorean) equated health with a balance of such qualities as warm and cold, moist and dry, and bitter and sweet. If one or more qualities dominates a person's system, sickness results. According to Alcmaeon, the physician's job is to help the patient regain a lost equilibrium, thereby regaining health. For example, a fever represented excess heat, and the treatment involved cooling the patient; excessive dryness was treated with moisture; and so forth. Diagnosis involved discovering the source of the disturbance of equilibrium, and treatment involved a procedure that would restore equilibrium. This Pythagorean view of health as a balance, or a harmony, was to have a profound influence on medicine and has persisted to the present time.

In addition to promoting naturalistic medicine, Alcmaeon was important for other reasons. He was among the first (if not *the* first) to dissect human bodies. One of the important things he learned from

these dissections was that the brain was connected to the sense organs. For example, he dissected the eye and traced the optic nerve to the brain. Unlike later thinkers such as Empedocles and Aristotle, who placed mental functions in the heart, Alcmaeon concluded that sensation, perception, memory, thinking, and understanding occurred in the brain. Alcmaeon's feats were truly remarkable, considering when they occurred. He did much to rid medicine of superstition and magic, and he used physiological information to reach conclusions concerning psychological functioning. As a physician interested in psychological issues, Alcmaeon started an illustrious tradition later followed by such individuals as Helmholtz, Wundt, James, and Freud.

Hippocrates

Hippocrates (ca. 460–377 B.C.) was born on the Greek island of Cos into a family of priests and physicians. He was educated at a famous school in Cos and received medical training from his father and other medical practitioners. By the time Hippocrates moved to Athens, he had acquired remarkable proficiency in the diagnosis, prognosis, and treatment of disease. He kept detailed records that gave precise accounts of mumps, epilepsy, hysteria, arthritis, and tuberculosis, to name only a few. From his training and observations, Hippocrates concluded that all disorders (both mental and physical) were caused by natural factors such as inherited susceptibility to disease, organic injury, and an imbalance of bodily fluids. Hippocrates is often referred to as the father of medicine, but this is only correct if we view him as "a culmination rather than a beginning" (Brett, 1912–1921/1965, p. 54). Several important physicians before Hippocrates (such as Alcmaeon and Empedocles) had challenged medical practices based on superstition and magic. However, Hippocrates' great accomplishment was that he took the development of naturalistic medicine to new heights.

As with Pythagoreans, it is difficult to separate what Hippocrates actually said from what his followers said. However, there is a corpus of ancient material consistent enough to be referred to as "Hippocratic writings" (see, for example, Lloyd, 1978). Therefore, I will hereafter refer to "the Hippocratics" rather than to Hippocrates.

The Hippocratics forcefully attacked the vestiges of supernatural medicine that still existed in their day. For example, epilepsy was called the "sacred disease," suggesting possession by an evil spirit. The Hippocratics disagreed, saying that all illness had natural and not supernatural causes. Supernatural causes, they said, were postulated in order to mask ignorance.

> I do not believe that the 'Sacred Disease' is any more divine or sacred than any other disease but, on the contrary, has specific characteristics and a definite cause. Nevertheless, because it is completely different from other diseases, it has been regarded as a divine visitation by those who, being only human, view it with ignorance and astonishment.... It is my opinion that those who first called this disease 'sacred' were the sort of people we now call witch-doctors, faith-healers, quacks and charlatans. These are exactly the people who pretend to be very pious and to be particularly wise. By invoking a divine element they were able to screen their own failure to give suitable treatment and so called this a 'sacred' malady to conceal their ignorance of its nature. (Lloyd, 1978, pp. 237–238)

The Hippocratics agreed with Empedocles that everything is made from four elements—earth, air, fire, and water—and that humans, too, are made up of these elements. In addition, however, the Hippocratics associated the four elements with four humors in the body. They associated earth with black bile, air with yellow bile, fire with blood, and water with phlegm. Individuals for whom the humors are properly balanced are healthy; an imbalance among the humors results in illness.

The Hippocratics strongly believed that the body has the ability to heal itself and that it is the physician's job to facilitate this natural healing. Thus, the "cures" the Hippocratics recommended included rest, proper diet, exercise, fresh air, massage, and baths. According to the Hippocratics the *worst* thing a physician could do would be to interfere with the body's natural healing power. They also emphasized treating the total, unique patient,

and not a disease. The Hippocratic approach to treatment emphasized an understanding physician and a trusting, hopeful patient. The Hippocratics also advised physicians not to charge a fee if a patient was in financial difficulty.

> Sometimes give your services for nothing, calling to mind a previous benefaction or present satisfaction. And if there be an opportunity of serving one who is a stranger in financial straits, give full assistance to all such. For where there is love of man, there is also love of the art. For some patients, though conscious that their condition is perilous, recover their health simply through their contentment with the goodness of the physician. (W. H. S. Jones, 1923, Vol. 1, p. 319)

Other maxims concerning the practice of medicine are contained in the famous Hippocratic oath which reads, in part, as follows:

> I will use my power to help the sick to the best of my ability and judgment; I will abstain from harming or wronging any man by it.
>
> I will not give a fatal draught to anyone if I am asked, nor will I suggest any such thing. Neither will I give a woman means to procure an abortion.
>
> I will be chaste and religious in my life and in my practice....
>
> Whenever I go into a house, I will go to help the sick and never with the intention of doing harm or injury. I will not abuse my position to indulge in sexual contacts with the bodies of women or of men, whether they be freemen or slaves.
>
> Whatever I see or hear, professionally or privately, which ought not to be divulged, I will keep secret and tell no one. (Lloyd, 1978, p. 67)

According to V. Robinson, the work of the Hippocratics "marks the greatest revolution in the history of medicine" (1943, p. 51). We will revisit the Hippocratics when we review the early treatment of the mentally ill in Chapter 15.

About 500 years after Hippocrates, **Galen** (ca. A.D. 130–200) associated the four humors of the body with four temperaments (the term *temperament* is derived from the Latin verb *temperare*, meaning "to mix"). If one of the humors dominates, the person displays the characteristics associated with that

Table 2.1

Galen's extension of Hippocrates' theory of humors.

Humor	Temperament	Characteristic
Phlegm	Phlegmatic	Sluggish, unemotional
Blood	Sanguine	Cheerful
Yellow bile	Choleric	Quick-tempered, fiery
Black bile	Melancholic	Sad

humor (see Table 2.1). Galen's extension of Hippocrates' views created a rudimentary theory of personality, as well as a way of diagnosing illness that was to dominate medicine for about the next 14 centuries. In fact, within the realm of personality theory Galen's ideas continue to be influential (see, for example, Eysenck and Eysenck, 1985; Kagan, 1994).

The Relativity of Truth

The step from supernatural explanations of things to natural ones was enormous, but perhaps too many philosophers took it. Various philosophers found the basic element (physis) to be water, fire, numbers, the atom, and the boundless, and some philosophers found more than one basic element. Some said that things are constantly changing, others that nothing changes, and still others that some things change and some do not. Furthermore, most of these philosophers and their disciples were outstanding orators who presented and defended their views forcefully and with convincing logic. Where does this leave the individual seeking the truth? Such an individual is much like the modern college student who goes to one class and is convinced of something (such as that psychology is a science), only to go to another class to be convinced of the opposite (psychology is not a science). Which is true?

In response to the confusion, one group of philosophers concluded that there is not just one truth but many. In fact, they believed that anything is true if you can convince someone that it is true. Nothing, they said, is inherently right or wrong, but believing makes it so. These philosophers were

called Sophists. The **Sophists** were professional teachers of rhetoric and logic who believed that effective communication determined whether an idea was accepted, rather than the idea's validity. Truth was considered relative, and therefore no single truth was thought to exist. This belief marked a major shift in philosophy. The question was no longer, What is the universe made of? but, What can humans know and how can they know it? In other words, there was a shift toward epistemological questions.

Protagoras

Protagoras (ca. 485–410 B.C.), the first and best-known Sophist, summarized the Sophists' position with his famous statement: "Man is the measure of all things—of the things that are, that they are, and of things that are not, that they are not." (Waterfield, 2000, p. 211) This statement is pregnant with meaning. First, truth depends on the perceiver rather than on physical reality. Second, because perceptions vary with the previous experiences of the perceiver, they will vary from person to person. Third, what is considered to be true will be, in part, culturally determined because one's culture influences one's experiences. Fourth, to understand why a person believes as he or she does, one must understand the person. According to Protagoras, therefore, each of the preceding philosophers was presenting his subjective viewpoint rather than the objective "truth" about physical reality. Paraphrasing Heraclitus' famous statement, Protagoras said, "Man never steps into the same river *once*," because the river is different for each individual *to begin with*. Protagoras emphasized the importance of rhetorical skills in getting one's point of view considered and, perhaps, to prevail. For a fee, which was typical of the Sophists, he taught his students to take both sides of an argument and created debating competitions where he introduced the disputants to the "tricks of the trade." Critics accused Protagoras of teaching how to "make the weaker argument stronger" or "to make the worse or morally more unsound argument defeat the more sound one" (Waterfield, 2000, pp. 205–206). However, Protagoras was primarily interested in teaching the skills necessary for effective communication and under the Periclean democracy in which he lived, the value of such skills was considerable.

> In the direct democracy that prevailed in Athens at the time, speeches could make or break a political career, and the constitution almost guaranteed that every prominent figure was likely to find himself in court at some time or other, where again a good speech could save his life, or at least prevent the loss of property and prestige. (Waterfield, 2000, p. 207)

Although Protagoras taught that nothing is false, he believed that some beliefs are more valuable than others. For example, in the political sphere, some beliefs are more conducive to utilitarian harmony than others and, he believed, effective argumentation would demonstrate this (Waterfield, 2000, p. 209).

Concerning the existence of the Greek gods, Protagoras was an agnostic. He said, "Where the gods are concerned, I am not in a position to ascertain that they exist, or that they do not exist. There are many impediments to such knowledge, including the obscurity of the matter and the shortness of human life" (Waterfield, 2000, p. 211).

With Protagoras, the focus of philosophical inquiry shifted from the physical world to human concerns. We now had a theory of *becoming* that was different from the one offered by Heraclitus. *Man is the measure of all things*, and therefore there is no universal Truth or code of ethics or anything else. In Chapter 21, we will see that the extreme relativism of the Sophists has much in common with the contemporary movement called postmodernism.

Gorgias

Gorgias (ca. 485–380 B.C.) was a Sophist whose position was even more extreme than Protagoras'. Protagoras concluded that, because each person's experience furnishes him or her with what seems to be true, "all things are equally true." Gorgias, however, regarded the fact that knowledge is subjective and relative as proof that "all things are equally false." Furthermore, because the individual can know only his or her private perceptions, there can

be no objective basis for determining truth. Gorgias' position, as well as Protagoras', exemplified **nihilism,** because it stated that there can be no objective way of determining knowledge or truth. The Sophist position also exemplifies **solipsism,** because the self can be aware of nothing except its own experiences and mental states. Thus, Gorgias reached his three celebrated conclusions: Nothing exists; if it did exist, it could not be comprehended; and if it could be comprehended, it could not be communicated to another person.

Insofar as Gorgias was referring to the physical world when he said, "Nothing exists," he was inconsistent, sometimes saying that it does (Waterfield, 2000, p. 223). However, on the last two points of his argument, he was entirely consistent. First, he argues if there is a physical world, we can only experience it through sense impressions, and the relationship between the physical world and sense impressions cannot be known. Second, we do not think in terms of sense impressions but in terms of the words used to describe those impressions. Therefore, there is an unbridgeable gap between the sensory events caused by the physical world and the words used to describe those events. And third, since the meaning of the words that are used to express thoughts are unique to each individual, there is an unbridgeable gap between one person's thoughts and those of another. Therefore, accurate communication between individuals is impossible.

Gorgias, like the other Sophists, emphasized the power of the spoken word. He likened the effect of words on the mind to the effect of drugs on the body (Waterfield, 2000, p. 223). He also believed that words were essentially deceitful. That is, words do not describe things as they are in the physical world but only beliefs about such things. Beliefs consist of words and therefore can be manipulated by words—thus, the importance of rhetorical techniques.

The Sophists clearly and convincingly described the gulf that exists between the physical world and the perceiving person. They also called attention to the difficulties in determining the relationships among terms, concepts, and physical things. In fact, as we have seen, the Sophists were well aware of the difficulty in demonstrating the external (physical) existence of anything. We saw in Chapter 1 that humans have always had a strong tendency toward reification—that is, to believe that because something has a name it exists. Concerning this belief Gorgias said:

> If things considered [thought about] are existent, all things considered exist, and in whatever way anyone considers them, which is absurd. For if one considers a flying man or chariot racing in the sea, a man does not straightway [*sic*] fly nor a chariot race in the sea. (Kennedy, 1972, p. 45)

The Sophists also raised the thorny question of what one human consciousness can know about another human consciousness. No satisfactory answer has ever been provided.

Xenophanes

Even before the Sophists, **Xenophanes** (ca. 560–478 B.C.) had attacked religion as a human invention. He noted that the Olympian gods acted suspiciously like humans; they lie, steal, philander, and even murder: "Homer . . . attributed to the gods all the things which among men are shameful and blameworthy—theft and adultery and mutual deception" (Barnes, 2001, p. 42). Xenophanes also noted that dark-skinned people had dark-skinned gods and light-skinned people had light-skinned gods. He went so far as to say that if animals could describe their gods, they would have the characteristics of the animals describing them:

> Mortals think that the gods are born, and have clothes and speech and shape like their own. . . . But if cows and horses or lions had hands and drew with their hands and made the things men make, then horses would draw the forms of gods like horses, cows like cows, and each would make their bodies similar in shape to their own. (Barnes, 2001, p. 43)

With regard to religion, Xenophanes can be seen as an early Sophist. Not only do humans create whatever "truth" exists, but they also create whatever religion exists. Moral codes, then, are not divinely inspired; they are human inventions.

The relativist nature of truth on which the Sophists insisted was distasteful to many who wanted truth to be more than the projection of one's subjective reality onto the world. As we will see, this debate became a constant theme in the history of philosophy and it continues to be.

Socrates was the first to provide a serious challenge to the relativism of the Sophists, with whom he both agreed and disagreed.

Socrates

Socrates (ca. 470–399 B.C.) agreed with the Sophists that individual experience is important. He took the injunction "know thyself," inscribed on the portals of the temple of Apollo at Delphi, to indicate the importance of knowing the contents of one's own mind or soul (Allen, 1991, p. 17). He went so far as to say, "The life which is unexamined is not worth living" (Jowett, 1988, p. 49). However,

Socrates

he disagreed with the Sophists' contention that no truth exists beyond personal opinion. In his search for truth, Socrates used a method sometimes called **inductive definition,** which started with an examination of instances of such concepts as beauty, love, justice, or truth and then moved on to such questions as, What is it that *all* instances of beauty have in common? In other words, Socrates asked what it is that makes something beautiful, just, or true. In this way, he sought to discover general concepts by examining isolated examples. It was thought that these concepts transcend their individual manifestations and are therefore stable and knowable. What Socrates sought was the **essence** of such things as beauty, justice, and truth. The essence of something is its basic nature, its identifying, enduring characteristics. To truly know something, according to Socrates, is to understand its essence. It is not enough to identify something as beautiful; one must know *why* it is beautiful. One must know what *all* instances of beauty have in common; one must know the essence of beauty. It is important to note that although Socrates sought the essence of various concepts, he did not believe that essences had abstract existence. For him, an essence was a universally acceptable definition of a concept—a definition that was both accurate and acceptable to all interested parties. Once such definitions were formulated, accurate communication among concerned individuals was possible. Contrary to the Sophists, who believed truth to be personal and noncommunicable, Socrates believed truth could be general and shared. Still, the essences that Socrates sought were verbal definitions, nothing more.

For Socrates, the understanding of essences constituted knowledge, and the goal of life was to gain knowledge. When one's conduct is guided by knowledge, it is necessarily moral. For example, if one knows what justice is, one acts justly. For Socrates, knowledge and morality were intimately related; knowledge is virtue, and improper conduct results from ignorance. Unlike most of the earlier philosophers, Socrates was concerned mainly with what it means to be human and the problems related to human existence. It is because of these concerns that Socrates is sometimes referred to as the first existential philosopher.

In 399 B.C., when Socrates was 70 years old, he was accused of disrespect for the city gods and of corrupting the youth of Athens. Socrates was charged with corrupting the youth of Athens because he caused them to question all things, including many cherished traditional beliefs. Perhaps on the latter charge he was guilty. In any case, Socrates was found guilty on both charges and sentenced to death. However, the end of his trial coincided with a religious observance during which executions were unlawful. During the month delay, Socrates was imprisoned but met regularly with his friends. Apparently it would have been easy for Socrates to escape from Athens at this time and he was encouraged by his friends to do so. It is even suggested that Socrates' escape would have been condoned by the authorities, "to whom the execution of such a prominent figure may well have been an embarrassment (Taylor, 1998, p. 11). Socrates preferred death over exile from his beloved Athens and, in the end, he consumed a drink containing deadly hemlock, thus fulfilling the order of the court.

What were the real reasons for Socrates' conviction? In the *Apology* (Jowett, 1988), Plato has Socrates, while awaiting his self-administered execution, recall a story explaining how he (Socrates) came to be considered the wisest of men. According to the story, a friend of Socrates went to the oracle of Delphi and asked if there was any man wiser than Socrates, and the oracle said no. Socrates was amazed to hear this because he considered himself ignorant. He set out to find men wiser than himself so that he could refute the oracle. In his quest Socrates questioned anyone who had the reputation of being wise. After many such encounters, Socrates concluded that these individuals really knew nothing, although they thought they did. Socrates, on the other hand, neither knew anything nor thought he did. Perhaps, Socrates reflected, it was for this reason that the oracle proclaimed him to be the wisest of men.

So why was Socrates convicted? After the defeat of Athens by Sparta, democracy in Athens was replaced by the regime of "thirty tyrants," some of whom were associated with Socrates. When democracy was restored in 403 B.C., Socrates may have been seen, because of his association with the tyrants, as a subversive (Roochnik, 2002, lecture 8). Also, Socrates' method of inquiry was abrasive. In his search for a person wiser than himself, Socrates questioned many of the leading citizens of Athens, including a number of politicians. As was the case with the youth of Athens, these encounters challenged many cherished beliefs, such as those concerning justice, courage, and even democracy. So, perhaps in addition to his being viewed as subversive, leading "Athenians may just have been sick and tired of Socrates' endless questioning" (Roochnik, 2002, lecture 8).

Following his death, it was Socrates' famous student, Plato, who perpetuated and greatly elaborated his philosophy.

Plato

The writings of **Plato** (ca. 427–347 B.C.) can be divided into two periods. During the first period, Plato essentially reported the thoughts and methods of his teacher, Socrates. When Socrates died, however, Plato went into self-imposed exile in southern Italy, where he came under the influence of the Pythagoreans. After he returned to Athens, he founded his own school, the Academy, and his subsequent writings combined the Socratic method with mystical Pythagorean philosophy. Like Socrates, Plato wished to find something permanent that could be the object of knowledge, but his search for permanence carried him far beyond the kind of essences for which Socrates had settled.

The Theory of Forms or Ideas

As we have seen, the Pythagoreans believed that although numbers and numerical relationships were abstractions (they could not be experienced through the senses), they were nonetheless real and could exert an influence on the empirical world. The result of the influence, however, was believed to be inferior to the abstraction that caused the influence. As already mentioned, the Pythagorean theorem is absolutely true when applied to abstract (imagined) triangles but is never completely true when applied

to a triangle that exists in the empirical world (for example, one that is drawn on paper). This discrepancy exists because, in the empirical world, the lines making up the right angle will never be exact.

Plato took an additional step. According to his **theory of forms,** everything in the empirical world is a manifestation of a pure form (idea) that exists in the abstract. Thus, chairs, chariots, rocks, cats, dogs, and people are inferior manifestations of pure **forms.** For example, the hundreds of cats that one encounters in a lifetime are but inferior copies of an abstract idea or form of "catness" that exists in pure form in the abstract. This is true for every object for which we have a name. What we experience through the senses results from the interaction of the pure form with matter; and because matter is constantly changing and is experienced through the senses, the result of the interaction must be less perfect than the pure idea before that idea interacts with matter. Plato replaced the essence that Socrates sought with the concept of form as the aspect of reality that was permanent and therefore knowable. That is, Socrates accepted the fact that a thorough definition specified an object's or a concept's essence; whereas for Plato, an object's or a concept's essence was equated with its form. For Plato, essence (form) had an existence separate from its individual manifestations. Socrates and Plato did agree, however, that knowledge could be attained only through reason.

The Analogy of the Divided Line

What, then, becomes of those who attempt to gain knowledge by examining the empirical world via sensory experience? According to Plato, they are doomed to ignorance or, at best, opinion. The only true knowledge involves grasping the forms themselves, and this can be done only by rational thought. Plato summarized this viewpoint with his famous **analogy of the divided line,** which is illustrated in Figure 2.1.

Imagining is seen as the lowest form of understanding because it is based on images—for example, a portrait of a person is once removed from the person. Reflections in the water are also images, because they are a step removed from the objects reflected. We are slightly better off confronting the

OBJECTS		STATES OF MIND
	The good	Intelligence (*noesis*) or knowledge (*episteme*)
INTELLIGIBLE WORLD	Forms	
	Mathematical Objects	Thinking (*dianoia*)
WORLD OF APPEARANCES	Visible things	Belief (*pistis*)
	Images	Imagining (*eikasia*)

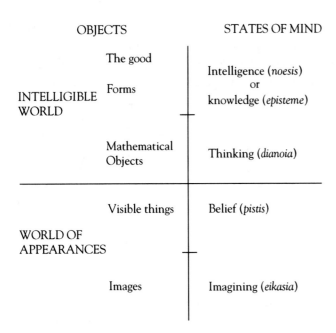

Figure 2.1
Plato's analogy of the divided line. (From Cornford's translation of Plato's *Republic*, 1941/1968, p. 222.)

objects themselves rather than their images, but the best we can do even when confronting objects directly is to form beliefs or opinions about them. Beliefs, however, do not constitute knowledge. Still better is the contemplation of mathematical relationships, but mathematical knowledge is still not the highest type because such knowledge is applied to the solution of practical (empirical) problems, and many of its relationships exist only by definition. That is, mathematical relationships are assumed to be true, but these assumptions could conceivably be false. To think about mathematics in the abstract, however, is better than dealing with images or empirical objects. The highest form of thinking involves embracing the forms themselves, and true intelligence or knowledge results *only* from an understanding of the abstract forms. The "good" or the "form of the good" constitutes the highest form of wisdom because it encompasses all other forms and shows their interrelatedness. The form of the good illuminates all other forms and makes them knowable. It is the highest truth. Later, in Christian theology, the form of the good is equated with God.

The Allegory of the Cave

In the **allegory of the cave** (Jowett, 1986), Plato described fictitious prisoners who have lived their entire lives in the depths of a cave. The prisoners are chained so that they can look only forward. Behind them is a road over which individuals pass, carrying a variety of objects. Behind the road a fire is blazing, causing a projection of shadows of the travelers and the objects onto the wall in front of the prisoners. For the prisoners, the projected shadows constitute reality. This corresponds to the lowest form of understanding in the divided line just discussed. Plato then described what might happen if one of the prisoners were to escape his bondage and leave the cave. Turning toward the fire would cause his eyes to ache, and he might decide to return to his world of shadows. If not, he would eventually adjust to the flames and see the individuals and objects of which he had previously seen only shadows. This represents an understanding of empirical events in the divided line. The fire is like the sun that illuminates those events. Plato then asks us to suppose that the prisoner continues his journey and leaves the cave. Once in the "upper world," the prisoner would be blinded by true reality. Only after a period of adjustment could he see things in this world and recognize that they were more real than the shadows that he had experienced in the cave. Finally, Plato asks us to imagine what might happen to the escaped prisoner if he went back into the cave to enlighten his fellow prisoners. Still partially blinded by such an illuminating experience, the prisoner would find it difficult to readjust to the previous life of shadows. He would make mistakes in describing the shadows and in predicting which objects would follow which. This would be evidence enough for his fellow prisoners that no good could come from leaving the world of shadows. In fact, anyone who attempted to lead the prisoners out of the shadowy world of the cave would be killed (Jowett, 1986, p. 257).

The bound prisoners represent humans who confuse the shadowy world of sense experience with reality. The prisoner who escapes represents the individual whose actions are governed by reason instead of sensory impressions. The escaped prisoner sees the real objects (forms) responsible for the shadows and objects in the cave (sensory information) and thus embraces true knowledge. After such an enlightening experience, an effort is often made to steer others away from ignorance and toward wisdom. The plight of Socrates is evidence of what can happen to the individual attempting to free others from the chains of ignorance.

The Reminiscence Theory of Knowledge

How does one come to know the forms if they cannot be known through sensory experience? The answer to this question involves the most mystical aspect of Plato's theory. Plato's answer was influenced by the Pythagorean notion of the immortality of the soul. According to the Pythagoreans, the highest form of thought was reason, which was a function of the immortal soul. Plato expanded this idea and said that before the soul was implanted in the body, it dwelled in pure and complete knowledge; that is, it dwelled among the forms. After the soul entered the body, sensory information began to contaminate this knowledge. The only way to arrive at true knowledge is to ignore sensory experience and focus one's thoughts on the contents of the mind. According to Plato's **reminiscence theory of knowledge,** all knowledge is innate and can be attained only through **introspection,** which is the searching of one's inner experiences. At most, sensory experience can only remind one of what was already known. Therefore, for Plato, all knowledge comes from reminiscence, from remembering the experiences the soul had before entering the body. In the *Meno,* Plato clearly presents his reminiscence theory of knowledge:

> Thus the soul, since it is immortal and has been born many times, and has seen all things both here and in the other world, has learned everything that is. So we need not be surprised if it can recall the knowledge of virtue or anything else which, as we see, it once possessed. All nature is akin, and the soul has learned everything, so that when a man has recalled a single piece of knowledge . . . there is no reason why he should not find out all the rest, if

he keeps a stout heart and does not grow weary of the search, for seeking and learning are in fact nothing but recollection. (Hamilton and Cairns, 1961, p. 364)

We see, then, that Plato was a nativist as well as a rationalist because he stressed mental operations as a means of arriving at the truth (rationalism) and that the truth ultimately arrived at was inborn (*nativism*). He was also an idealist because he believed that ultimate reality consisted of ideas or forms.

The Nature of the Soul

Plato believed not only that the soul had a rational component that was immortal but also that it had two other components: the courageous (sometimes translated as emotional or spirited) and the appetitive. The courageous and appetitive aspects of the soul were part of the body and thus mortal. With his concept of the three-part soul, Plato postulated a situation in which humans were almost always in a state of conflict, a situation not unlike the one Freud described many centuries later. According to Plato, the body has appetites (needs such as hunger, thirst, and sex) that must be met and that play a major motivational role in everyday life. Humans also have varied emotions such as fear, love, and rage. However, if true knowledge is to be attained, the person must suppress the needs of the body and concentrate on rational pursuits, such as introspection. Because bodily needs do not go away, the person must spend considerable energy keeping them under control—but they must be controlled. It is the job of the rational component of the soul to postpone or inhibit immediate gratifications when it is to a person's long-term benefit to do so. The person whose rational soul dominates is not impulsive. His or her life is dominated by moral principles and future goals, not the immediate satisfaction of biological or emotional needs. The supreme goal in life, according to Plato, should be to free the soul as much as possible from the adulterations of the flesh. In this he agreed with the Pythagoreans.

Plato realized that not everyone was capable of intense rational thought; he believed that in some individuals the appetitive aspect of the soul would dominate, in others the courageous (emotional) aspect of the soul would dominate, and in still others the rational aspect would dominate. In his *Republic*, he created a utopian society in which the three types of individuals would have special functions. Those in whom the appetitive aspect dominated would be workers and slaves, those in whom courage (emotion) dominated would be soldiers, and those in whom reason dominated would be philosopher-kings. In Plato's scheme, an inverse relationship exists between concern with bodily experiences and one's status in society. In Book V of the *Republic*, Plato forcibly stated his belief that societies have little chance of survival unless they are led by individuals with the wisdom of philosophers:

> Until philosophers are kings, or the kings and princes of this world have the spirit and power of philosophy, and political greatness and wisdom meet in one, and those of commoner natures who pursue either to the exclusion of the other are compelled to stand aside, cities will never have rest from their evils.... Then only will this our state have a possibility of life and behold the light of day. (Jowett, 1986, p. 203)

We see that Plato was a nativist not only where knowledge was concerned but also where character or intelligence was concerned. He felt that education was of limited value for children of low aptitude. To a large extent then, whether one was destined to be a slave, a soldier, or a philosopher-king was a matter of inheritance. With his discussion of the three character types, Plato created a rudimentary theory of personality. He also had a highly developed philosophy of education that combined his theory of forms with his belief in character types. This philosophy is prominently featured in his *Republic* (Jowett, 1986).

Plato's Legacy

Because science depends on empirical observation, Plato's philosophy did little to promote science and much to inhibit it. Plato created a dualism that divided the human into a body, which was material and imperfect, and a mind (soul), which contained pure knowledge. Furthermore, the rational soul was immortal. Had philosophy remained unencumbered by theological concerns, perhaps Plato's theory would have been challenged by subsequent philosophers and gradually displaced by more tempered philosophic views. Aristotle, in fact, went a long way in modifying Plato's position, but the challenge was aborted. The mysticism of early Christianity was combined with Platonic philosophy, creating unchallengeable religious dogma. When Aristotle's writings were rediscovered centuries later, they were also carefully modified and assimilated into church dogma. It was not until the Renaissance that Platonism (and Aristotelianism) was finally questioned openly and largely discarded.

Aristotle

Aristotle (384–322 B.C.) was born in the obscure Macedonian city of Stagira, located between the Black Sea and the Aegean Sea. His father was court physician to King Amyntas II of Macedon. Although his father died when Aristotle was a young boy and he was raised by a guardian, it is assumed that he received training in medicine. In 367 B.C., Aristotle journeyed to Athens and soon established himself as one of Plato's most brilliant students; he was 17 years old at the time, and Plato was 60. Aristotle continued to study at the Academy until he was 37 years old. When Plato died in 347 B.C., Aristotle moved to Asia Minor, where he engaged in biological and zoological field work. In 343 B.C., Aristotle returned to Macedon, where he tutored the son of King Philip II, the future Alexander the Great, for about four years. After a few more journeys, Aristotle returned to Athens and, at the age of 48, founded his own school called the Lyceum. Because the Lyceum had many teachers, regular lectures, a substantial library, and large natural science collections, it is considered the world's first university (Esper, 1964, p. 128). When Alexander the Great died in 323 B.C., Aristotle fled Athens, and he died a year later in Challis at the age of 63.

Why did Aristotle flee Athens? Macedon, where Aristotle was born, was an ancient Greek-speaking

Aristotle

CORBIS-BETTMANN

country to the north of Greece. With the goal of unifying diverse Greek communities into a powerful Graeco-Macedonian nation, King Philip II of Macedon invaded and conquered a number of Greek city-states, including Athens. When Philip II was assassinated in 336 B.C. his 19-year-old son Alexander (Aristotle's ex-student) became ruler, and his subsequent military accomplishments are legendary. Although Aristotle had many disagreements with Alexander, both preferred "Greek solidarity to city patriotism" (Durant, 1926/1961, p. 94). When Alexander died in 323 B.C. at the age of 32, the Macedonian party was overthrown in Athens, and Athenian independence was again proclaimed. Undoubtedly because of Aristotle's association with the Macedonians, the trumped-up charge of impiety was brought against him. He was accused of having taught that prayer and sacrifice were ineffective. This, of course, is reminiscent of what happened to

Socrates. Unlike Socrates, however, Aristotle chose to flee Athens rather than meet his inevitable fate, saying, "He would not give Athens a chance to sin a second time against philosophy" (Durant, 1926/1961, p. 94).

Aristotle was the first philosopher to extensively treat many topics that were later to become part of psychology. In his vast writings, he covered memory, sensation, sleep, dreams, geriatrics, and learning. He also began his book *De Anima* (*On the Soul*) with what is considered to be the first history of psychology. Taken alone, Aristotle's contributions to psychology were truly impressive. It must be realized, however, that with the possible exception of mathematics, he made contributions to every branch of knowledge. The influence of his thoughts on such philosophical and scientific topics as logic, metaphysics, physics, biology, ethics, politics, rhetoric, and poetics have lasted to the present time. It is often said that Aristotle was the last human to know everything that was knowable during his lifetime.

The Basic Difference Between Plato and Aristotle

Both Plato and Aristotle were primarily interested in essences or truths that went beyond the mere appearance of things, but their methods for discovering those essences were distinctly different. For Plato, essences corresponded to the forms that existed *independently* of nature and that could only be arrived at by ignoring sensory experience and turning one's thoughts inward (that is, by introspection). For Aristotle, essences existed but could become known only by studying nature. He believed that if enough individual manifestations of a principle or phenomenon were investigated, eventually one could infer the essence that they exemplified. In the opening passage of his *Metaphysics*, Aristotle demonstrates that his attitude toward sensory information was much friendlier than was Plato's.

All men by nature desire to know. An indication of this is the delight we take in our senses; for even apart from their usefulness they are loved for themselves; and above all others the sense of sight. For not only with a view to action, but even when we are not going to do anything, we prefer sight to almost everything else. The reason is that this, most of all the senses, makes us know and brings to light many differences between things. (Barnes, 1984, Vol. 2, p. 1552)

Aristotle's philosophy shows the difficulty that is often encountered when attempting to clearly separate the philosophies of rationalism and empiricism. As was noted in Chapter 1, the rationalist claims that logical, mental operations must be used to gain knowledge, and the empiricist emphasizes the importance of sensory information in gaining knowledge. Aristotle embraced both rationalism and empiricism. He believed that the mind must be employed before knowledge can be attained (rationalism) but that the object of rational thought was the information furnished by the senses (empiricism). Aristotle's position is not unique, however. Throughout history most rationalists have recognized and accepted the importance of sensory experience, and most empiricists have postulated one or more mental operations that are presumed to act on sensory information. In other words, finding a *pure* rationalist or empiricist is very difficult, and a philosopher is usually categorized as one or the other, depending on whether he or she emphasizes mental operations or sensory experience. With this in mind, we can say that Aristotle was more of a rationalist than an empiricist.

The general principles that Plato and Aristotle (and other philosophers) thought were real and knowable have been referred to in different ways through the years—for example, as first principles, essences, or universals. In each case, it was assumed that something basic existed that could not be discovered by studying only individual instances or manifestations of the abstract principle involved. Some type of rational activity was needed to find the principle (essence) underlying individual cases. The search for first principles, essences, or universals characterized most early philosophy and, in a sense, continues in modern science as the search for laws governing nature. For Plato, first principles were arrived at by pure thought; for Aristotle, they were attained by examining nature directly. For Plato, all knowledge existed independently of nature; for

Aristotle, nature and knowledge were inseparable. In Aristotle's view, therefore, the body was not a hindrance in the search for knowledge, as it was for Plato and the Pythagoreans. Also, Aristotle disagreed with Plato on the importance of mathematics. For Aristotle, mathematics was essentially useless, his emphasis being on the careful examination of nature by observation and classification. Here we see again the empirical component of Aristotle's philosophy. In Aristotle's Lyceum, an incredibly large number of observations of physical and biological phenomena were made. Categories into which the observations fit were then determined. Through this method of observation, definition, and classification, Aristotle compiled what has been called an encyclopedia of nature. He was interested in studying the things in the empirical world and learning their functions. Because Aristotle sought to explain several psychological phenomena in biological terms, he can be considered the first physiological psychologist (D. N. Robinson, 1986, pp. 81–82).

Plato's philosophy followed in the Pythagorean, mathematical tradition, and Aristotle's in the Hippocratic, biological tradition. The views of Plato and Aristotle concerning the sources of knowledge set the stage for epistemological inquiry that has lasted to the present time. Almost every philosopher, and most psychologists, can be evaluated in terms of their agreement or disagreement with the views of Plato or Aristotle.

Causation and Teleology

To truly understand anything, according to Aristotle, we must know four things about it. That is, everything has the following four causes:

- **Material cause** is the kind of matter of which an object is made. For example, a statue is made of marble.

- **Formal cause** is the particular form, or pattern, of an object. For example, a piece of marble takes on the form of Venus.

- **Efficient cause** is the force that transforms the matter into a certain form—for example, the energy of the sculptor.

- **Final cause** is the purpose for which an object exists. In the case of a statue, the purpose may be to bring pleasure to those who view it. The final cause is "that for the sake of which something exists." Thus, although I have listed it last, the final cause (a thing's purpose) actually precedes the other three causes.

Aristotle's philosophy exemplified **teleology** because, for him, everything in nature exists for a purpose. By "purpose," however, Aristotle did not mean conscious intention. Rather, he meant that everything in nature had a function built into it. This built-in purpose, or function, is called **entelechy.** Entelechy keeps an object moving or developing in its prescribed direction until its full potential is reached. For example, the eye exists to provide vision, and it continues developing until it does so. The final cause of living things is part of their nature; it exists as a potentiality from the organism's very inception. An acorn has the potential to become an oak tree, but it cannot become a frog or an olive tree. In other words, the purpose, or entelechy, of an acorn is to become an oak tree. Nature is characterized by the change and motion that occurs as objects are slowly transformed from their potentialities to their actualities—that is, as objects move toward their final causes or purposes, such as when an acorn becomes an oak tree. Aristotle also saw the final cause, or purpose, of something as its essence.

According to Aristotle, all natural things, both animate and inanimate, have a purpose built into them. In addition, however, nature itself has a grand design or purpose. Although Aristotle believed that the categories of things in nature remain fixed, thus denying evolution, he spoke of a grand hierarchy among all things. The *scala naturae* refers to the idea that nature is arranged in a hierarchy ranging from neutral matter to the **unmoved mover,** which is pure actuality and is the cause of everything in nature. For Aristotle, the unmoved mover is what gives all natural objects their purposes. In his scala naturae, the closer to the unmoved mover something is, the more perfect it is. Among animals, humans were closest to the unmoved mover, with all other animals at various distances behind us.

Although Aristotle did not accept evolution, his scala naturae does create a phylogenetic scale of sorts, making it possible to study "lower" animals in order to understand humans. Such information will always be of limited value, however, because for Aristotle, humans were unique among the animals. Again, Aristotle's position was thoroughly teleological: all objects in nature have a purpose, and nature itself has a purpose.

The Hierarchy of Souls

For Aristotle, as for most Greek philosophers, a soul was that which gives life; therefore, all living things possess a soul. According to Aristotle, there were three types of souls, and a living thing's potential (purpose) is determined by what type of a soul it possesses.

- A **vegetative** (or nutritive) **soul** is possessed by plants. It allows only growth, the assimilation of food, and reproduction.
- A **sensitive soul** is possessed by animals but not plants. In addition to the vegetative functions, organisms that possess a sensitive soul sense and respond to the environment, experience pleasure and pain, and have a memory.
- A **rational soul** is possessed only by humans. It provides all the functions of the other two souls but also allows thinking or rational thought.

Because it is the soul that gives a living organism its distinctive properties, to ask whether body and soul exist independently was, for Aristotle, a meaningless question: "We can dismiss as unnecessary the question whether the soul and the body are one: it is as though we were to ask whether the wax and its shape are one" (Barnes, 1984, Vol. 1, p. 657).

Sensation

Aristotle said that information about the environment is provided by the five senses: sight, hearing, taste, touch, and smell. Unlike earlier philosophers (such as Empedocles and Democritus), Aristotle did not believe objects sent off tiny copies of themselves (eidola). Rather, he thought that perception was explained by the motion of objects that stimulate one of the senses. The movement of environmental objects created movements through different media, and each of the five senses was maximally sensitive to movements in a certain medium. For example, seeing resulted from the movement of light caused by an object, hearing and smelling resulted from the movement of air, and taste and touching resulted from movement of the flesh. In this way, Aristotle explained how we could actually sense environmental objects without those objects sending off physical copies of themselves. Unlike Plato, Aristotle believed we could trust our senses to yield an accurate representation of the environment.

Common Sense, Passive Reason, and Active Reason

As important as sensory information was to Aristotle, it was only the first step in acquiring knowledge. In other words, *sensory experience was a necessary, but not a sufficient, element in the attainment of knowledge.* In the first place, each sensory system provides isolated information about the environment that by itself is not very useful. For example, seeing a baby tossing and turning provides a clue as to its condition, hearing it cry provides another clue, smelling it may give a clue as to why it is so uncomfortable, and touching may reveal that it has a fever. It is the combined information from all the senses that allows for the most effective interactions with the environment.

Aristotle postulated a **common sense** as the mechanism that coordinated the information from all the senses. The common sense, like all other mental functions, was assumed to be located in the heart. The job of common sense was to synthesize sensory experience, thereby making it more meaningful. However, sensory information, even after it was synthesized by common sense, could provide information only about particular instances of things. **Passive reason** involved the utilization of synthesized experience for getting along effectively in everyday life, but it did not result in an understanding of essences, or first principles. The abstraction of first principles from one's many experiences could be accomplished only by **active reason,** which

was considered the highest form of thinking. Aristotle therefore delineated levels of knowing or understanding much like Plato's divided line:

- Active reason: The abstraction of principles, or essences, from synthesized experience
- Passive reason: Utilization of synthesized experience
- Common sense: Synthesized experience
- Sensory information: Isolated experiences

To see how these levels of understanding are related, consider how electricity is experienced through the various senses: sight (seeing an electrical discharge), pain (being shocked), and hearing (hearing the electrical discharge). These experiences would correspond to the level of sense reception. The common sense would indicate that all these experiences had a common source—electricity. Passive reason would indicate how electricity could be used in a variety of practical ways, whereas active reason would seek the laws governing electricity and an understanding of its essence. What started as a set of empirical experiences ends as a search for the principles that can explain those experiences.

The active reason part of the soul provides humans with their highest purpose. That is, it provides their entelechy. Just as the ultimate goal of an acorn is to become an oak tree, the ultimate goal of humans is to engage in active reason. Aristotle also believed that acting in accordance with one's nature caused pleasure and that acting otherwise brought pain. In the case of humans, engaging in active reason was the source of greatest pleasure. On this matter, Aristotle was essentially in agreement with Socrates and Plato. Also, because Aristotle postulated an inner potential in humans that may or may not be reached, his theory represents psychology's first self-actualization theory. The self-actualization theories of Jung, Maslow, and Rogers reflect Aristotle's thoughts on the human entelechy.

With his concept of active reason, Aristotle inserted a mystical or supernatural component into an otherwise naturalistic philosophy. The active reason part of the soul was considered immortal, but when it left the body upon death, it carried no recollections with it. It was considered a mechanism for pure thought and was believed to be identical for all humans. It was not judged in accordance with the moral character of its prior possessor, and there was no union or reunion with God. The active reason part of the soul went neither to heaven nor to hell. Later, however, the Christianized version of the Aristotelian soul was to be characterized by all these things.

Another mystical component in Aristotle's theory was his notion of the unmoved mover. As stated earlier, for Aristotle, everything in nature had a purpose that was programmed into it. This purpose, or entelechy, explained why a thing was the way it was and why it did what it did. But if everything in nature has a purpose, what causes that purpose? As we have seen, Aristotle postulated an unmoved mover, or that which caused everything else but was not caused by anything itself. For Aristotle, the unmoved mover set nature in motion and did little else; it was a logical necessity, not a deity. Along with Aristotle's notion of the immortal aspect of the soul, the Christians also found his unmoved mover very much to their liking.

Memory and Recall

In keeping with the empirical aspect of his philosophy, Aristotle, in his *On Memory*, explained memory and recall as the results of sense perception. This contrasts with Plato's explanation, which was essentially nativistic. **Remembering,** for Aristotle, was a spontaneous recollection of something that had been previously experienced. For example, you see a person and remember that you saw that person before and perhaps engaged in a certain conversation. **Recall,** however, involves an actual mental search for a past experience. It was in conjunction with recall that Aristotle postulated what have been called his **laws of association.** The most basic law of association is the **law of contiguity,** which states that when we think of something, we also tend to think of things that were experienced along with it. The **law of similarity** states that when we think of something, we tend to think of things similar to it.

The **law of contrast** states that when we think of something, we also tend to think of things that are its opposite. Aristotle said that on rare occasions a strong association can be formed between two events after experiencing them together just once. More typically, however, the more often events are experienced together, the stronger will be their association. Thus, Aristotle implied the **law of frequency,** which states, that, in general, the more often experiences occur together, the stronger will be their association. According to Aristotle, events can be associated naturally, such as when thunder follows lightning, or by custom, such as learning the letters of the alphabet or associating a certain name with a certain person. In both cases, it is generally the frequency of occurrence that determines the strength of association. In *On Memory* Aristotle said, "For as one thing follows another by nature, so too that happens by custom, and frequency creates nature" (Barnes, 1984, Vol. 1, pp. 718–719).

Aristotle's laws of association were to become the basis of learning theory for more than 2,000 years. In fact, the concept of mental association is still at the heart of most theories of learning. The belief that one or more laws of association can be used to explain the origins of ideas, the phenomena of memory, or how complex ideas are formed from simple ones came to be called **associationism.**

Imagination and Dreaming

We have seen that Aristotle's philosophy had both rational and empirical components. For example, his account of memory and recall was empirical. We see that component again in his explanation of **imagination** and **dreaming.** According to Aristotle, when sensations occur, they create images that long outlast the stimulation that caused them. The retention of these images is what constitutes memory. These images also create the important link between sensation and rational thought, because it is the images provided by experience that are pondered by the passive and active intellects. Imagination, then, is explained as the lingering effects of sensory experience. Aristotle did question the reliability of the products of imagination. Sensations, he said, tend to be free of error because of the close relationship between objects of sense and the sense organs. Because imagination is removed from this relationship, it is much more susceptible to error.

Aristotle also explained dreaming in terms of the images of past experience. During sleep, the images of past experience may be stimulated by events inside or outside the body. The reasons that our residual impressions (images) may seem odd during a dream are (1) during sleep the images are not organized by reason, and (2) while awake our images are coordinated with or controlled by ongoing sensory stimulation, which interacts with the images of previous experience; during sleep this does not occur.

Aristotle was extremely skeptical about a dream's ability to provide information about future events. Most often we dream about activities in which we have recently engaged, but it is possible that a course of action is dreamed about so vividly that it will suggest an actual course of action in the dreamer's life. However, according to Aristotle, most cases of apparent prophecy by dreams are to be taken as mere coincidences:

> [Just as] mentioning a particular person is neither token nor cause of this person's presenting himself, so, in the parallel instance, the dream is, to him who has seen it, neither token nor cause of its fulfillment, but a mere coincidence. Hence the fact that many dreams have no "fulfillment," for coincidences do not occur according to any universal or general law. . . . For the principle which is expressed in the gambler's maxim: "If you make many throws your luck must change," holds good [for dreams] also. (Barnes, 1984, Vol. 1, p. 737)

It is interesting to note that the eminent Roman statesman and philosopher Cicero (106–43 B.C.) agreed with Aristotle's analysis of dreams:

> From the visions of drunkards and madmen one might, doubtless, deduce innumerable consequences by conjecture, which might seem to be presages of future events. For what person who aims at a mark all day long will not sometimes hit it? We sleep every night; and there are very few on which we do not dream; can we wonder then that what we dream sometimes comes to pass? (Yonge, 1997, p. 251)

There was a sense, however, in which Aristotle believed dreams were capable of predicting important future events. Because sensations are often exaggerated in dreams, subtle bodily changes may be reflected in dreams but not during wakefulness. For this reason, it makes sense for physicians to analyze dreams to detect the early signs of disease (Barnes, 1984, Vol. 1, pp. 736–737).

Motivation and Happiness

Happiness, for Aristotle, was doing what is natural because doing so fulfills one's purpose. For humans, our purpose is to think rationally, and therefore doing so brings the greatest happiness. However, humans are also biological organisms characterized by the functions of nutrition, sensation, reproduction, and movement. That is, although humans are distinct from other animals (because of our reasoning ability), we do share many of their motives. As with other animals, much of human behavior is motivated by appetites. Action is always directed at the satisfaction of an appetite. That is, behavior is motivated by such internal states as hunger, sexual arousal, thirst, or the desire for bodily comfort. Because the existence of an appetite causes discomfort, it stimulates activity that will eliminate it. If the activity is successful, the animal or person experiences pleasure. Much human behavior, then, like all animal behavior, is hedonistic; its purpose is to bring pleasure or to avoid pain.

Unlike other animals, however, we can use our rational powers to inhibit our appetites. Furthermore, our greatest happiness does not come from satisfying our biological needs. Rather, it comes from exercising our rational powers to their fullest. Given the fact that humans have both appetites and rational powers, conflict often arises between the immediate satisfaction of our appetites and more remote rational goals. On the portals of the temple of Apollo at Delphi, were two inscriptions. One was "Know thyself" which, as we have seen, so inspired Socrates. The other was "Nothing in excess." The latter reflects the high esteem with which the Greeks held self-control, and Aristotle was no exception. In *The Nicomachean Ethics* (Ross, 1990), Aristotle described the best life as one lived in moderation; that is, one lived according to the **golden mean.** As examples, he described courage as the mean between cowardice and foolhardiness, temperance as the mean between abstinence and self-indulgence, and generosity as the mean between meanness (stinginess) and extravagance. A life of moderation requires the rational control of one's appetites. Even the best of humans, however, are capable of acting hedonistically rather than rationally: "For desire is a wild beast, and passion perverts the minds of rulers, even when they are the best of men" (Barnes, 1984, Vol. 2, p. 2042). According to Aristotle, the lives of many humans are governed by nothing more than the pleasure and pain that comes from the satisfaction and frustration of appetites. These people are indistinguishable from animals. Appetites and reason are part of every human, but his or her character is revealed by which of the two dominates.

The Emotions and Selective Perception

In general, in Aristotelian philosophy, the emotions had the function of amplifying any existing tendency. For example, people might run more quickly if they were frightened than if they were merely jogging for exercise. Also, the emotions provide a motive for acting—for example, people might be inclined to fight if they are angry. However, the emotions may also influence how people perceive things; that is, they may cause *selective perception.* Aristotle gave the following examples:

> We are easily deceived respecting the operations of sense-perception when we are excited by emotion, and different persons according to their different emotions; for example, the coward when excited by fear and the amorous person by amorous desire; so that with but little resemblance to go upon, the former thinks he sees his foes approaching, the latter that he sees the object of his desire; and the more deeply one is under the influence of the emotion, the less similarity is required to give rise to

these impressions. Thus, too, in fits of anger, and also in all states of appetite, all men become easily deceived, and more so the more their emotions are excited. (Barnes, 1984, Vol. 1, p. 732)

We can engage here in a bit of presentism and note that Aristotle made several mistakes. For example, he assigned thinking and common sense to the heart and claimed that the main function of the brain was to cool the blood. He believed that the number of species of living things in the world was fixed and thereby denied evolution. He also believed the earth to be the center of the universe. However, compared to his many positive contributions, his mistakes are minor. Although many of his observations were incorrect, he did promote empirical observation as a means of attaining knowledge, and in doing so, he brought Greek philosophy to new heights.

The Importance of Early Greek Philosophy

To realize the importance of the early Greek philosophers, remembering Popper's philosophy of science is important. As we saw in Chapter 1, Popperian science consists of specifying a problem, proposing solutions to the problem, and attempting to refute the proposed solutions. What survives in such a process is a solution to a problem that, at the moment, cannot be refuted. Again, the highest status that a proposed solution to a problem can ever attain is *not yet disconfirmed.* The assumption in Popper's view of science is that all scientific "facts" and "theories" eventually will be found to be false.

What has this to do with the importance of early Greek philosophy? In Popper's view, science began when humans first began to question the stories they were told about themselves and the world. According to Brett, "The Greek cosmologists were important because they broke loose from the accepted religious traditions and produced what they considered to be better stories about the origin and stuff of the world. They speculated" (1912–1921/1965, p. 38). Not only did the Greek philosophers speculate, but they also respected the speculations of others.

With the exception of the Pythagoreans, who created a secretive cult designed to perpetuate dogma, the Greek philosophers engaged in open, critical discussion of each other's ideas. For Popper, this willingness to engage in critical discussion was the beginning of an extremely important tradition:

> Here is a unique phenomenon, and it is closely connected with the astonishing freedom and creativeness of Greek philosophy. How can we explain this phenomenon? *What we have to explain is the rise of a tradition.* It is a tradition that allows or encourages critical discussions between various schools and, more surprisingly still, within one and the same school. For nowhere outside the Pythagorean school do we find a school devoted to the preservation of a doctrine. Instead we find changes, new ideas, modifications, and outright criticism of the master. (1958, p. 27)

As we have seen, Popper attributed the founding of this new tradition of freedom to Thales, who not only tolerated criticism but encouraged it. According to Popper, this was a "momentous innovation" because it broke with the dogmatic tradition that permitted only one true doctrine and allowed a plurality of doctrines, all attempting to approach the truth via critical discussion. Coupled with this tradition of free, critical discussion is the realization that our inquiries are never final but always tentative and capable of improvement. Popper said of this tradition:

> It . . . leads, almost by necessity, to the realization that our attempts to see and to find the truth are not final, but open to improvement; that our knowledge, our doctrine, is conjectural; that it consists of guesses, of hypotheses, rather than of final and certain truths; and that criticism and critical discussion are our only means of getting nearer to the truth. It thus leads to the tradition of bold conjectures and of free criticism, the tradition which created the rational or scientific attitude, and with it our Western civilization. (1958, p. 29)

Aristotle's death, in 322 B.C., marked the end of the Golden Age of Greece, which had started about 300 years earlier with the philosophy of Thales. Most, if not all, of the philosophical concepts that have been pursued since the Golden Age were produced during this period. After Aristotle's death, philosophers either began to rely on the teaching of past authorities or they turned their attention to questions concerning models for human conduct. It was not until the Renaissance, many centuries after Aristotle's death, that the critical tradition of the early Greek philosophers was rediscovered and revived.

Summary

Primitive humans looked upon everything in nature as if it were alive; there was no distinction between the animate and the inanimate—this view was called animism. Moreover, there was a tendency to project human feelings and emotions onto nature, and this was called anthropomorphism. A spirit or ghost was thought to reside in everything, giving it life. An array of magical practices evolved that were designed to influence various spirits. These practices gave humans the feeling that they had some control over nature. Early Greek religion was of two main types: Olympian, which consisted of a number of gods whose activities were very much like those of upper-class Greeks, and Dionysiac-Orphic, which preached that the soul was a prisoner of the body and that it longed to be released so that it could once again dwell among the gods. Whereas Olympian religion tended to be the favorite of the wealthier Greeks, Dionysiac-Orphic religion tended to be favored by the lower classes.

The first philosophers emphasized natural explanations instead of supernatural ones. They sought a primary element, called the physis, from which everything was made. For Thales, the physis was water; for Anaximander, it was the boundless; for Heraclitus, it was fire; for Parmenides, it was the "one" or "changelessness"; for Pythagoras, it was numbers; for Democritus, it was the atom; and for Hippocrates and Empedocles, there were four primary elements: water, earth, fire, and air; and for Anaxagoras there was an infinite number of elements. The earliest Greek philosophers were called cosmologists, because they sought to explain the origin, structure, and processes of the universe (cosmos). Along with the four elements, Empedocles postulated the forces of love, which tends to bring the elements together, and strife, which tends to separate them. When the mixture of elements and forces is just right, parts of animals and humans form and combine into almost all possible arrangements. Only a limited number of the random arrangements were capable of survival, and humans were among them.

The debate between Heraclitus, who believed everything was constantly changing, and Parmenides, who believed nothing ever changed, raised a number of epistemological questions, such as, What, if anything, is permanent enough to be known with certainty? and, If sensory experience provides information only about a continually changing world, how can it be a source of knowledge? These and related questions have persisted to the present.

Most of the first philosophers were monists because they made no distinction between the mind and the body; whatever element or elements they arrived at were supposed to account for everything. In Pythagoras, however, we have a full-fledged dualism between the mind and the body and between the physical and the abstract. Numbers were abstractions but were real, and they could be known only by rational thought, not by sensory experience. Sensory experience could only inhibit attainment of abstract knowledge and was to be avoided. The mind, or soul, was thought to be immortal.

Early Greek medicine was temple medicine based on superstition and magical practices. Through the efforts of such individuals as Alcmaeon and Hippocrates, medical practice became objective and naturalistic. Displacing such beliefs as that illness was due to the possession of spirits was the belief that health resulted from a balance among bodily elements or processes and illness from an imbalance.

The Sophists concluded that there were many equally valid philosophical positions. "Truth" was believed to be a function of a person's education, personal experiences, culture, and beliefs; and

whether this "truth" was accepted by others depended on one's communicative skills. There is much in common between what the Sophists taught and contemporary postmodernism. Socrates agreed with the Sophists that truth was subjective, but he also believed that a careful examination of one's subjective experiences would reveal certain concepts that were stable and knowable and which, when known, would generate proper conduct.

Plato, influenced by the Pythagoreans, took Socrates' belief an additional step by saying that ideas, or concepts had an independent existence, just as the Pythagorean number did. For Plato, ideas or forms were the ultimate reality, and they could be known only by reason. Sensory experience leads only to ignorance—or at best, opinion—and should be avoided. The soul, before becoming implanted in the body, dwells in pure and complete knowledge, which can be remembered if one turns one's thoughts inward and away from the empirical world. For Plato, knowledge results from remembering what the soul experienced prior to its implantation in the body. This is called the reminiscence theory of knowledge. Plato believed that the rational powers of the mind (rationalism) should be turned inward (introspection) to rediscover ideas that had been present at birth (nativism).

Aristotle was also interested in general concepts instead of isolated facts; but unlike Plato, he believed that the way to arrive at these concepts was to examine nature. Instead of urging the avoidance of sensory experience, he claimed that it was the source of all knowledge. Aristotle's brand of rationalism relied heavily on empiricism because he believed that concepts are derived from the careful scrutiny of sensory observations. He believed that all things contained an entelechy, or purpose. An acorn, for example, has the potential to become an oak tree, and its purpose is to do so. There were three categories of living things: those possessing a vegetative soul, those possessing a sensitive soul, and those possessing a rational soul. Humans alone possess a rational soul, which has two functions: passive reason and active reason. Passive reason ponders information from the five senses and from the common sense, which synthesizes sensory information. Active reason is used to isolate enduring concepts (essences) that manifest themselves in sensory experience. Aristotle considered active reason immortal. He also postulated an unmoved mover that was the entelechy for all of nature; it caused everything else but was not itself caused by anything. Aristotle believed that nature was organized on a grand scale ranging from formless matter to plants, to animals, to humans, and finally to the unmoved mover. Because humans have much in common with other animals, we can learn about ourselves by studying them.

Aristotle distinguished between memory, which was spontaneous, and recall, which was the active search for a recollection of a past experience. It was with regard to recall that Aristotle postulated his laws of association—the laws of contiguity, similarity, contrast, and frequency. Aristotle explained imagination and dreaming as the pondering of images that linger after sensory experience has ceased. Contrary to what almost everyone else at the time believed, Aristotle believed that dreams do not foretell the future, and if they appear to do so it is simply coincidence. However, because minute bodily events are exaggerated in dreams, dreams can be used to detect the early signs of disease. Humans are motivated by their very nature to engage their rational powers in an effort to attain knowledge. In addition, however, humans have appetites not unlike those of other animals. The presence of an appetite stimulates behavior that will satisfy it. When an appetite is satisfied, the person or animal experiences pleasure; when it is not satisfied, pain is experienced. Human rationality can and should be used to control appetites and emotions, but both sometimes overwhelm even the best of humans. The best life is one lived in accordance with the golden mean—a life of moderation. Emotions amplify ongoing thoughts and behavior and sometimes cause people to selectively perceive or misperceive events in the environment. Although Aristotle made several mistakes, his accomplishments far exceeded his failures.

Early Greek philosophy was significant because it replaced supernatural explanations with naturalistic ones and because it encouraged the open criticism and evaluation of ideas.

Discussion Questions

1. Describe some of the events that may have concerned primitive humans and discuss how they accounted for and attempted to control those events.
2. Summarize the major differences between Olympian and Dionysiac-Orphic religion.
3. What distinguishes the attempts of the first philosophers to understand nature from the attempts of those who preceded them?
4. What did the cosmologists attempt to do?
5. Why were the first philosophers called physicists? List the physes arrived at by Thales, Anaximander, Heraclitus, Parmenides, Pythagoras, Empedocles, Anaxagoras, and Democritus.
6. Summarize Empedocles' view of the universe.
7. Summarize Empedocles' view of how species of animals, including humans, came into existence.
8. What important epistemological question did Heraclitus' philosophy raise?
9. Give examples of how logic was used to defend Parmenides' belief that change and motions were illusions.
10. Differentiate between elementism and reductionism and give an example of each.
11. What were the major differences between temple medicine and the type of medicine practiced by Alcmaeon and the Hippocratics?
12. How did the Sophists differ from the philosophers who preceded them? What was the Sophists' attitude toward knowledge? In what way did Socrates agree with the Sophists, and in what way did he disagree?
13. What observations did Xenophanes make about religion?
14. What, for Socrates, was the goal of philosophical inquiry? What method did he use in pursuing that goal?
15. What are the charges brought against Socrates by the Athenians? What were perhaps the real reasons Socrates was convicted and sentenced to death?
16. Describe Plato's theory of forms or ideas.
17. In Plato's philosophy, what was the analogy of the divided line?
18. Summarize Plato's cave allegory. What points was Plato making with this allegory?
19. Discuss Plato's reminiscence theory of knowledge.
20. Compare Aristotle's attitude toward sensory experience with that of Plato.

21. Provide evidence that Aristotle's philosophy had both rational and empirical components.
22. According to Aristotle, what were the four causes of things?
23. Discuss Aristotle's concept of entelechy.
24. Describe Aristotle's concept of scala naturae and indicate how that concept justifies a comparative psychology.
25. Discuss Aristotle's concept of soul.
26. Discuss the relationship of sensory experience, common sense, passive reason, and active reason.
27. Summarize Aristotle's views on imagination and dreaming.
28. Discuss Aristotle's views on happiness. What for him provided the greatest happiness? What characterized the life lived in accordance with the golden mean?
29. Discuss Aristotle's views on emotions.
30. In Aristotle's philosophy, what was the function of the unmoved mover?
31. Describe the laws of association that Aristotle proposed.
32. Summarize the reasons Greek philosophy was important to the development of Western civilization.

InfoTrac College Edition

 Explore InfoTrac College Edition, your online library. Go to *http://infotrac.cengage.com/*

Search term:
Aristotle

Suggestions for Further Reading

Allen, R. E. (Ed.). (1991). *Greek philosophy from Thales to Aristotle* (3rd ed.). New York: Free Press.

Annas, J. (2003). *Plato: A very short introduction.* New York: Oxford University Press.

Barnes, J. (2001). *Early Greek philosophy* (rev. ed). New York: Penguin Putnam.

Bremmer, J. N. (1993). *The early Greek concept of the soul.* Princeton, NJ: Princeton University Press.

Cartledge, P. (1999). *Democritus.* New York: Routledge.

Guthrie, K. S. (Comp. and Trans.). (1987). *The Pythagorean sourcebook and library.* Grand Rapids, MI: Phanes Press.

Hicks, R. D. (Trans.). (1991). *Aristotle: De anima.* Buffalo, NY: Prometheus Books.

McLeish, K. (1999). *Aristotle.* New York: Routledge.

Robinson, D. N. (1989). *Aristotle's psychology.* New York: Columbia University Press.

Robinson, T. M. (1995). *Plato's psychology.* (2nd ed.). Toronto: University of Toronto Press.

Ross, D. (Trans.). (1990). *Aristotle: The Nicomachean ethics.* New York: Oxford University Press.

Taylor, C. C. W. (1998). *Socrates.* New York: Oxford University Press.

Waterfield, R. (2000). *The first philosophers: The Presocratics and the Sophists.* New York: Oxford University Press.

Glossary

Active reason According to Aristotle, the faculty of the soul that searches for the essences or abstract concepts that manifest themselves in the empirical world. Aristotle thought that the active reason part of the soul was immortal.

Alcmaeon (fl. ca. 500 B.C.) One of the first Greek physicians to move away from the magic and superstition of temple medicine and toward a naturalistic understanding and treatment of illness.

Allegory of the cave Plato's description of individuals who live their lives in accordance with the shadows of reality provided by sensory experience instead of in accordance with the true reality beyond sensory experience.

Analogy of the divided line Plato's illustration of his contention that there is a hierarchy of understanding. The lowest type of understanding is based on images of empirical objects. Next highest is an understanding of empirical objects themselves, which results only in opinion. Next is an understanding of abstract mathematical principles. Then comes an understanding of the forms. The highest understanding (true knowledge) is an understanding of the form of the good and includes a knowledge of all forms and their organization.

Anaxagoras (ca. 500–428 B.C.) Postulated an infinite number of elements (seeds) from which everything is made. He believed that everything contained all the elements and that a thing's identity is determined by which elements predominate. An exception is the mind, which contains no other element but may combine with other elements, thereby creating life.

Anaximander (ca. 610–547 B.C.) Suggested the "infinite" or "boundless" as the physis and formulated a rudimentary theory of evolution.

Animism The belief that everything in nature is alive.

Anthropomorphism The projection of human attributes onto nonhuman things.

Aristotle (384–322 B.C.) Believed sensory experience to be the basis of all knowledge, although the five senses and the common sense provided only the information from which knowledge could be derived. Aristotle also believed that everything in nature had within it an entelechy (purpose) that determined its potential. Active reason, which was considered the immortal part of the human soul, provided humans with their greatest potential, and therefore fully actualized humans engage in active reason. Because everything was thought to have a cause, Aristotle postulated an unmoved mover that caused everything in the world but was not itself caused. (See also **Unmoved mover.**)

Associationism The philosophical belief that mental phenomena, such as learning, remembering, and imagining, can be explained in terms of the laws of association. (*See also* **Laws of association.**)

Becoming According to Heraclitus, the state of everything in the universe. Nothing is static and unchanging; rather, everything in the universe is dynamic—that is, becoming something other than what it was.

Being Something that is unchanging and thus, in principle, is capable of being known with certainty. Being implies stability and certainty; becoming implies instability and uncertainty.

Common sense According to Aristotle, the faculty located in the heart that synthesizes the information provided by the five senses.

Cosmology The study of the origin, structure, and processes governing the universe.

Democritus (ca. 460–370 B.C.) Offered atoms as the physis. Everything in nature, including humans, was explained in terms of atoms and their activities. His was the first completely materialistic view of the world and of humans.

Dionysiac-Orphic religion Religion whose major belief was that the soul becomes a prisoner of the body because of some transgression committed by the soul. The soul continues on a circle of transmigrations until it has been purged of sin, at which time it can escape its earthly existence and return to its pure, divine existence among the gods. A number of magical practices were thought useful in releasing the soul from its bodily tomb.

Dreaming According to Aristotle, the experience of images retained from waking experience. Dreams are often bizarre because the images experienced during sleep are neither organized by our rational powers nor supported by ongoing sensory experience. That dreams sometimes correspond to future events was, for Aristotle, mere coincidence. However, because bodily processes are exaggerated in dreams, physicians can sometimes use dreams to detect the early signs of disease.

Efficient cause According to Aristotle, the force that transforms a thing.

Eidola (singular, **eidolon**) A tiny replication that some early Greek philosophers thought emanated from the surfaces of things in the environment, allowing the things to be perceived.

Elementism The belief that complex processes can be understood by studying the elements of which they consist.

Empedocles (ca. 490–430 B.C.) Postulated earth, fire, air, and water as the four basic elements from which everything is made and two forces, love and strife, that alternately synthesize and separate those elements. He was also the first philosopher to suggest a theory of perception, and he offered a theory of evolution that emphasized a rudimentary form of natural selection.

Entelechy According to Aristotle, the purpose for which a thing exists and which remains a potential until actualized. Active reason, for example, is the human entelechy, but it exists only as a potential in many humans.

Essence Those indispensable characteristics of a thing that give it its unique identity.

Final cause According to Aristotle, the purpose for which a thing exists.

Formal cause According to Aristotle, the form of a thing.

Forms According to Plato, the pure, abstract realities that are unchanging and timeless and therefore knowable. Such forms create imperfect manifestations of themselves when they interact with matter. It is these imperfect manifestations of the forms that are the objects of our sense impressions. (*See also* **Theory of forms.**)

Galen (ca. A.D. 130–200) Associated each of Hippocrates' four humors with a temperament, thus creating a rudimentary theory of personality.

Golden mean The rule Aristotle suggested people follow to avoid excesses and to live a life of moderation.

Gorgias (ca. 485–380 B.C.) A Sophist who believed the only reality a person can experience is his or her subjective reality and that this reality can never be accurately communicated to another individual.

Heraclitus (ca. 540–480 B.C.) Suggested fire as the physis because in its presence nothing remained the same. He viewed the world as in a constant state of flux and thereby raised the question of what could be known with certainty.

Hippocrates (ca. 460–377 B.C.) Considered the father of modern medicine because he assumed that disease had natural causes, not supernatural ones. Health prevails when the four humors of the body are in balance, disease when there is an imbalance. The physician's task was to facilitate the body's natural tendency to heal itself.

Imagination According to Aristotle, the pondering of the images retained from past experiences.

Inductive definition The technique used by Socrates that examined many individual examples of a concept to discover what they all had in common.

Introspection The careful examination of one's inner experiences.

Law of contiguity A thought of something will tend to cause thoughts of things that are usually experienced along with it.

Law of contrast A thought of something will tend to cause thoughts of opposite things.

Law of frequency In general, the more often events are experienced together, the stronger they become associated in memory.

Law of similarity A thought of something will tend to cause thoughts of similar things.

Laws of association Those laws thought responsible for holding mental events together in memory. For Aristotle, the laws of association consisted of the laws of contiguity, contrast, similarity, and frequency.

Magic Various ceremonies and rituals that are designed to influence spirits.

Material cause According to Aristotle, what a thing is made of.

Nihilism The belief that because what is considered true varies from person to person, any search for universal (interpersonal) truth will fail. In other words, there is no Truth, only truths. The Sophists were nihilists.

Olympian religion The religion based on a belief in the Olympian gods as they were described in the Homeric odes. Olympian religion tended to be favored by the privileged classes, whereas peasants, laborers, and slaves tended to favor the more mys-

tical Dionysiac-Orphic religion. (*See also* **Dionysiac-Orphic religion.**)

Parmenides (born ca. 515 B.C.) Believed that the world was solid, fixed, and motionless, and therefore that all apparent change or motion was an illusion.

Passive reason According to Aristotle, the practical utilization of the information provided by the common sense.

Physicists Those who search for or postulate a physis.

Physis A primary substance or element from which everything is thought to be derived.

Plato (ca. 427–347 B.C.) First a disciple of Socrates, came under the influence of the Pythagoreans, and postulated the existence of an abstract world of forms or ideas that, when manifested in matter, make up the objects in the empirical world. The only true knowledge is that of the forms, a knowledge that can be gained only by reflecting on the innate contents of the soul. Sensory experience interferes with the attainment of knowledge and should be avoided.

Protagoras (ca. 485–410 B.C.) A Sophist who taught that "Man is the measure of all things." In other words, what is considered true varies with a person's personal experiences; therefore, there is no objective truth, only individual versions of what is true.

Pythagoras (ca. 580–500 B.C.) Believed that an abstract world consisting of numbers and numerical relationships exerted an influence on the physical world. He created a dualistic view of humans by saying that in addition to our body, we have a mind (soul), which through reasoning could understand the abstract world of numbers. Furthermore, he believed the human soul to be immortal. Pythagoras' philosophy had a major influence on Plato and, through Christianity, on the entire Western world.

Rational soul According to Aristotle, the soul possessed only by humans. It incorporates the functions of the vegetative and sensitive souls and allows thinking about events in the empirical world (passive reason) and the abstraction of the concepts that characterize events in the empirical world (active reason).

Recall For Aristotle, the active mental search for the recollection of past experiences.

Reductionism The attempt to explain objects or events in one domain by using terminology, concepts, laws, or principles from another domain.

Explaining observable phenomena (domain$_1$) in terms of atomic theory (domain$_2$) would be an example; explaining human behavior and cognition (domain$_1$) in terms of biochemical principles (domain$_2$) would be another. In a sense, it can be said that events in domain$_1$ are *reduced* to events in domain$_2$.

Remembering For Aristotle, the passive recollection of past experiences.

Reminiscence theory of knowledge Plato's belief that knowledge is attained by remembering the experiences the soul had when it dwelled among the forms before entering the body.

Scala naturae Aristotle's description of nature as being arranged in a hierarchy from formless matter to the unmoved mover. In this grand design, the only thing higher than humans was the unmoved mover.

Sensitive soul According to Aristotle, the soul possessed by animals. It includes the functions provided by the vegetative soul and provides the ability to interact with the environment and to retain the information gained from that interaction.

Socrates (ca. 470–399 B.C.) Disagreed with the Sophists' contention that there is no discernible truth beyond individual opinion. Socrates believed that by examining a number of individual manifestations of a concept, the general concept itself could be defined clearly and precisely. These general definitions were stable and knowable and, when known, generated moral behavior.

Solipsism The belief that a person's subjective reality is the only reality that exists and can be known.

Sophists A group of philosopher-teachers who believed that "truth" was what people thought it to be. To convince others that something is "true," one needs effective communication skills, and it was those skills that the Sophists taught.

Teleology The belief that nature is purposive. Aristotle's philosophy was teleological.

Temple medicine The type of medicine practiced by priests in early Greek temples that was characterized by superstition and magic. Individuals such as Alcmaeon and Hippocrates severely criticized temple medicine and were instrumental in displacing such practices with naturalistic medicine—that is, medicine that sought natural causes of disorders rather than supernatural causes.

Thales (ca. 625–547 B.C.) Often called the first philosopher because he emphasized natural instead of supernatural explanations of things. By encouraging the critical evaluation of his ideas and those of others, he is thought to have started the Golden Age of Greek philosophy. He believed water to be the primary element from which everything else was derived.

Theory of forms Plato's contention that ultimate reality consists of abstract ideas or forms that correspond to all objects in the empirical world. Knowledge of these abstractions is innate and can be attained only through introspection.

Transmigration of the soul The Dionysiac-Orphic belief that because of some transgression, the soul is compelled to dwell in one earthly prison after another until it is purified. The transmigration may find the soul at various times in plants, animals, and humans as it seeks redemption.

Unmoved mover According to Aristotle, that which gave nature its purpose, or final cause, but was itself uncaused. In Aristotle's philosophy, the unmoved mover was a logical necessity.

Vegetative soul The soul possessed by plants. It allows only growth, the intake of nutrition, and reproduction.

Xenophanes (ca. 560–478 B.C.) Believed people created gods in their own image. He noted that dark-skinned people created dark-skinned gods and light-skinned people created light-skinned gods. He speculated that the gods created by nonhuman animals would have the characteristics of those animals.

Zeno's paradox The assertion that in order for an object to pass from point A to point B, it must first traverse half the distance between those two points, and then half of the remaining distance, and so forth. Because this process must occur an infinite number of times, Zeno concluded that an object could logically never reach point B.

3

Physiological Influences on Psychology

David K. Makes a Mistake: The Importance of the Human Observer

David Kinnebrook got his shoes shined every night, but that was the only perk he received from his job. Otherwise his work was lonely, tedious, and highly demanding. He had to live in the same building where he worked and to be available from 7 in the morning until 10 at night, seven days a week. In addition, many nights an alarm bell rang in his tiny bedroom, summoning him to work again. For this he was paid a tiny salary, given three meals a day, and, oh yes, he had his shoes shined.

What were the qualifications for this dream job? One of the scientists who operated the facility wrote, "I want indefatigable, hard-working, and above all obedient drudges, men who will be contented to pass their day in using their hands and eyes in the mechanical act of observing and the remainder of it in the dull process of calculations" (quoted in Croarken, 2003, p. 286).

After Kinnebrook finally left, his replacement described the job as follows:

Nothing can exceed the tediousness and *ennui* of the life the assistant leads in this place, excluded from all society, except perhaps that of a poor mouse which may occasionally sally forth from a hole in the wall. . . . Here forlorn, he spends his days, weeks, and months, in the

In Their Own Words:
Original Source
Material on
Psychophysics from
*Elements of
Psychophysics*
(1860), by Gustav
Fechner

The Formal Founding of Psychology

same long wearisome computations, without a friend to shorten the tedious hours, or a soul with whom he can converse" (quoted in Croarken, 2003, p. 285)

The place was the Royal Observatory in Greenwich, England; the year was 1795. Kinnebrook worked as assistant to the Reverend Nevil Maskelyne (1732–1811), the Royal Astronomer. He held the job 1 year, 8 months, and 22 days before he was fired. And he never knew how losing his job would play such an important role in the founding of the new science of psychology.

It all began with a difference of five-tenths of a second. That's not much, you may be thinking, but it was too much for the Royal Astronomer. Maskelyne, when he noticed that Kinnebrook's observations of the time required for a star to pass from one point to another were slower than his own, rebuked the man for his mistakes and warned him to be more careful. Kinnebrook tried, but the differences increased. Maskelyne wrote:

> I think it necessary to mention that my assistant, Mr. David Kinnebrook, who had observed the transits of the stars and planets very well, in agreement with me, all the year 1794, and for the great part of the present year, began, from the beginning of August last, to set them down half a second of time later than he should do, according to my observations; and in January of the succeeding year, 1796, he increased his error to eight-tenths of a second.
>
> As he had unfortunately continued a considerable time in this error before I noticed it, and did not seem to me likely ever to get over it, and return to a right method of observing, therefore, though with reluctance, as he was a diligent and useful assistant to me in other respects, I parted with him (quoted in Howse, 1989, p. 169).

And so Kinnebrook was fired. He passed into that crowded place known as obscurity, never to know that he had not really made errors after all.

For 20 years the Kinnebrook incident was ignored, until the phenomenon was investigated by Friedrich Wilhelm Bessel (1784–1846), a German astronomer interested in errors of measurement. He suspected that the so-called mistakes made by Maskelyne's assistant were attributable to individual differences—personal differences among people over which they have no control. If so, Bessel reasoned, then differences in observation times would be found among all astronomers, a phenomenon that came to be called the "personal equation." Bessel proceeded to test his hypothesis and found it to be correct. Even among the most experienced astronomers, disagreements were common.

Bessel's finding led to two conclusions: (1) astronomers would have to take into account the nature of the human observer, because

Old Royal Observatory, Greenwich, England.

personal characteristics and perceptions would necessarily influence the reported observations; and (2) if the role of the human observer had to be considered in astronomy, then surely it was also important in every other science that relied on observational methods.

Empirical philosophers such as Locke and Berkeley had discussed the subjective nature of human perception, arguing that there is not always—or even often—an exact correspondence between the nature of an object and our perception of it. Bessel's work provided data from a hard science—astronomy—to illustrate and support that point. As a result, scientists were forced to focus on the role of the human observer to account fully for the results of their experiments. They began to study the human sense organs—those physiological mechanisms through which we receive information about our world—as a way of investigating the psychological processes of sensing and perceiving. Once the physiologists began to study sensation in this manner, a science of psychology was but a short and inevitable step away.

Developments in Early Physiology

The physiological research that stimulated and guided the new psychology was a product of the scientific work of the late nineteenth century. As with all such endeavors, it had its antecedents—earlier work on which it built. Physiology became an experimentally oriented discipline during the 1830s, primarily under the influence of the German physiologist Johannes Müller (1801–1858), who advocated the use of the experimental method. Müller held the prestigious position of professor of anatomy and physiology at the University of Berlin. He was phenomenally productive, publishing, on the average, one scholarly paper every seven weeks. He maintained this pace for 38 years before committing suicide during a bout of depression.

One of his most influential publications was the *Handbook of the Physiology of Mankind,* published between 1833 and 1840. These volumes summarized the physiological research of the period and systematized a large body of knowledge. They cited many new studies, indicating the rapid growth in experimental work. The first volume was translated into English in 1838 and the second in 1842, which attests to the interest in physiological research shown by scientists in many countries outside Germany.

Müller is also noteworthy in physiology and psychology for his theory of the specific energies of nerves. He proposed that the stimulation of a particular nerve always leads to a characteristic sensation, because each sensory nerve has its own specific energy. This idea stimulated a great deal of research aimed at localizing functions within the nervous system and pinpointing sensory receptor mechanisms on the periphery of the organism.

Research on Brain Functions: Mapping from the Inside

Several early physiologists made substantial contributions to the study of brain functions by conducting research directly on brain tissue. Their efforts constituted the first attempts to map the brain's functions, that is, to determine the specific parts of the brain that controlled different cognitive functions. This work is significant for psychology not only because it delimited the brain's specialized areas, but also because it refined the research methods that later became widespread in physiological psychology.

A pioneer in the investigation of reflex behavior was Marshall Hall (1790–1857), a Scottish physician working in London. Hall observed that decapitated animals would continue to move for some time when he stimulated various nerve endings. He concluded that different levels of behavior arise from different parts of the brain and nervous system. Specifically, Hall postulated that voluntary movement depends on the cerebrum, reflex movement on the spinal cord, involuntary movement on direct stimulation of the muscles, and respiratory movement on the medulla.

The research of Pierre Flourens (1794–1867), a professor of natural history at the Collège de France in Paris, involved systematically destroying parts of the brain and spinal cord in pigeons and observing the consequences. Flourens concluded that the cerebrum controls higher mental processes, parts of the midbrain control visual and auditory reflexes, the cerebellum controls coordination, and the medulla governs heartbeat, respiration, and other vital functions.

The findings of Hall and Flourens, although generally considered valid, are for our purposes second in importance to their use of the **extirpation** method. In extirpation, the researcher attempts to determine the function of a given part of the brain by removing or destroying it and observing the resulting changes in the animal's behavior.

The mid-nineteenth century saw the introduction of two additional experimental approaches to brain research: the clinical method and the electrical stimulation technique. The **clinical method** was developed in 1861 by Paul Broca (1824–1880), a surgeon at a hospital for the insane near Paris. Broca performed an autopsy on a man who for many years had been unable to speak intelligibly. The clinical examination revealed a lesion in the third frontal convolution of the left hemisphere of the cerebral cortex. Broca labeled this section of the brain the speech center; later it came to be known, appropriately, as *Broca's area*.[1] The clinical method is a useful supplement to extirpation because it is difficult to secure human subjects who agree to the removal of parts of their brain. As a sort of "posthumous extirpation," the clinical method provides the opportunity to examine the damaged area of the brain, the area assumed to be responsible for a behavioral condition that existed while the patient was still alive.

The **electrical stimulation** technique for studying the brain was first promoted in 1870 by Gustav Fritsch and Eduard Hitzig. This technique involves the use of weak electrical currents to explore the cerebral cortex. Fritsch and Hitzig found that stimulating certain cortical areas in rabbits and dogs resulted in motor responses, such as movements of the front and back legs. With the development of increasingly sophisticated electronic equipment, electrical stimulation has become a productive technique for studying brain functions.

Research on Brain Functions: Mapping from the Outside

Among the scientists attempting to map the brain from the inside was the German physician Franz Josef Gall (1758–1828), who dissected

Extirpation: A technique for determining the function of a given part of an animal's brain by removing or destroying it and observing the resulting behavior changes.

Clinical method: Posthumous examination of brain structures to detect damaged areas assumed to be responsible for behavioral conditions that existed before the person died.

Electrical stimulation: A technique for exploring the cerebral cortex with weak electric current to observe motor responses.

---

[1] Broca's brain has been preserved in the Musée de l'Homme in Paris.

the brains of deceased animals and humans. His work confirmed the existence of both white and gray matter in the brain, the nerve fibers connecting each side of the brain to the opposite side of the spinal cord, and the fibers connecting both halves of the brain.

After completing this painstaking research program, Gall turned his attention to the outside of the brain. He wanted to find out if the size and shape of the brain would reveal information about brain faculties. With regard to brain size, his studies on animals showed the tendency for species with larger brains to display more intelligent behavior than species with smaller brains. However, when he began to investigate the shape of the brain, Gall ventured into controversial territory. He founded a movement called cranioscopy, later known as phrenology, which proposed that the shape of a person's skull revealed his or her intellectual and emotional characteristics. In promoting this idea, Gall's reputation plummeted; he was no longer viewed by his colleagues as a respected scientist but rather as a quack and a fraud.

Gall believed that when a mental characteristic—such as conscientiousness, benevolence, or self-esteem—was particularly well developed, there would be a corresponding protrusion or bulge on the surface of the skull in the area controlling that characteristic. If that ability was weak, there would be an indentation in the skull. After examining the bumps and dents of a great many people, Gall mapped the location of 35 human attributes (see Figure 3.1).

Johann Spurzheim, a student of Gall, and George Combe, a Scottish phrenologist, did much to popularize the movement. They traveled throughout Europe and the United States, giving lectures and demonstrations on phrenology. Their success was rapidly overshadowed by two brothers, Orson and Lorenzo Fowler, well-educated sons of a farmer in upstate New York. The Fowler brothers became interested in phrenology from reading the works of Spurzheim and Combe and went on to develop an amazingly successful business enterprise. As described by psychologists Ludy Benjamin and David Baker, millions of Americans had their heads examined and the bumps on their skulls read by the Fowlers and their associates. The brothers

> opened clinics in New York, Boston, and Philadelphia in the late 1830s. They franchised their business to other cities, principally through the training of phrenological examiners, and provided phrenological supplies . . . such as busts for display and teaching, calipers of varying sizes for measurements, display charts for the wall, manuals to sell, and, for the itinerant phrenologists, carrying cases for tools and supplies (Benjamin & Baker, 2004, pp. 4–5).

Theirs was an incredibly profitable business that remained successful well into the twentieth century. They started a magazine, the

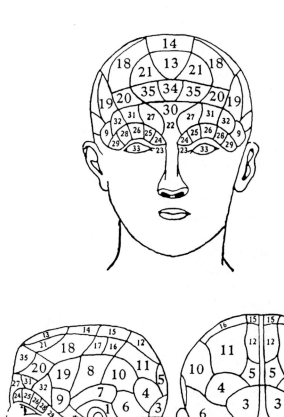

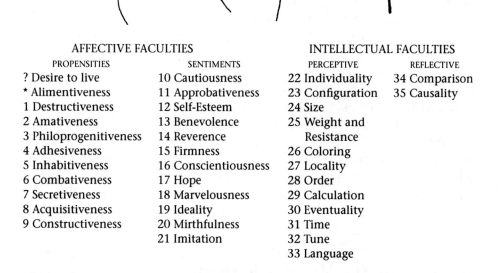

AFFECTIVE FACULTIES

PROPENSITIES	SENTIMENTS
? Desire to live	10 Cautiousness
* Alimentiveness	11 Approbativeness
1 Destructiveness	12 Self-Esteem
2 Amativeness	13 Benevolence
3 Philoprogenitiveness	14 Reverence
4 Adhesiveness	15 Firmness
5 Inhabitiveness	16 Conscientiousness
6 Combativeness	17 Hope
7 Secretiveness	18 Marvelousness
8 Acquisitiveness	19 Ideality
9 Constructiveness	20 Mirthfulness
	21 Imitation

INTELLECTUAL FACULTIES

PERCEPTIVE	REFLECTIVE
22 Individuality	34 Comparison
23 Configuration	35 Causality
24 Size	
25 Weight and Resistance	
26 Coloring	
27 Locality	
28 Order	
29 Calculation	
30 Eventuality	
31 Time	
32 Tune	
33 Language	

Figure 3.1   The power and organs of the mind.

Suggested by J. Spurzheim. *Phrenology, or the Doctrine of Mental Phenomena*, 1834.

American Phrenological Journal, in 1838, which was published for more than 70 years. Clients arrived in such huge numbers that the practice often resembled a carnival sideshow. Phrenologists went from town to town, "visiting during market days, setting themselves up for a short time, and offering their services for a fee. . . . they sold books and charts, much as today's rock groups sell T-shirts and posters at their concerts" (Sokal, 2001, p. 25).

Phrenological societies were formed, and the reading of heads become so widespread that many American businesses used the technique to select their employees. Phrenology practitioners claimed they could use it to assess a child's level of intelligence and to counsel couples experiencing marriage difficulties. Thus, the belief that phrenology could be applied to practical problems was a major reason for its success in the United States.

The most effective criticism of Gall's original cranioscopy theory grew out of the brain research conducted by Pierre Flourens. By systematically destroying parts of the brain (using the method of extirpation), Flourens found that the shape of the skull did not match the contours of the underlying brain tissue. In addition, brain tissue was too soft to produce changes such as bulges and dents in the bony surface of the skull. Flourens and other physiologists also demonstrated that the areas Gall designated for specific mental functions were in error. So while you may now be feeling your own skull for bumps, you can be assured that they do not reveal anything about your intellectual or emotional functioning.

Gall failed in his attempt to map the brain from the outside, but his ideas reinforced the growing belief among scientists that through the application of extirpation, clinical, and electrical stimulation methods, it was possible to localize specific brain functions.

There is a lesson to be learned from the success and later failure of phrenology that is applicable to all movements in all time periods. There is not necessarily a relationship between the popularity of an idea, trend, or school of thought and its validity. Daniel Robinson, a noted historian of psychology, observed that "Gall's phrenology flourished as long as has psychoanalytic theory [and] its findings and sayings filled a score of journals. . . . Educated citizens in all the right and interesting centers of culture were serious about palpating each other's heads. Thus does another moral lesson intrude itself: Impact *per se* establishes nothing regarding the validity or adequacy of works" (Robinson, 2003, p. 200). In other words, just because something is popular does not mean it is true.

Research on the Nervous System

Considerable research on the structure of the nervous system and the nature of neural activity also was being conducted during this period.

Recall the two early descriptions of neural activity: Descartes's nerve tube theory and Hartley's theory of vibrations.

Toward the end of the eighteenth century, the Italian researcher Luigi Galvani (1737–1798) had suggested that nerve impulses were electrical. Galvani's work was continued by his nephew, Giovanni Aldini. One historian wrote that Aldini "mixed serious research with showmanship. One of the more gruesome of Aldini's displays, designed to emphasize the effectiveness of electrical stimulation for obtaining spasmodic movements from muscles, involved using the recently severed heads of two criminals" (Boakes, 1984, p. 96).

Experimental work proceeded so rapidly that by the middle of the nineteenth century, scientists accepted as fact the electrical nature of nerve impulses. They came to believe that the nervous system was essentially a conductor of electrical impulses and that the central nervous system functioned like a switching station, shunting the impulses onto either sensory or motor nerve fibers.

Although this position was a great advance over Descartes's nerve tube theory and Hartley's theory of vibrations, it was conceptually similar. Both the newer and the older viewpoints were reflexive: Something from the external world (a stimulus) made an impact on a sense organ and thereby excited a nerve impulse. The nerve impulse traveled to the appropriate place in the brain or central nervous system. There, in response to the impulse, a new impulse was generated and transmitted along the motor nerves to trigger the organism's response.

The direction of travel for nerve impulses in the brain and spinal cord was revealed by the Spanish physician Santiago Ramón y Cajal (1852–1934), a professor of anatomy at the medical school of the University of Zaragoza and director of the Zaragoza Museum. For his discoveries, he received the Helmholtz Medal from the Royal Academy of Sciences in Berlin in 1905 and the Nobel Prize in 1906. Because the Spanish language was not used in the scientific journals of the day, however, Ramón y Cajal had difficulty communicating his findings to the scholarly community. Frustrated, he "was often saddened to read of 'new' discoveries in English, German, or French journals that were really rediscoveries of his own work published much earlier in Spanish" (Padilla, 1980, p. 116). His situation presents another instructive example of the barriers faced by scientists who work outside the mainstream culture.

Researchers also were investigating the anatomical structure of the nervous system. They found that nerve fibers were composed of separate structures (neurons) that somehow were connected at specific points (synapses). These findings were consistent with a mechanistic image of human functioning. Scientists believed that the nervous system, like the mind, was made up of atomistic structures—bits of matter that combined to produce a more complex product.

The Mechanistic Spirit

The spirit of mechanism was dominant in nineteenth-century physiology, as it was in the philosophy of that time. Nowhere was this spirit more pronounced than in Germany. In the 1840s, a group of scientists, many of them former students of Johannes Müller, founded the Berlin Physical Society. These scientists, all in their twenties, were committed to a single proposition: that all phenomena could be accounted for by the principles of physics.

What they hoped to do was connect physiology with physics, that is, to develop a physiology in the framework of mechanism. In a dramatic gesture, four of the scientists swore a solemn oath, signing it, according to legend, with their own blood. Their declaration stated that the only forces active within an organism are the common physicochemical ones. And so the threads came together in nineteenth-century physiology: materialism, mechanism, empiricism, experimentation, and measurement.

The developments in early physiology indicate the kinds of research techniques and the discoveries that supported a scientific approach to the psychological investigation of the mind. While philosophers were paving the way for an experimental attack on the mind, physiologists were experimentally investigating the mechanisms that underlie mental phenomena. The next step was to apply the experimental method to the mind itself.

The British empiricists had argued that sensation was the only source of knowledge. The astronomer Bessel had demonstrated the impact on observation of individual differences in sensation and perception. Physiologists were defining the structure and function of the senses. It was time to experiment with and to quantify this doorway to the mind: the subjective, mentalistic experience of sensation. Techniques had been available to investigate the body; now they were being developed to explore the mind. Experimental psychology was ready to begin.

The Beginnings of Experimental Psychology

Four scientists can be credited with the initial applications of the experimental method to the mind, the subject matter of the new psychology: Hermann von Helmholtz, Ernst Weber, Gustav Theodor Fechner, and Wilhelm Wundt. All were German scientists who had been trained in physiology, and all were aware of the impressive developments in modern science.

Why Germany?

The sciences were developing in most of Western Europe in the nineteenth century, particularly in England, France, and Germany. No one nation had a monopoly on the enthusiasm, conscientiousness, or optimism with which the tools of science were being applied to a variety of research problems. Why, then, did experimental psychology begin in Germany and not in England, France, or elsewhere? The answer seems to lie in certain unique characteristics that made German science a more fertile breeding ground for the new psychology.

The German approach to science. For a century, German intellectual history had paved the way for an experimental science of psychology. Experimental physiology was firmly established and recognized to a degree not yet achieved in France and England. The so-called German temperament was well suited to the precise description and classification work needed in biology, zoology, and physiology. Whereas scientists in France and England favored the deductive, mathematical approach, German scientists—with their emphasis on the careful, thorough collection of observable facts—adopted an inductive approach.

Because biological and physiological sciences do not lend themselves to grand generalizations from which facts can be deduced, biology was accepted only slowly by the scientific communities of England and France. In contrast, Germany, with its faith in taxonomic description and classification, welcomed biology to its family of sciences.

Further, the Germans defined science broadly. Science in France and England was limited to physics and chemistry, which could be approached quantitatively. Science in Germany included such areas as phonetics, linguistics, history, archaeology, esthetics, logic, even literary criticism. French and English scholars were skeptical about applying science to the complex human mind. Not so the Germans, and they plunged ahead, unconstrained, using the tools of science to explore and measure all facets of mental life.

The reform movement in German universities. In the early nineteenth century, a wave of educational reform swept over German universities devoted to the principles of academic freedom. Professors were encouraged to teach whatever they wished, without outside interference, and to conduct research on topics of their choice. Students were free to take whatever courses they preferred, unrestricted by a fixed curriculum. This freedom—unknown in English and French universities—also extended to the consideration of new areas of scientific inquiry, such as psychology.

The German style of university provided the ideal environment for the flourishing of scientific inquiry. Professors could not only lecture on whatever interested them, but they could also direct students in experimental research in well-equipped laboratories. No other country actively promoted such an approach to science.

Germany also provided greater opportunities to learn and practice new scientific techniques; here we see the impact of prevailing economic conditions (a contextual factor). Germany had many universities. Prior to 1870, the year it became a unified nation with a central government, Germany had consisted of a loose confederation of autonomous kingdoms, duchies, and city-states. Each of these districts had a well-financed university with a highly paid faculty and state-of-the-art laboratory equipment.

England at that time had only two universities—Oxford and Cambridge—and neither facilitated, encouraged, or supported scientific research in any discipline. Further, they opposed adding new fields of study to the curriculum. In 1877, Cambridge vetoed a request to teach experimental psychology because it would "insult religion by putting the human soul on a pair of scales" (Hearnshaw, 1987, p. 125). Experimental psychology would not be taught at Cambridge for another 20 years and was not offered at Oxford until 1936. The only way to practice science in England was in the manner of the gentleman-scientist, living on an independent income, the way of Charles Darwin or Francis Galton (chapter 6). The situation was similar in France.

The United States had no universities devoted to research until 1876, when Johns Hopkins University was founded in Baltimore, Maryland. This new university was based strongly on the German model. Its primary goal was to make scientific research the core and focus of graduate student training. Indeed, Baltimore itself was considered "a little fragment of Germany that had resettled on the eastern seaboard." According to the psychologist and philosopher John Dewey (see chapter 7), "students and teachers [in the club room at Hopkins] met to drink German beer and sing German songs" (quoted in Martin, 2002, p. 56).

Nevertheless, there were more opportunities for scientific research in Germany than in other countries. In pragmatic terms, we may say that a person could make a living as a research scientist in Germany but not in France, England, or the United States. Thus, the chances of becoming a well-paid, respected professor were higher in Germany than elsewhere, although it remained difficult to attain the very top positions. The promising university scientist was required to produce research judged by peers to be a major contribution, research more significant than the typical doctoral dissertation. Consequently, most of the people selected for university careers were of extremely high caliber, and once these scientists joined the faculty, the pressure on them to publish was fierce.

Although the competition was intense and the demands high, the rewards were more than worth the effort. Only the best succeeded in nineteenth-century German science, and the result was a series of breakthroughs in all sciences, including the new psychology. Thus, it is no coincidence that the people directly responsible for the growth of scientific psychology were German university professors.

Hermann von Helmholtz (1821–1894)

Archives of the History of American Psychology/University of Akron

One of the greatest scientists of the nineteenth century, Hermann von Helmholtz was a prolific researcher in physics and physiology. Psychology ranked third among his areas of scientific contribution, yet his work, together with that of Fechner and Wundt, was instrumental in beginning the new psychology. He emphasized a mechanistic and deterministic approach, assuming that the human sense organs functioned like machines. He also liked technical analogies— for example, comparing the transmission of nerve impulses to the operation of the telegraph (see Ash, 1995).

Hermann von Helmholtz

Helmholtz's Life

Born in Potsdam, Germany, where his father taught at the *Gymnasium* (in Europe, a high school/junior college preparatory for the university), Helmholtz was tutored at home because of his delicate health. At 17, he enrolled in a Berlin medical institute where no tuition was charged to students who agreed to become army surgeons after graduation. Helmholtz served for seven years, during which time he continued his studies in mathematics and physics and published several articles. In a paper on the indestructibility of energy, he mathematically formulated the law of the conservation of energy. After leaving the army, Helmholtz accepted a position as associate professor of physiology at the University of Königsberg. Over the next 30 years, he held academic appointments in physiology at universities in Bonn and Heidelberg, and in physics at Berlin.

The tremendously energetic Helmholtz delved into several scholarly areas. In doing research on physiological optics, he invented the ophthalmoscope, a device still used to examine the retina of the eye. This revolutionary instrument made possible diagnosis and treatment of retinal disorders. As a result, Helmholtz's name "spread quickly throughout the academic and public worlds. At a stroke he achieved career advancement and worldly recognition" (Cahan, 1993, p. 574). All by the age of 30.

Helmholtz's three-volume work on physiological optics (*Handbook of Physiological Optics*, 1856–1866) proved to be so influential and

The Helmholtz motor, powered by an electromagnetic device, generated energy for many laboratory instruments.

Archives of the History of American Psychology/University of Akron.

enduring that it was translated into English 60 years later. He published research on acoustical problems in *On the Sensations of Tone* (1863), which summarized his own findings plus the rest of the available literature. He also wrote on such diverse subjects as afterimages, color blindness, the Arabian-Persian musical scale, human eye movements, the formation of glaciers, geometrical axioms, and hay fever. In later years, Helmholtz contributed indirectly to the invention of wireless telegraphy and radio.

In the fall of 1893, returning from a trip to the United States that included a visit to the Chicago World's Fair, Helmholtz suffered a fall aboard ship. Less than a year later, he had a stroke that left him semiconscious and delirious. His wife wrote: "His thoughts ramble on confusedly, real life and dream life, time and scene, all float mistily by in his brain. . . . It is as if his soul were far, far away, in a beautiful ideal world, swayed only by science and the eternal laws" (quoted in Koenigsberger, 1965, p. 429).

Helmholtz's Contributions: The Neural Impulse, Vision, and Audition

Of major importance to psychology are Helmholtz's investigations of the speed of the neural impulse and his research on vision and hearing. Scientists had assumed that the nerve impulse was instantaneous, or at least that it traveled too fast to be measured. Helmholtz provided the first empirical measurement of the rate of conduction by stimulating a motor nerve and the attached muscle in the leg of a frog. He arranged the demonstration so that the precise moment of stimulation and of the resulting movement could be recorded. Working with nerves of different length, he recorded the delay between stimulation of the nerve near the muscle and the muscle's response, and did the same for stimulation farther from the muscle. These measurements yielded the conduction speed of the neural impulse: 90 feet per second.

Helmholtz also experimented on the reaction times for sensory nerves in human subjects, studying the complete circuit from stimulation of a sense organ to the resulting motor response. The findings showed such enormous individual differences—as well as differences for the same person from one trial to the next—that he abandoned the research.

Helmholtz's demonstration that the speed of conduction was not instantaneous suggested that thought and movement follow each other at a measurable interval and do not occur simultaneously, as had been thought. Helmholtz was interested, however, in the measurement itself and not its psychological significance. Later, the implications of his research for the new psychology were recognized by others, who made reaction-time experiments a fruitful line of research. Helmholtz's work was one of the earliest instances of experimentation and measurement for a psychophysiological process.

His studies on vision also had an impact on the new psychology. Helmholtz investigated the external eye muscles and the mechanism by which internal eye muscles focus the lens. He revised and extended a theory of color vision published in 1802 by Thomas Young; this work is now known as the Young-Helmholtz theory of color vision. No less important is Helmholtz's research on audition, specifically, the perception of tones, the nature of harmony and discord, and the problem of resonance. The enduring influence of his ideas and experiments is evident from the fact that they are still cited in modern psychology textbooks.

He focused on the applied or practical benefits of scientific research. He did not believe in conducting experiments just to accumulate data. In his view, the mission of a scientist was to gather information and to extend or apply that growing body of knowledge to practical problems. We see the further development of this approach in the functionalist school of psychology that took root in the United States (chapters 7 and 8).

Helmholtz was not a psychologist, nor was psychology his major interest, but he contributed a large and important body of knowledge to the study of the human senses and thus helped to strengthen the experimental approach to the study of psychological issues.

ERNST WEBER

Archives of the History of American Psychology/University of Akron.

Ernst Weber (1795–1878)

Ernst Weber, the son of a theology professor, was born in Wittenberg, Germany. He earned his doctorate at the University of Leipzig in 1815 and taught anatomy and physiology there from 1817 until his retirement in 1871. His primary research interest was the physiology of the sense organs, an area in which he made outstanding contributions. Thus, he applied physiology's experimental methods to problems of a psychological nature. Previous research on the sense organs had been conducted almost exclusively on the higher senses of vision and hearing. Weber explored new fields, notably cutaneous (skin) senses and muscular sensations.

Two-Point Thresholds

A significant contribution to the new psychology involved Weber's experimental determination of the accuracy of the two-point discrimination of the skin—that is, the distance between two points that must be spanned before subjects report feeling two distinct sensations. Without looking at the apparatus, which resembles a drawing compass, subjects are asked to report whether they feel one or two points touching the skin. When the two points of stimulation are close together, subjects report a sensation of being touched at only one point. As the distance between the two sources of stimulation is increased, subjects report uncertainty about whether they feel one or two sensations. Finally, a distance is reached where subjects report two distinct points of touch.

This procedure demonstrates the **two-point threshold**, the point at which the two separate sources of stimulation can be distinguished. Weber's research marks the first systematic, experimental demonstration of the concept of threshold (the point at which a psychological effect begins to be produced), an idea widely used in psychology from its beginnings to the present day. (In chapter 13 we discuss the concept of threshold as it applies to consciousness—to that point at which unconscious ideas in the mind become conscious.)

Just Noticeable Differences

Two-point threshold: The threshold at which two points of stimulation can be distinguished as such.

Just noticeable difference: The smallest difference that can be detected between two physical stimuli.

Weber's research led to the formulation of psychology's first quantitative law. He wanted to determine the **just noticeable difference** (jnd)—that is, the smallest difference between weights that could be detected. He asked his subjects to lift two weights—a standard weight and a comparison weight—and to report whether one felt heavier than the other. Small differences between the weights resulted in judgments of sameness; large differences resulted in judgments of disparity between the weights.

As his research program progressed, Weber found that the just noticeable difference between two weights was a constant ratio, 1:40, of the standard weight. In other words, a weight of 41 grams was reported to be "just noticeably different" from a standard weight of 40 grams, and an 82-gram weight was just noticeably different from a standard weight of 80 grams.

Weber then asked how muscle sensations might contribute to a person's ability to distinguish between the weights. He found that subjects could make such discriminations much more accurately when they lifted the weights themselves (by receiving muscular sensations in hands and arms) than when the experimenter placed the weights in their hands. Actually hefting the weights involved tactile (touch) and muscular sensations, whereas when the weights were placed in the palms, only tactile sensations were experienced.

Because subjects could detect smaller differences between the weights when the weights were lifted (a ratio of 1:40) than when the weights were placed in the hand (a ratio of 1:30), Weber concluded that the internal muscular sensations in the first instance must have an influence on the subjects' ability to discriminate.

From these experiments, Weber suggested that discrimination among sensations depended not on the absolute difference between two weights but on their relative difference or ratio. His experiments on visual discrimination found that the ratio was smaller than for the muscle sense experiments. He then proposed a constant ratio for the just noticeable difference between two stimuli that would be consistent for each of the human senses.

Weber's research showed that there is not a direct correspondence between a physical stimulus and our perception of it. Like Helmholtz, however, Weber was interested only in the physiological processes and did not appreciate the significance of his work for psychology. His research provided a method for investigating the relationship between body and mind—between the stimulus and the resulting sensation. This was a vital breakthrough; what was required now was for someone to act on its importance.

Weber's experiments stimulated additional research and focused the attention of later physiologists on the usefulness of the experimental method for studying psychological phenomena. Weber's research on thresholds and the measurement of sensations was of paramount importance to the new psychology and has influenced virtually every aspect of psychology to the present day.

Gustav Theodor Fechner (1801–1887)

Gustav Theodor Fechner was a scholar who followed diverse intellectual pursuits during a remarkably active life. He was a physiologist for 7 years, a physicist for 15, a psychophysicist for 14, an experimental

GUSTAV THEODOR FECHNER

estheticist for 11, a philosopher for 40—and an invalid for 12. Of these endeavors, the work on psychophysics brought his greatest fame, although he did not wish to be so remembered by posterity.

Fechner's Life

Fechner was born in a village in southeastern Germany where his father was the minister. He began medical studies at the University of Leipzig in 1817 and while there attended Weber's lectures on physiology. Fechner remained at Leipzig for the rest of his life.

Even before he graduated from medical school, Fechner's humanistic viewpoint rebelled against the prevailing mechanism of his scientific training. Under the pen name "Dr. Mises" he wrote satirical essays ridiculing medicine and science. This conflict between the two sides of his personality persisted throughout his life—his interest in science and his interest in the metaphysical. Obviously troubled by the current atomistic approach to science, he subscribed to what he called his "day view"—that the universe can be regarded from the standpoint of consciousness. This stood in opposition to the prevailing "night view"—that the universe, including consciousness, consisted of nothing but inert matter.

After completing his medical studies, Fechner began a career in physics and mathematics at Leipzig and also translated handbooks of physics and chemistry from French into German. By 1830, he had translated more than a dozen volumes, and this activity brought him recognition as a physicist. In 1824, he began lecturing in physics at the university and conducting his own research. By the late 1830s, he had become interested in the problem of sensation, and while investigating visual afterimages, he seriously injured his eyes by looking directly at the sun through colored glasses.

In 1833, Fechner obtained the prestigious appointment of professor at Leipzig, whereupon he fell into a depression that endured for several years. He complained of exhaustion and had difficulty sleeping. He could not digest food, and even though his body approached starvation, he felt no hunger. He was unusually sensitive to light and spent most of his time in a darkened room whose walls were painted black, listening while his mother read to him through a narrowly opened door.

He tried to take long walks—at first only at night, when it was dark, and then in daylight with his eyes bandaged—hoping to ease the boredom and gloom. As a form of catharsis, he composed riddles and poems. He dabbled in alternative medical therapies, including laxatives, electric shock, steam treatments, and the application of burning substances to the skin; none of them provided a cure.

Fechner's illness may have been neurotic in nature. This idea is supported by the bizarre way in which he recovered. A friend reported a dream in which she prepared him a meal of raw spiced ham marinated in Rhine wine and lemon juice. The next day she fixed the dish and brought it to Fechner. He tasted it, reluctantly, but ate more and more of the ham every day, declaring that he felt somewhat better. The improvement in his condition was short lived, and after 6 months, the symptoms worsened to the point where he feared for his sanity. Fechner wrote: "I had the distinct feeling that my mind was hopelessly lost unless I could stem the flood of disturbing thoughts. Often the least important matters bothered me in this manner and it took me often hours, even days, to rid myself of these worries" (Kuntze, 1892, quoted in Balance & Bringmann, 1987, p. 42).

Fechner forced himself to undertake routine chores—a sort of occupational therapy—but was limited to tasks that did not make demands on his mind or his eyes. "I made strings and bandages, dipped candles . . . rolled yarn and helped in the kitchen sorting [and] cleaning lentils, making bread crumbs, and grinding a sugarloaf into powdered sugar. I also peeled and chopped carrots and turnips . . . a thousand times I wished to be dead" (Fechner in Kuntze, 1892, quoted in Balance & Bringmann, 1987, p. 43).

In time, Fechner's interest in the world around him revived, and he maintained the diet of wine-soaked ham. He had a dream in which the number 77 appeared, persuading him that he would be well in 77 days. And of course he was. His depression turned to euphoria and delusions of grandeur, and he claimed God had chosen him to solve all the world's mysteries. Out of this experience he developed the notion of the pleasure principle, which many years later influenced the work of Sigmund Freud (see chapter 13).

Fechner lived to the age of 86, in excellent health, and made major contributions to science, despite the fact that more than 40 years earlier the University of Leipzig had declared him an invalid and paid him an annual pension for the rest of his life.

Mind and Body: A Quantitative Relationship

October 22, 1850, is a significant date in the history of psychology. While lying in bed that morning, Fechner had a flash of insight about the connection between mind and body: It could be found, he said, in a quantitative relationship between a mental sensation and a material stimulus.

An increase in the intensity of a stimulus, Fechner argued, does not produce a one-to-one increase in the intensity of the sensation. Rather, a geometric series characterizes the stimulus and an arithmetic series characterizes the sensation.

For example, adding the sound of one bell to that of an already ringing bell produces a greater increase in sensation than adding one bell to 10 others already ringing. Therefore, the effects of stimulus intensities are not absolute but are relative to the amount of sensation that already exists.

What this simple yet brilliant revelation means is that the amount of sensation (the mental quality) depends on the amount of stimulation (the physical quality). To measure the change in sensation, we must measure the change in stimulation. Thus, it is possible to formulate a quantitative or numerical relationship between the mental and material worlds. Fechner crossed the barrier between body and mind by relating one to the other empirically, making it possible to conduct experiments on the mind.

Although the concept was now clear to Fechner, how was he to proceed? A researcher would have to measure precisely both the subjective and the objective, the mental sensation and the physical stimulus. To measure the physical intensity of the stimulus—such as the level of brightness of a light or the weight of a standard object—was not difficult, but how to measure sensation, the conscious experiences the subjects reported when they responded to the stimulus?

Fechner proposed two ways to measure sensations. First, we can determine whether a stimulus is present or absent, sensed or not sensed. Second, we can measure the stimulus intensity at which subjects report that the sensation first occurs; this is the **absolute threshold** of sensitivity—a point of intensity below which no sensation is reported and above which subjects do experience a sensation.

Although the idea of an absolute threshold is useful, its usefulness is limited because only one value of a sensation—its lowest level—can be determined. To relate both intensities, we must be able to specify the full range of stimulus values and their resulting sensation values. To accomplish this, Fechner proposed the **differential threshold** of sensitivity: the least amount of change in a stimulus that gives rise to a change in sensation. For example, by how much must a weight be increased or decreased before subjects will sense the change—before they will report a just noticeable difference in sensation?

To measure how heavy a particular weight feels to a person (how heavy a subject senses it to be), we cannot use the physical measurement of the object's weight. But we can use that physical measurement as a basis for measuring the sensation's psychological intensity.

Absolute threshold: The point of sensitivity below which no sensations can be detected and above which sensations can be experienced.

Differential threshold: The point of sensitivity at which the least amount of change in a stimulus gives rise to a change in sensation.

First, we measure by how much the weight must be decreased in intensity before a subject is barely able to discriminate the difference. Second, we change the weight of the object to this lower value and measure the size of the differential threshold again. Because both weight changes are just barely noticeable to the subject, Fechner assumed they were subjectively equal.

This process can be repeated until the object is barely felt by the subject. If every decrease in weight is subjectively equal to every other decrease, then the number of times the weight must be decreased—the number of just noticeable differences—can be taken as an objective measure of the subjective magnitude of the sensation. In this way we are measuring the stimulus values necessary to create a difference between two sensations.

Fechner suggested that for each of the human senses there is a certain relative increase in stimulus intensity that always produces an observable change in the intensity of the sensation. Thus, the sensation (the mind or mental quality), as well as the stimulus (the body or material quality), can be measured. The relationship between the two can be stated in the form of an equation: $S = K \log R$, in which S is the magnitude of the sensation, K is a constant, and R is the magnitude of the stimulus. The relationship is logarithmic; one series increases arithmetically and the other geometrically.

In his later writings, Fechner noted that this idea for describing the mind-body relationship had not been suggested to him by Weber's work, even though he had attended Weber's lectures at the University of Leipzig and Weber had published on the topic a few years earlier. Fechner maintained that he did not discover Weber's work until after he had begun the experiments designed to test his hypothesis. It was only some time later that Fechner realized that the principle to which he gave mathematical form was essentially what Weber's work had shown.

Methods of Psychophysics

The immediate result of Fechner's insight was his research on **psychophysics.** (The word defines itself: the relationship between the mental [*psycho-*] and material [*physics*] worlds.) In the course of this work, which included experiments on lifted weights, visual brightness, visual distance, and tactile distance, Fechner developed one and systematized two of the three fundamental methods used in psychophysics research today.

The method of average error, or method of adjustment, consists in having subjects adjust a variable stimulus until they perceive it to be equal to a constant standard stimulus. Over a number of trials, the mean, or average, value of the differences between the standard stimulus and the subjects' setting of the variable stimulus represents the error of observation. This technique is useful for measuring reaction times as well as visual and auditory discriminations. In a larger sense, it is basic to much psychological research; every time we calculate a mean we are essentially using the method of average error.

The method of constant stimuli involves two constant stimuli, and the aim is to measure the stimulus difference required to produce a given proportion of correct judgments. For example, subjects first lift a standard weight of 100 grams and then lift a comparison weight of, say, 88, 92, 96, 104, or 108 grams. The subjects must judge whether the second weight is heavier, lighter, or equal to the first.

Psychophysics: The scientific study of the relations between mental and physical processes.

In the method of limits, two stimuli (for example, two weights) are presented to the subjects. One stimulus is increased or decreased until subjects report that they detect a difference. Data are obtained from a number of trials, and the just noticeable differences are averaged to determine the differential threshold.

Fechner's psychophysics research program lasted seven years. He published two brief papers in 1858 and 1859, and in 1860 offered the complete exposition in the *Elements of Psychophysics,* a textbook of the exact science of the "functionally dependent relations . . . of the material and the mental, of the physical and psychological worlds" (Fechner, 1860/1966, p. 7). This book is an outstanding original contribution to the development of scientific psychology. Fechner's statement of the quantitative relationship between stimulus intensity and sensation was considered, at the time, to be of comparable importance to the discovery of the laws of gravity.

The following material is a portion of *Elements of Psychophysics,* in which Fechner discussed the difference between matter and mind, between the stimulus and the resulting sensation. In the section reprinted here, Fechner also distinguishes between what he called "inner" and "outer" psychophysics. Inner psychophysics refers to the relationship between the sensation and the accompanying brain and nerve excitation. It was not possible, in Fechner's day, to measure precisely such physiological processes. Therefore, he chose to deal with outer psychophysics, the relationship between the stimulus and the subjective intensity of the sensation, as measured by his psychophysical methods.

 In Their Own Words

Original Source Material on Psychophysics from *Elements of Psychophysics* (1860)
Gustav Fechner

Psychophysics should be understood here as an exact theory of the functionally dependent relations of body and soul or, more generally, of the material and the mental, of the physical and the psychological worlds.

We count as mental, psychological, or belonging to the soul, all that can be grasped by introspective observation or that can be abstracted from it; as bodily, corporeal, physical, or material, all that can be grasped by observation from the outside or abstracted from it. These designations refer only to those aspects of the world of appearance, with whose relationships psychophysics will have to occupy itself, provided that one understands inner and outer observation in the sense of everyday language to refer to the activities through which alone existence becomes apparent.

In any case, all discussions and investigations of psychophysics relate only to the apparent phenomena of the material and mental worlds, to a world that either appears directly through introspection or through outside observation, or that can be deduced from its appearance or grasped as a phenomenological relationship, category, association, deduction, or law. Briefly, psychophysics refers to the *physical* in the sense of physics and chemistry, and to the *psychical* in the sense of experiential psychology, without referring back in any way to the nature of the body or of the soul beyond the phenomenal in the metaphysical sense.

In general, we call the psychic a dependent function of the physical, and vice versa, insofar as there exists between them such a constant or lawful relationship that, from the presence and changes of one, we can deduce those of the other.

The existence of a functional relationship between body and mind is, in general, not denied; nevertheless, there exists a still unresolved dispute over the reasons for this fact, and the interpretation and extent of it.

With no regard to the metaphysical points of this argument (points which concern rather more the so-called essence than the appearance), psychophysics undertakes to determine the actual functional relationship between the modes of appearance of body and mind as exactly as possible.

What things belong together quantitatively and qualitatively, distant and close, in the material and in the mental world? What are the laws governing their changes in the same or in opposite directions? These are the questions in general that psychophysics asks and tries to answer with exactitude.

In other words, but still with the same meaning: what belong together in the inner and outer modes of appearance of things, and what laws exist regarding their respective changes?

Insofar as a functional relationship linking body and mind exists, there is actually nothing to prevent us from looking at it and pursuing it from the one direction rather than from the other. One can illustrate this relationship suitably by means of a mathematical function, an equation between the variables x and y, where each variable can be looked upon at will as a function of the other, and where each is dependent upon the changes of the other. There is a reason, however, why psychophysics prefers to make the approach from the side of the dependence of the mind on the body rather than the contrary, for it is only the physical that is immediately open to measurement, whereas the measurement of the psychical can be obtained only as dependent on the physical. . . .

By its nature, psychophysics may be divided into an outer and an inner part, depending on whether consideration is focused on the relationship of the psychical to the body's external aspects, or on those internal functions with which the psychic are closely related. . . .

The truly basic empirical evidence for the whole of psychophysics can be sought only in the realm of outer psychophysics, inasmuch as it is only this part that is available to immediate experience. Our point of departure therefore has to be taken from outer psychophysics. However, there can be no development of outer psychophysics without constant regard to inner psychophysics, in view of the fact that the body's external world is functionally related to the mind only by the mediation of the body's internal world. . . .

Psychophysics, already related to psychology and physics by name, must on the one hand be based on psychology, and on the other hand promises to give psychology a mathematical foundation. From physics outer psychophysics borrows aids and methodology; inner psychophysics leans more to physiology and anatomy, particularly of the nervous system, with which a certain acquaintance is presupposed. . . .

Sensation depends on stimulation; a stronger sensation depends on a stronger stimulus; the stimulus, however, causes sensation only via the intermediate action of some internal process of the body. To the extent that lawful relationships between sensation and stimulus can be found, they must include lawful relationships between the stimulus and this inner physical activity, which obey the same general laws of interaction of bodily processes and thereby give us a basis for drawing general conclusions about the nature of this inner activity. . . .

Quite apart from their import for inner psychophysics, these lawful relationships, which may be ascertained in the area of outer psychophysics, have their own importance. Based on them, as we shall see, physical measurement yields a psychic measurement, on which we can base arguments that in their turn are of importance and interest.

At the beginning of the nineteenth century, the German philosopher Immanuel Kant insisted that psychology could never be a science because it was impossible to experiment on or measure psychological processes. Because of Fechner's work—which, indeed, made it possible to measure mental phenomena—Kant's assertion could no longer be taken seriously. And it was largely because of Fechner's psychophysical research that Wilhelm Wundt conceived his plan for an experimental psychology. Fechner's methods have proved applicable to a wider range of psychological problems than he ever imagined. Most important, he gave psychology what every discipline must possess if it is to be called a science: precise and elegant techniques of measurement.

The Formal Founding of Psychology

By the middle of the nineteenth century, the methods of the natural sciences were being used to investigate purely mental phenomena. Techniques had been developed, apparatus devised, important books written, and widespread interest aroused. British empirical philosophers and astronomers emphasized the importance of the senses, and

German scientists were describing how the senses functioned. The positivist intellectual spirit of the times, the Zeitgeist, encouraged the convergence of these two lines of thought. Still lacking, however, was someone to bring them together, someone to "found" the new science. This final touch was provided by Wilhelm Wundt.

Discussion Questions

1. What was David Kinnebrook's role in the development of the new psychology?
2. What was the significance of Bessel's work for the new psychology? How did it relate to the work of Locke, Berkeley, and other empirical philosophers?
3. How did developments in early physiology support the mechanistic image of human nature?
4. Discuss the methods that scientists developed to map brain functions.
5. Describe Gall's cranioscopy method and the popular movement that derived from it. How were they discredited?
6. What was the ultimate goal of the Berlin Physical Society?
7. Explain how developments in physiology combined with British empiricism to produce the new psychology.
8. For what reasons did experimental psychology emerge in Germany and not elsewhere?
9. What is the significance of Helmholtz's research on the speed of the neural impulse?
10. Describe Weber's research on two-point thresholds and on just noticeable differences. What was the importance of these ideas for psychology?
11. What was Fechner's insight on October 22, 1850? How did Fechner measure sensations?
12. What is the relationship between the intensity of the stimulus and the intensity of the sensation, as represented by the equation $S = K \log R$?
13. What psychophysical methods did Fechner use? How did psychophysics influence the development of psychology?
14. Do you think experimental psychology would have developed when it did without Fechner's work? Without Weber's work? Why?
15. What is the difference between inner psychophysics and outer psychophysics? Which was Fechner forced to focus on? Why?

Suggested Readings

Burrell, B. (2004). *Postcards from the Brain Museum: The improbable search for meaning in the matter of famous minds.* New York: Broadway Books.
Offers a tour of brain collections held in various museums and explores scientific attempts (both the credible and the fantastic) to explain brain structures and functions.

Cahan, D. (Ed.). (1993). *Hermann von Helmholtz and the foundations of nineteenth-century science.* Berkeley: University of California Press.
Presents and assesses the popular lectures and speeches Helmholtz delivered between 1853 and 1892. These cover the nature and purpose of scientific research, the optimum intellectual and social conditions for scientific advances, and the impact of science on society.

Dobson, V., & Bruce, D. (1972). The German university and the development of experimental psychology. *Journal of the History of the Behavioral Sciences, 8,* 204–207.
Describes the climate of academic freedom in German universities as a necessary condition for the growth of modern psychology.

Marshall, M. E. (1969). Gustav Fechner, Dr. Mises, and the comparative anatomy of angels. *Journal of the History of the Behavioral Sciences, 5,* 39–58.
Analyzes the wide range of essays Fechner wrote under the pen name "Dr. Mises."

Zimmer, C. (2004). *Soul made flesh: The discovery of the brain and how it changed the world.* New York: Free Press.
Examines 200 years of evolving scientific thought about the human soul, the brain, and consciousness.

Contemporary Developments in Psychology

Chess Champion Capitulates to Cunning Computer

Garry Kasparov wasn't just another great chess player, the master of all grandmasters. By universal agreement, he was the greatest chess player in history. In the spring of 1997, at the age of 34, at the peak of the long boom, he had held his world championship for 12 years. Never once had he lost a multi-game match against an individual opponent. Never once had he displayed anything but absolute assurance in his chess genius. His attitude toward any rival bordered on the contemptuous, a trait he displayed again after winning, as expected, the first of six games in his heralded rematch that May in New York against an opponent he had soundly defeated just a year before.

As the match resumed, chess experts who gathered to watch the great champion crush his foe witnessed something so unexpected that they were left speechless. They were not alone. Millions of observers intently following the contest over the Internet and via worldwide television hookups were astonished to see Kasparov show uncharacteristic signs of confusion. First, he displayed growing doubt, followed by dismay, despair, and loss of control. Finally, he seemed to be having an emotional breakdown. He appeared to be terror stricken.

The first sign that the champion was on the verge of a crackup came during the second game. It was then that Kasparov encountered something unique in his experience.

In the past, he was always able to exploit an opponent's weaknesses by understanding the pattern of thought being employed against him. This time he could not.

That second game ended in a draw. Another draw followed. Then his opponent won a game. When the contestants resumed play on a Saturday, the match was dead even. Kasparov began aggressively, brilliantly; he knew he was winning. His opponent fought back with a series of inspired, indeed brutal, moves that left Kasparov visibly shaken.

Grandmasters were shocked to see the champion, for the first time, seem pitiful. He was forced to accept another draw. After a day's break in the match, the denouement came on Monday.

Worldwide attention intensified. Television networks assigned correspondents to cover the event for their lead prime-time broadcasts. Newspapers dispatched top writers, not just their chess analysts, and prepared to open their front pages to report the final results. They and millions more watching on TV and the Internet saw the great Garry Kasparov, the consummate champion whose supreme confidence was matched only by his arrogance, replaced by a nervous, hollowed-out player, his eyes darkened, his manner brooding. He appeared beaten before making his first move.

Kasparov grew even more dispirited as his opponent's swift, ruthless moves drove him into a corner. In a riveting moment captured on television screens, and later on newspaper front pages, the champion leaned forward over the chessboard. He placed his hands over his face and eyes, and lowered his head dejectedly. It became an enduring portrait of human despair. Moments later Kasparov suddenly stood up. He was resigning the game and match, he announced. Only nineteen moves had been played.

Grandmasters were amazed at the way the champion abruptly crumbled. "It had the impact of a Greek tragedy," said the chairman of the chess committee responsible for officiating the match. Kasparov reacted more simply. "I lost my fighting spirit," he said. "I was not in the mood of playing at all."

Asked to explain why, at a tumultuous news conference minutes later, he replied, "I'm a human being. When I see something that is well beyond my understanding, I'm afraid."[1]

What did Kasparov see that was beyond his understanding? What had spooked him so much that he could no longer play the game at which he was master? And what does this have to do with the history of psychology? Be patient. All will be revealed in time. For now, let us follow the ever-changing nature of psychology into the twenty-first century.

---

[1] "Deep (RS/6000 SP) Blue" from *The Best of Times*, © 2001 by Haynes Johnson, reprinted by permission of Harcourt, Inc.

Schools of Thought in Perspective

We have seen how each of the schools of thought in psychology developed, prospered for a time, and then—with the exception of psychoanalysis—became part of mainstream contemporary psychological thought. We have also seen that each movement drew strength from its opposition to an earlier school. And when there was no longer a need to protest, when the new school had ousted its opposition, it ceased to be a revolutionary movement and became the established order, at least for a while.

Each school attained success in its own way, and each made substantial contributions to psychology's evolution. This is true even for structuralism, although it has left little direct imprint on psychology as we know it today. There are no longer structuralists of Titchener's sort in modern psychology, nor have there been for nearly a century. Yet structuralism was an enormous success in promoting the enterprise Wundt began, the establishing of an independent science of psychology free of the strictures of philosophy. That structuralism failed to dominate psychology more than a short time does not detract from its revolutionary achievement as the first school of thought of a new science and a vital source of opposition for the systems that followed.

Consider the success of functionalism, which also has not endured as a separate school. As an attitude or viewpoint, however, which is all its advocates hoped it would be, functionalism permeated American psychological thought. To the extent that American psychology today is as much profession as science and applies its findings to virtually every aspect of modern life, the functional, utilitarian attitude has indeed changed the nature of psychology.

What of Gestalt psychology? It, too, on a more modest scale, accomplished its mission. The opposition to elementism, the support of a "wholes" approach, and the interest in consciousness have influenced psychologists in clinical psychology, learning, perception, social psychology, and thinking. Although the Gestalt school did not transform psychology the way its founders expected, it had considerable impact and can therefore be described as a success.

As noteworthy as the accomplishments of structuralism, functionalism, and Gestalt psychology are, they take second place to the phenomenal impact of behaviorism and psychoanalysis. The effects of these movements have been profound, and they have maintained their identities as separate and unique schools of thought.

We discussed how behaviorism and psychoanalysis splintered into various positions after the days of their founders, Watson and Freud. No single form of behaviorism or of psychoanalysis has won allegiance from all members of either school. The emergence of subschools divided the systems into competing factions, each with its own map of the path to truth. But despite this internal diversity, behaviorists and psychoanalysts stand firmly opposed to each other in their approaches to psychology. For example, Skinnerian behaviorists have more in common with sociobehaviorist followers of Bandura and Rotter than they do with followers of Jung's or Horney's psychoanalysis. The vitality of these two schools of thought is evident in their continuing evolution.

We have seen that Skinner's psychology was not the last stage in the development of behaviorism any more than Adler's individual psychology was the final stage of psychoanalysis. We also saw that humanistic psychology, although failing to make an impact as a separate school of thought, nevertheless influenced contemporary psychology through the growth of the positive psychology movement.

By the 1960s and 1970s, two other movements arose within American psychology, and each attempted to shape a new definition for the field. These are cognitive psychology and evolutionary psychology.

The Cognitive Movement in Psychology

In Watson's behaviorist manifesto in 1913, he insisted that psychology drop all references to mind, consciousness, or conscious processes. And indeed the psychologists who followed Watson's dictates eliminated mention of these concepts and banished all mentalistic terminology. For decades, introductory psychology textbooks described the functioning of the brain but refused to discuss any conception of the mind. People joked that psychology had "lost consciousness" or "lost its mind," seemingly forever.

Then suddenly (though the trend actually had been building for some time) psychology regained consciousness. Words that once were politically incorrect were being uttered at meetings and appearing in print. In 1979, the *American Psychologist* published an article entitled "Behaviorism and the Mind: A (Limited) Call for a Return to Introspection" (Lieberman, 1979), invoking not only mind but also the suspect technique of introspection. A few months earlier, the journal had published an article with the simple title "Consciousness." "After decades of deliberate neglect," its author wrote, "consciousness is again coming under scientific scrutiny, with discussions of the topic appearing at entirely respectable locations in psychology's literature" (Natsoulas, 1978, p. 906).

In 1976, in his annual address, the APA president told the assembled audience that psychology was changing and that the new conception included a refocus on consciousness. Psychology's image of human nature was becoming "human rather than mechanical" (McKeachie, 1976, p. 831). When an officer of the APA and a prestigious journal discuss consciousness so openly and optimistically, it seems obvious that a revolution—another new movement—is under way. Revisions in introductory textbooks followed, redefining psychology as the science of behavior and mental processes instead of only behavior, a science seeking to explain overt behavior and its relationship to mental processes. Thus it became clear that psychology had progressed far beyond the desires and designs of Watson and Skinner. A new school of thought was taking hold.

Antecedent Influences on Cognitive Psychology

Like all revolutionary movements in psychology, cognitive psychology did not spring up overnight. Many of its features had been anticipated. Interest in consciousness was evident in the earliest days of psychology before it became a formal science. The writings of the Greek philosophers Plato and Aristotle deal with thought processes, as do the theories of the British empiricists and associationists.

When Wundt founded psychology as a separate scientific discipline, his work centered on consciousness. He may be considered a forerunner of contemporary cognitive psychology because of his emphasis on the mind's creative activity. The structuralist and functionalist schools of thought dealt with consciousness, studying its elements and functions. Behaviorism, however, brought fundamental change, dismissing consciousness for nearly 50 years.

The return to consciousness, and the formal beginning of the cognitive psychology movement, can be traced to the 1950s, although signs were apparent as early as the 1930s. The behaviorist E. R. Guthrie, toward the end of his career, deplored the mechanistic model and argued that stimuli cannot always be reduced to physical terms. He suggested that psychologists describe stimuli in perceptual or cognitive terms so that they will be meaningful for the responding organism (Guthrie, 1959). The concept of meaning cannot be described solely in behaviorist terms because it is a mentalistic or cognitive process.

The purposive behaviorism of E. C. Tolman (chapter 11) was another precursor of the cognitive movement. His form of behaviorism recognized the importance of cognitive variables and contributed to the decline of the stimulus-response approach. Tolman proposed cognitive maps, attributed purposive behavior to animals, and emphasized intervening variables as a way to operationally define internal unobservable states.

Rudolf Carnap, a positivist philosopher, called for a return to introspection. In 1956, Carnap wrote, "a person's awareness of his own state of imagining, feeling, et cetera, must be recognized as a kind of observation, in principle not different from external observation, and therefore as a legitimate source of knowledge" (quoted in

Koch, 1964, p. 22). Even Bridgman, the physicist who gave behaviorism the notion of operational definitions, denounced behaviorism and insisted that introspective reports be used to give meaning to operational analyses.

Gestalt psychology influenced the cognitive movement with its focus on "organization, structure, relationships, the active role of the subject, and the important part played by perception in learning and memory" (Hearst, 1979, p. 32). The Gestalt school of thought helped keep alive at least a token interest in consciousness during the years that behaviorism dominated American psychology.

Another anticipator of cognitive psychology is the Swiss psychologist Jean Piaget (1896–1980),[2] who wrote his first scientific paper at age 10 and later studied with Jung. Piaget also worked with Théodore Simon who, with Alfred Binet, developed the first psychological test of mental abilities (see chapter 8). Piaget assisted in administering the tests to children. He later became important for his work on child development not in psychosexual stages as proposed by Freud, but in cognitive stages. Piaget's clinical method of interviewing children and his insistence on highly detailed note-taking during the interviews were seen as a major inspiration for the famous Hawthorne studies of industrial workers in the 1920s, which we described in chapter 8 (see Hsueh, 2004).

However, Piaget's work on cognitive development, published in the 1920s and 1930s, although highly influential in Europe, was not so widely accepted in the United States because of its incompatibility with the behaviorist position. The early cognitive theorists, however, welcomed Piaget's emphasis on cognitive factors. And as the ideas of the cognitive psychologists took hold in American psychology, the relevance of Piaget's ideas became clearer. In 1969, he became the first European psychologist to receive the APA's Distinguished Scientific Contribution Award. Because his work focused on children, it helped broaden the range of behavior to which cognitive psychology would be applied.

The Changing Zeitgeist in Physics

When we find a major shift in the evolution of a science, we know it is reflecting changes that are already part of its intellectual Zeitgeist. We have seen that a science, like a living species, adapts to the conditions and demands of its environment. What intellectual climate fostered the cognitive movement and moderated behaviorist ideas by readmitting consciousness? Once again we look to the Zeitgeist in physics, long psychology's role model, for it has influenced the field since its beginnings as a science.

---

[2] Piaget enjoyed hiking in the mountains to hunt for snails while eating stale bread covered with mayonnaise and garlic.

Early in the twentieth century, a viewpoint developed within physics arising from the work of Albert Einstein, Neils Bohr, and Werner Heisenberg. They rejected the mechanistic model of the universe stemming from the days of Galileo and Newton, the prototype for the mechanistic, reductionistic, and deterministic view of human nature embraced by psychologists from Wundt to Skinner. The new look in physics discarded the requirement of total objectivity and the complete separation of external world from observer.

Physicists recognized that any observation we make of the natural world is likely to disturb it. They would have to attempt to bridge the artificial gap between observer and observed, between inner world and outer world, between mental and material. Thus, scientific investigation shifted from an independent and objectively knowable universe to one's observation of that universe. Modern scientists would no longer be so detached from the focus of their observation. In a sense, they would become "participant-observers."

As a result, the ideal of a totally objective reality was no longer considered attainable. Physics came to be characterized by the belief that objective knowledge is actually subjective, dependent on the observer. This idea that all knowledge is personal sounds suspiciously like what Berkeley proposed 300 years ago: Knowledge is subjective because it depends on the nature of the person perceiving it. One writer noted that our picture of the world, "far from being a genuine photographic reproduction of an independent reality 'out there,' [is] rather more on the order of a painting: a subjective creation of the mind which can convey a likeness but can never produce a replica" (Matson, 1964, p. 137).

The physicists' rejection of an objective, mechanistic subject matter and their concurrent recognition of subjectivity restored the vital role of conscious experience as a way of obtaining information about our world. This revolution in physics was an effective argument for again making consciousness a legitimate part of psychology's subject matter. Although the scientific psychology establishment resisted the new physics for a half century, clinging to an outdated model by stubbornly defining itself as an objective science of behavior, it eventually responded to the Zeitgeist and modified itself sufficiently to readmit cognitive processes.

The Founding of Cognitive Psychology

A retrospective look at the cognitive movement gives the impression of a rapid transition that undermined psychology's behaviorist foundations in a few short years. At the time, of course, this transition was not at all apparent. The change that now seems so dramatic came about slowly and quietly, with no beating drums, no fanfare. One psychologist wrote, "The term 'revolution' is probably inappropriate.

There were no cataclysmic events; the change occurred slowly in different subfields over some 10 to 15 years; there was no identifiable flashpoint or leader" (Mandler, 2002a, p. 339).

Often, the progression of history is clear only after the event. The founding of cognitive psychology did not occur overnight, nor could it be attributed to the charisma of one individual who, like Watson, changed the field almost single-handedly. Like functional psychology, the cognitive movement claims no solitary founder, perhaps because none of the psychologists working in the area had the personal ambition to lead the new movement. Their interest was pragmatic: simply getting on with the work of redefining psychology.

In retrospect, history identifies two scholars who are not founders in the formal sense but who contributed groundbreaking work in the form of a research center and books now considered milestones in the development of cognitive psychology. They are George Miller and Ulric Neisser. Their stories highlight some of the personal factors involved in shaping new schools of thought.

George Miller (1920–)

George Miller majored in English and speech at the University of Alabama, where he received his master's degree in speech in 1941. While there, he expressed an interest in psychology and was offered an instructorship to teach 16 sections of introductory psychology, even though he had never taken a course in the field. He said that after teaching the same material 16 times a week, he began to believe in it.

Miller went on to Harvard University, where he worked in the psychoacoustic laboratory on problems in vocal communication. In 1946, he received his Ph.D. Five years later, he published a landmark book on psycholinguistics, *Language and Communication* (1951). Miller accepted the behaviorist school of thought, noting that he had little choice because behaviorists held the leadership positions in major universities and professional associations.

GEORGE MILLER

> The power, the honors, the authority, the textbooks, the money, everything in psychology was owned by the behavioristic school. . . . those of us who wanted to be scientific psychologists couldn't really oppose it. You just wouldn't get a job. (Miller, quoted in Baars, 1986, p. 203)

By the mid-1950s, after investigating statistical learning theory, information theory, and computer-based models of the mind, Miller concluded that behaviorism was not, as he put it, "going to work out." The similarities between computers and the operation of the human mind impressed him, and his view of psychology became more cognitively oriented. At the same time, he developed an annoying allergy to animal hair and dander, so he could no longer conduct research with laboratory rats. Working only with human subjects was a disadvantage in the world of the behaviorists.

Miller's shift toward a cognitive psychology was also helped by his rebellious nature, so typical of many of his generation of psychologists. They were primed to revolt against the psychology then being taught and practiced, ready to offer their new approach, their focus on cognitive rather than behavioral factors. But as Miller wrote, some 50 years later, "At the time it was happening, I did not realize that I was, in fact, a revolutionary" (2003, p. 141).

In 1956, Miller published an article, which has since become a classic, entitled "The Magical Number Seven, Plus or Minus Two: Some Limits on our Capacity for Processing Information." In this work, Miller demonstrated that our conscious capacity for short-term memory of numbers (or, similarly, for words or colors) is limited to approximately seven "chunks" of information. That is all we are able to process at any given point. The importance, and impact, of this finding lies in the fact that it deals with a conscious, or cognitive, experience at a time when behaviorism still dominated psychological thought. In addition, Miller's use of the phrase "processing information" indicated the influence of a computer-based model of the human mind.

The Center for Cognitive Studies

With Jerome Bruner (1915–), his colleague at Harvard, Miller established a research center to investigate the human mind. Miller and Bruner asked the university president for space and in 1960 were given the house in which William James had once lived. This was considered an appropriate site because James had dealt so exquisitely in his *Principles* book with the nature of mental life. Choosing a name for the new enterprise was not a trivial matter. Being associated with Harvard, the center had the potential for exerting an enormous influence on psychology. They selected the word "cognition" to denote their subject matter and decided to call the facility the Center for Cognitive Studies.

> In using the word "cognition" we were setting ourselves off from behaviorism. We wanted something that was *mental*—but "mental psychology" seemed terribly redundant. "Common-sense psychology" would have suggested some sort of anthropological investigation, and "folk psychology" would have suggested Wundt's social psychology. What word do you use to label this set of views? We chose cognition. (Miller, quoted in Baars, 1986, p. 210)

Two students at the center later recalled that no one could tell them what cognition really meant at that time or what ideas they were supposed to be promoting. The center "was not set up to be for anything in particular; it was set up to be against things. What was important was what it was not" (Norman & Levelt, 1988, p. 101).

It was not behaviorism. It was not the ruling authority, the establishment, or the psychology of the present. In defining the center, its founders were demonstrating how greatly they differed from behaviorism. As we have seen, every new movement proclaims that its position or attitude differs from the current school of thought; this is a necessary preliminary stage to defining what they are about and what changes they propose. Miller, however, gave due credit to the Zeitgeist. "Neither of us should take too much credit for the Center's success. It was an idea whose time had come" (Miller, 1989, p. 412).

Miller did not consider cognitive psychology to be a true revolution, despite its differences from behaviorism. He called it an "accretion," a change by slow growth or accumulation. He saw the movement as more evolutionary than revolutionary and believed it was a return to a commonsense psychology that recognized and affirmed psychology's concern with mental life as well as behavior.

Researchers at the center investigated a wide range of topics: language, memory, perception, concept formation, thinking, and developmental psychology. Most of these areas had been eliminated from the behaviorists' vocabulary. Miller later established a program for cognitive sciences at Princeton University.

Miller became president of the APA in 1969 and received the Distinguished Scientific Contribution Award and the American Psychological Foundation's Gold Medal Award for Life Achievement in the Application of Psychology. In 1991, he was awarded the National Medal of Science. In 2003, he was given the APA's Outstanding Lifetime Contribution to Psychology Award. Additional acknowledgment of the significance of his work is the number of cognitive psychology laboratories modeled on his center and the rapid development and formalization of the approach he did so much to define.

Ulric Neisser (1928–)

Born in Kiel, Germany, Ulric Neisser was brought to the United States by his parents at the age of 3. He began his college studies at Harvard, majoring in physics. Impressed with a young psychology professor by the name of George Miller, Neisser decided that physics did not excite him. He switched to psychology and took an honors course with Miller on the psychology of communications and information theory. He reports also being influenced by Koffka's book, *Principles of Gestalt Psychology.* After receiving his bachelor's degree from Harvard in 1950, Neisser earned his master's degree at Swarthmore College, studying under Gestalt psychologist Wolfgang Köhler. Neisser returned to Harvard for his Ph.D., which he completed in 1956.

© Emory University

ULRIC NEISSER

Despite his growing attraction to a cognitive approach to psychology, Neisser saw no escape from behaviorism if he wanted an academic career. "It was what you had to learn. That was the age when it was supposed that no psychological phenomenon was real unless you could demonstrate it in a rat" (quoted in Baars, 1986, p. 275). It was fortunate for Neisser that his first academic job was at Brandeis University, where the psychology department chair was Abraham Maslow. At the time, Maslow was moving away from his own behaviorist training to develop the humanistic approach to the field. Maslow was not successful in turning Neisser into a humanistic psychologist, or in turning humanistic psychology into psychology's third force, but he provided the opportunity for Neisser to pursue his interest in cognitive issues. (Neisser later claimed that cognitive psychology, not humanistic psychology, was the third force.)

In 1967, Neisser published *Cognitive Psychology*. He reported that the book was a personal one, an attempt to define himself and the kind of psychologist he wanted to be. The book was also a landmark in the history of psychology, an attempt to define a new approach to the field. It became extremely popular, and Neisser was embarrassed to find himself designated the "father" of cognitive psychology. Although he had no desire to found a school of thought, his writings helped push psychology away from behaviorism and toward cognition. Nevertheless, Neisser emphasized that the study of cognitive issues should be only a part of psychology and not characterize the entire field.

Neisser defined cognition as those processes by which "sensory input is transformed, reduced, elaborated, stored, recovered, and used. . . . cognition is involved in everything a human being might possibly do" (Neisser, 1967, p. 4). Thus, cognitive psychology is concerned with sensation, perception, imaging, memory, problem solving, thinking, and related mental activities.

Just nine years later, Neisser published *Cognition and Reality* (1976), which expressed dissatisfaction with the narrowing of the cognitive position and its reliance on laboratory situations instead of real-world settings from which to collect data. He insisted that the results of psychological research should have ecological validity. By that he meant that they should be generalizable to situations beyond the confines of the laboratory. In addition, Neisser insisted that cognitive psychologists should be able to apply their findings to practical problems, helping people deal with the everyday issues in their work and in their lives. Thus, Neisser had become disillusioned, concluding that the cognitive psychology movement had little to contribute to psychology's understanding of how people cope. And so this major figure in the founding of cognitive psychology became an outspoken critic, challenging the movement as he had earlier challenged behaviorism.

After 17 years at Cornell University, where his office was not far from where Titchener's pickled brain was housed, Neisser moved to Emory University in Atlanta. He returned to Cornell in 1996.

The Computer Metaphor

Clocks and automata were the seventeenth-century metaphors for the mechanical view of the universe and, by extension, for the human mind. Those machines were widespread, easily understood models of how the mind was believed to work. Today, the mechanical model of the universe and the behavioral psychology that derived from it have been superseded by other viewpoints such as the acceptance of subjectivity in physics and the cognitive movement in psychology.

As a result, the clock is no longer a useful example for the modern view of the mind. A twentieth-century machine, the computer, has emerged to serve as our model, as a new metaphor for the functioning of the mind. One historian of science wrote, "The vehicle for the reintroduction of mind, and a vital agent of behaviorism's overthrow, was the idea that the brain is a computer. This assertion has become a commonplace one in the historical literature on the 'cognitive revolution'" (Crowther-Heyck, 1999, p. 37). Psychologists invoke the operations of the computer to explain cognitive phenomena. Computers, said to display artificial intelligence, are often described in human terms. The storage capacity is its memory, programming codes are languages, and new generations of computers are said to be evolving.

Computer programs, essentially sets of instructions for dealing with symbols, may be seen to function similarly to the human mind. Both the computer and the mind receive from the environment and process large amounts of information (sensory stimuli or data). They digest this information, manipulating, storing, and retrieving it, and acting on it in various ways. Thus, computer programming has been proposed as the basis for the cognitive view of human information processing, reasoning, and problem solving. It is the program (the software), not the computer itself (the hardware), that serves as the explanation for mental operations.

Cognitive psychologists are interested in the sequence of symbol manipulation that underlies human thought processes. In other words, they are concerned with how the mind processes information. Their goal is to discover the programs each of us has stored in our memory, those patterns of thinking that allow us to understand and articulate ideas, to remember and recall events and concepts, and to grasp and solve new problems. In nearly 125 years of history, psychology has progressed from simple clocks to sophisticated computers as the models for its subject matter, but it is significant that both are machines. This demonstrates the historical continuity in psychology's evolution from older to newer schools of thought. We can also see a historical continuity in the evolution of computers themselves.

The Development of the Modern Computer

We have already discussed the work of Charles Babbage and Henry Hollerith to develop machines that would "think" like humans. But it was a practical problem during the early days of World War II that led to the beginning of the modern age of computers. In 1942, the U.S. Army desperately needed to find a faster way to make the rapid calculations required to fire artillery pieces. To aim a cannon accurately, so that the shell hits its target, was (and still is) a difficult process, far more complex than a soldier aiming a rifle and squeezing the trigger. Here's one description: "To aim a cannon, a gunner had to adjust the gun to several settings. That required [mathematical] tables to account for all the variables that affect the trajectory of an artillery shell; wind speed and direction, humidity, temperature, elevation, even the temperature of the gunpowder" (Keiger, 1999, p. 40).

The book of settings for each type of artillery piece contained hundreds, even thousands, of tables of settings. This work was being done by women, newly employed during wartime, using mechanical calculating machines. (The women holding these jobs were called "computers.") Within a year, however, they had fallen behind; they could not keep up with the demand. The situation was so critical that some cannons had to be withdrawn from combat because there were no firing tables available.

This need spurred the development of the first giant computer, ENIAC (Electronic Numerical Integrator and Calculator). Completed in 1943, the horseshoe-shaped machine took up three walls of a huge room with "arms 80 feet long. It would stand 8 feet tall and weigh 30 tons. It would contain 17,468 vacuum tubes . . . as well as 10,000 capacitors, 70,000 resistors, 1,500 relays, and 6,000 manual switches—an array of electronics so vast that large blowers would be required to dissipate the heat it produced" (Waldrop, 2001, p. 45).

Machines that can perform mental operations have come a long way from Babbage's calculating engine. You need only to compare the size and capacity of your laptop or handheld computer to realize how primitive ENIAC was. The evolution of machines to perform mental functions continues at a rapid pace, which leads, inevitably, to the question of whether these machines truly demonstrate intelligence.

Artificial Intelligence

We noted that cognitive psychologists accepted computers as a model for human cognitive functioning, suggesting that the machines display artificial intelligence and process information similarly to the way people do. Does it follow that the computer's intelligence is the same as human intelligence? Can computers think? In the seventeenth century, automata simulated human movements and speech. In the future, will new generations of computers simulate human thought?

Initially computer scientists and cognitive psychologists enthusiastically embraced the notion of artificial intelligence. As early as 1949, when computers were relatively primitive, the author of a book entitled *Giant Brains* declared, "a machine can handle information; it can calculate, conclude, and choose; it can perform reasonable operations with information. A machine, therefore, can think" (quoted in Dyson, 1997, p. 108).

In 1950, the British computer genius Alan Turing (1912–1954) proposed a way to examine the proposition that computers can think. Called the Turing Test, it involved persuading a subject that the computer with which he or she is communicating is really another person, not a machine. If the subject cannot distinguish the computer's responses from human responses, then the computer must be displaying intelligence at a human level. The Turing Test works as follows.

> The interrogator [the subject] has two different "conversations" with an interactive computer program. The goal of the interrogator is to figure out which of the two parties is a person communicating through the computer and which is the computer itself. The interrogator can ask the two parties any questions at all. However, the computer will try to fool the interrogator into believing that it is human, whereas the human will be trying to show the interrogator that she or he truly is human. The computer passes the Turing Test if an interrogator is unable to distinguish the computer from the human. (Sternberg, 1996, pp. 481–482)

Not everyone agreed with the premise of the Turing Test. One of the most effective objections was offered by John Searle (1932–), an American philosopher, who advanced the Chinese Room problem (Searle, 1980). Imagine you are sitting at a desk. In the wall in front of you are two slots. Slips of paper appear one at a time from the slot on the left. Each paper contains a group of Chinese characters. Your job is to match by shape the set of symbols with those in a book. When you find the matching set, you are directed to copy another set of symbols from the book onto a piece of paper and feed the paper through the slot on the right.

What is happening here? You are receiving inputs from the left slot and writing outputs for the right slot, following the instructions (the program) you have been given. If you are like most subjects in the United States, you would not be expected to read or understand Chinese. All you are doing is mechanically following your instructions.

However, if a Chinese psychologist were on the far side of the wall containing the slots, he or she would not know you were unfamiliar with the Chinese language. Communications are going to you in Chinese and you are responding with appropriate answers in Chinese, copied from your book. But no matter how many messages you receive and respond to, you still do not know Chinese. You are not thinking; you are merely following instructions. You are not displaying intelligence but simply following orders.

Searle argued that computer programs that may appear to comprehend different kinds of inputs and respond to them in an intelligent manner are operating like the subject in the Chinese Room puzzle. A computer no more understands the messages it receives than you may have understood Chinese. In these instances, both you and the computer are operating strictly in accordance with a set of programmed rules.

Many cognitive psychologists came to agree that computers may pass the Turing Test and simulate intelligence without actually *being* intelligent. We may conclude, then, that computers cannot yet think. They can perform as if they were thinking, however. And that brings us back to the 1997 chess match that so devastated the world champion Garry Kasparov. What caused him to become so dispirited and abandon the game was that his opponent was a computer.

Manufactured by IBM, the computer's name was Deep Blue. It weighed almost three tons, and each of its two towers was more than six feet tall. It was capable of processing 200 million chess positions every second; within three minutes it could process 50 billion moves. No wonder even the greatest chess master gave up in despair. But for all its capacity, was Deep Blue really thinking?

The general conclusion is that the machine was not, even though it "behaved" as if it were. A British science writer with an interest in chess-playing machines concluded, "Despite the relentless improvement in computer performance, there has been little progress toward general-purpose machine intelligence. . . . Deep Blue showed that building a computer capable of playing chess as well as any human reveals very little about intelligence in general" (Standage, 2002, p. 241). The computer, for all its spectacular performance, still had to be programmed in advance by a thinking human being. In 2003, Kasparov played against Deep Junior, a new generation of chess-playing computer. Before the match he said, "I'm here representing the human race. I promise I'll do my utmost."

But Kasparov had a hard time of it again. An observer for *Wired* magazine wrote:

> while Kasparov is nearly worn out, Deep Junior just keeps on going. Like a homicidal robot, the computer absolutely will not stop. Ever. Garry has become more and more exhausted. He's trying to stay calm and focused so he can upset the machine and not blunder [but] upsetting the machine is not an option. It doesn't rankle. (wired. com/news.7/6/2006)

And when Kasparov agreed to a 3-3 tie, he was booed by the crowd. Nevertheless, his performance showed that artificial intelligence has not attained the level and complexity of human intelligence—yet.

The Nature of Cognitive Psychology

In chapter 11 we noted how the inclusion of cognitive factors in the social learning theories of Albert Bandura and Julian Rotter altered American behaviorism. Today it is not only in behavioral psychology that the cognitive movement has an impact. Cognitive factors are considered by researchers in virtually all areas: attribution theory in social psychology, cognitive dissonance theory, motivation and emotion, personality, learning, memory, perception, problem solving, creativity, and information processing in human intelligence and in artificial intelligence. Applied areas such as clinical, community, school, and industrial-organizational psychology have also seen an emphasis on cognitive factors.

Cognitive psychology differs from behaviorism on several points. First, cognitive psychologists focus on the process of knowing rather than merely responding to stimuli. The important factors are mental processes and events, not stimulus-response connections; the emphasis is on the mind, not behavior. This does not mean that cognitive psychologists ignore behavior, but behavioral responses are not the sole focus of their research. Behavioral responses are sources for making inferences and drawing conclusions about the mental processes accompanying them.

Second, cognitive psychologists are interested in how the mind structures or organizes experience. Gestalt psychologists, as well as Piaget, argued in favor of an innate tendency to organize conscious experience (sensations and perceptions) into meaningful wholes and patterns. The mind gives form and coherence to mental experience; this process is the subject matter of cognitive psychology. British empiricists and associationists and their twentieth-century derivatives, the Skinnerian behaviorists, insisted that the mind did not possess inherent organizational abilities.

Third, cognitive psychologists believe that the individual actively and creatively arranges the stimuli received from the environment. We are capable of participating in the acquisition and application of knowledge, deliberately attending to some events and choosing to commit them to memory. We are not, as the behaviorists claimed, passive responders to external forces or blank slates on which sensory experience will write.

Cognitive Neuroscience

Research on mapping brain functions dates from the eighteenth and nineteenth centuries and the work of Hall, Flourens, and Broca (see chapter 3). Using methods such as extirpation and electrical stimulation, early physiologists attempted to determine the specific parts of the brain that controlled various cognitive functions.

That quest continues today in the discipline called cognitive neuroscience, a hybrid of cognitive psychology and the neurosciences. The goals of this field are to determine "how brain functions give rise to mental activity" and to "correlate specific aspects of information processing with specific brain regions" (Sarter, Bernston, & Cacioppo, 1996, p. 13).

Researchers in cognitive neuroscience have made striking advances in mapping the brain, largely due to the development and application of sophisticated imaging techniques. For example, the electroencephalogram (EEG) records variations in electrical activity in selected parts of the brain. Computerized axial tomography (CAT) scans reveal detailed cross sections of the brain. Magnetic resonance imagery (MRI) scans produce three-dimensional pictures of the brain. Whereas these techniques produce still images, positron emission tomography (PET) scans provide live pictures of various cognitive activities as they occur. These and other imaging techniques are providing scientists with a degree of precision and detail that was not previously attainable.

In 2006, cognitive neuroscientists demonstrated that the human brain could exert control over a computer. Thought could be translated into movement by electrical impulses alone. The subject was a 25-year-old man who had been totally paralyzed for the last three years. Electronic sensors, implanted in the motor cortex of his brain, were interfaced with a computer allowing him to control not only the computer but also a television set and a robot—all by using only his thoughts.

Within minutes he had learned to move the computer's cursor, allowing him to open e-mail, move objects using a robotic arm, play a simple video game, and draw a crude circle on the screen. He exercised this control by thinking about—that is, by willing or intending to make—such movements. He could not, of course, move any control with his hands.

This application of cognitive neuroscience, called neuroprosthetics, offers the hope that people with these types of disabilities could one day be able to interact with and exercise control over objects in their environment (Hochberg et al., 2006; Pollack, 2006).

The Role of Introspection

Cognitive psychologists' acceptance of conscious experiences led them to reconsider scientific psychology's first research approach, the introspective method introduced by Wundt more than a century ago. In a statement that could have been uttered by Wundt or Titchener, a psychologist writing in the late twentieth century noted the obvious fact that "if we are to study consciousness we must use introspection and introspective reports" (Farthing, 1992, p. 61).

Psychologists have attempted to quantify introspective reports to render them more objective and amenable to statistical analyses. One approach, retrospective phenomenological assessment, involves asking subjects to rate the intensity of their subjective experiences while responding to a previous stimulus situation. In other words, subjects retrospectively evaluate the subjective experiences that occurred during an earlier period when they were asked to respond to a given stimulus.

A leading cognitive psychologist noted that not only is introspection widely used but that the conscious states revealed by introspection are "often good predictors of people's behavior" (Wilson, 2003, p. 131).

Although some form of introspection constitutes the most frequently used research method in contemporary psychology, even its most ardent adherents recognize the limitations to its validity. For example, some subjects may give socially desirable introspective reports by telling researchers what they think the researchers want to hear in an effort to please them. Another problem with introspection is that subjects may not be able to access some of their thoughts or feelings because these reside deep in the unconscious, a topic to which psychologists are devoting increasing attention.

Unconscious Cognition

The study of conscious mental processes sparked a renewed interest in unconscious cognitive activities. "After 100 years of neglect, suspicion, and frustration, unconscious processes have now taken a firm hold on the collective mind of psychologists" (Kihlstrom, Barnhardt, & Tataryn, 1992, p. 788). Increasingly, cognitive psychologists agree that the unconscious is able to accomplish many functions that were once thought to require deliberation, intention, and conscious awareness. Research suggests that most of our thinking and information processing takes place in the unconscious, which may operate more quickly and efficiently than does the conscious mind (see Hassin, Uleman, & Margh, 2005; Wilson, 2002).

However, this is not the unconscious mind of which Freud spoke, overflowing with repressed desires and memories brought into conscious awareness only through psychoanalysis. The new unconscious is more rational than emotional and is involved in the first stage of cognition in responding to a stimulus. Thus, unconscious processes form an integral part of learning and can be studied experimentally.

To distinguish the modern version of the cognitive unconscious from the psychoanalytic version (and from the physical states of being unaware, asleep, or comatose), some cognitive psychologists prefer the term "nonconscious." In general, cognitive researchers agree that most human mental processing occurs at a nonconscious level. "It now appears that the unconscious is 'smarter' than first thought, capable of processing complex verbal and visual information and even anticipating (and planning for) future events. . . . No longer simply a repository for drives and impulses, the unconscious appears to play a role in problem solving, hypothesis testing, and creativity" (Bornstein & Masling, 1998, p. xx).

In both laboratory experiments and observational studies of consumer purchasing behavior, researchers have found that unconscious thought (called here "deliberation-without-attention") was more creative and diverse and led to purchases with which people were more satisfied than when the laboratory responses and purchasing behavior were directed by conscious thought (Dijksterhuis, Bos, Nordgren, & van Baaren, 2006; Dijksterhuis & Meurs, 2006).

A popular approach to studying nonconscious processing involves subliminal perception (or subliminal activation), in which stimuli are presented below the subjects' levels of conscious awareness. Despite the subjects' inability to perceive those stimuli, the stimuli activate the subjects' conscious processes and behavior. Thus, this type of research shows that we can be influenced by stimuli we cannot see or hear. These and similar findings have persuaded cognitive psychologists that the process of acquiring knowledge (in or out of the laboratory setting) takes place at both conscious and nonconscious levels but that most of the mental work involved in learning occurs at the nonconscious level.

Animal Cognition

The cognitive movement restored consciousness not only to humans but to animals as well. Indeed, animal psychology and comparative psychology have come full circle, from observations of animal mental life reported by Romanes and Morgan in the 1880s and 1890s, through the mechanical stimulus-response conditioning research of Skinnerian behaviorists in the 1950s and 1960s, to the contemporary restoration of consciousness by cognitive psychologists.

Since the 1970s, animal psychologists have attempted to demonstrate how animals "encode, transform, compute, and manipulate symbolic representations of the real world's spatial, temporal, and causal textures for the purposes of adaptively organizing their behavior" (Cook, 1993, p. 174). In other words, the computer-like information processing system believed to be operating in humans is being studied in animals. The early animal cognition research used simple stimuli such as colored lights, tones, and clicks. These stimuli may have been too basic to permit an understanding of animal cognitive processes because they did not allow the animals to display the full range of their information-processing abilities. Later research has used more complex and realistic stimuli, such as color photographs of familiar objects. These pictorial stimuli have revealed conceptual abilities not previously attributed to animals.

Animal memory has been shown to be complex and flexible, and at least some cognitive processes may operate similarly in animals and humans. Laboratory animals are capable of learning diverse and sophisticated concepts. They display mental processes such as coding and organizing symbols, the ability to form abstractions about space, time, and number and to perceive cause-and-effect relationships. In addition, their use of tools and other implements implies a basic sense of reasoning (Wynne, 2001).

Studies of animals ranging from insects to mammals (including rats, pigeons, chimps, parrots, dolphin, and crows) suggest that animals can perform a variety of cognitive functions. These include forming cognitive maps, sensing the motives of others, planning by taking into account past experiences, understanding the concept of numbers, and solving problems through the use of reason (see, for example, Emery & Clayton, 2005; Pennisi, 2006).

As you might expect, however, the idea of animal cognition is still controversial. Some animal psychologists maintain that the research to date does not sufficiently support the generalization that animal cognition operates similarly to human cognition. The gap between human and animal functioning proposed by Descartes in the seventeenth century retains its appeal.

Behavioral psychologists still reject the notion of consciousness, in animals as well as humans. One behaviorist wrote about cognitive animal psychologists, "They are the George Romaneses of today. Speculating about memory, reasoning, and consciousness in animals is no less ridiculous today than it was a hundred years ago" (Baum, 1994, p. 138). A noted historian offered a contradictory view:

> Do animals show all the observable aspects of consciousness? The biological evidence points to a clear yes. Are they then likely to have the subjective side as well? Given the long and growing list of similarities, the weight of evidence, it seems to me, is inexorably moving toward yes. . . . My sense is that the scientific community has now swung decisively in its favor. The basic facts have come home at last. We are not the only conscious beings on earth. (Baars, 1997, p. 33)

If animals are conscious beings and can perform cognitive functions similar to humans, is it reasonable to ask whether they also display common personality characteristics? A growing number of psychologists believe the answer is yes.

Animal Personality

In the early 1990s two psychologists decided to study the 44 red octopuses at the aquarium in Seattle, Washington, where staff scientists and keepers had often noticed what they thought were differing personalities among their charges. Indeed, they had given the creatures names to match their natures. A shy female octopus was called Emily Dickinson, after the poet. Another was so aggressive and destructive she was called Lucretia McEvil (Siebert, 2006).

The psychologists observed the behavior of the octopuses in three experimental situations and found that they differed on three factors: activity, reactivity, and avoidance. Their answer to the question, "Do octopuses have personalities?" was a qualified yes (Mather & Anderson, 1993).

Since the time of that research, studies have documented personality characteristics in a variety of animals including fish, spiders, farm animals, hyenas, chimps, and dogs. For example, hyenas in a zoo were observed by their keepers to have such distinct human-like characteristics as excitability, sociability, curiosity, and assertiveness. Mice showed some degree of empathy for other mice in pain, as did chimps, elephants, and dolphin. Orangutans that rated high in extraversion and agreeableness and low in neuroticism were also rated high in subjective well-being. In addition, personality traits exhibited by dogs have been measured as accurately as those in humans (see Gosling, Kwan, & John, 2003; Miller, 2006; Siebert, 2006; Weiss, King, & Perkins, 2006).

"With the emergency of animal personality studies, we are gaining an even fuller appreciation not only of the distinctiveness of birds and beasts and their behaviors but also of their deep resemblances to us and our own behaviors" (Siebert, 2006, p. 51). If animals are so similar to humans in cognitive processing, temperament, and personality, does this lend additional support to the importance of evolution in all living creatures? As we shall see, the relatively new field of evolutionary psychology is dedicated to investigating this question.

Current Status of Cognitive Psychology

With the cognitive movement in experimental psychology and the emphasis on consciousness within humanistic psychology and post-Freudian psychoanalysis, we can see that consciousness has reclaimed the central position it held when the field formally began. An analysis of 95 APA presidential addresses shows that the dominant view of psychology's subject matter has swung from subjective to objective and again to subjective events (Gibson, 1993). Consciousness has made a substantial and vigorous return.

As a school of thought, cognitive psychology boasts the trappings of success. Within the decade of the 1970s, the movement had so many adherents that it could support its own journals: *Cognitive Psychology* (first published in 1970), *Cognition* (1971), *Cognitive Science* (1977), *Cognitive Therapy and Research* (1977), *Journal of Mental Imagery* (1977), and *Memory and Cognition* (1983). *Consciousness and Cognition* began publication in 1992 and the *Journal of Consciousness Studies* in 1994.

Jerome Bruner once described cognitive psychology as "a revolution whose limits we still cannot fathom" (Bruner, 1983, p. 274). Nobel Prize–winning scientist Roger Sperry commented that compared to the behaviorist and psychoanalytic revolutions in psychology, the cognitive or consciousness revolution is the "most radical turnaround; the most revisionary and transformative" (Sperry, 1995, p. 35).

The impact of cognitive psychology has been felt in most areas of interest to psychologists. Further, cognitive psychologists have attempted to extend and consolidate the work of several major disciplines in a unified study of how the mind acquires knowledge. This perspective, dubbed *cognitive science,* is an amalgam of cognitive psychology, linguistics, anthropology, philosophy, computer sciences, artificial intelligence, and the neurosciences. Although George Miller questioned just how united such disparate fields of study could become (cognitive sciences, he suggested, rather than cognitive science), there is no denying the growth of the multidisciplinary approach. Cognitive science laboratories and institutes have been established at universities throughout the United States; some psychology departments have been renamed cognitive science departments. By whatever name, the cognitive approach to the study of mental phenomena and mental processes has come to dominate psychology and allied disciplines.

No revolution, however successful, lacks critics. For example, most Skinnerian behaviorists oppose the cognitive movement. Even those who support it point out weaknesses and limitations, noting that there are few concepts that the majority of cognitive psychologists agree upon or consider important, and there remains considerable confusion about terminology and definitions.

Another criticism is directed at an overemphasis on cognition at the expense of other influences on thought and behavior, such as motivation and emotion. The professional literature on motivation and emotion has declined over the last few decades, whereas publications on cognition have increased. Ulric Neisser suggested that the result is a narrow, sterile approach to the field. "Human thinking is passionate and emotional, people operate from complex motives. A computer program, by contrast . . . has no emotion and is monomaniacal in its single-mindedness" (Neisser, quoted in Goleman, 1983, p. 57). He sensed a danger that cognitive psychology was fixated on thought processes to the same extreme that behaviorism focused only on overt behavior. Jerome Bruner warned that cognitive science was becoming more restricted to increasingly narrow, even trivial, concerns (Bruner, 1990). A harsher judgment deals with the failure to unify the disparate fields of study concerned with cognitive functioning. One critic noted that there is, as yet, "no common view of the mind" (Erneling, 1997, p. 381).

Despite such criticisms, the primacy of the cognitive position in psychology is widely accepted. This was recently supported by an empirical analysis covering 19 years of doctoral dissertations and articles published and cited in four mainstream psychology periodicals: *American Psychologist, Annual Review of Psychology, Psychological Bulletin,* and *Psychological Review* (Robins, Gosling, & Craik, 1999).

Cognitive psychology is not finished. Because it is still developing, still history in the making, it is too soon to judge its ultimate contribution. It has the characteristics of a school of thought: its own journals, laboratories, meetings, jargon, and convictions, as well as the zeal of righteous believers. We may speak of cogniti*vism,* as we do of functionalism and behaviorism. Cognitive psychology has already become what other schools of thought became in their time, part of psychology's mainstream. And that, as we have seen, is the natural progression of revolutions when they become successful.

Evolutionary Psychology

The most recent approach to psychology, evolutionary psychology, argues that people are biological creatures that have been wired or programmed by evolution to behave, think, feel, and learn in ways that have fostered survival over many past generations. This approach is based on the assumption that people with certain behavioral, cognitive, and affective tendencies were more likely to survive and bear and raise children.

As one evolutionary psychologist commented, "Humans who defended territory, nurtured children, and strove for domination were more likely to successfully reproduce than humans who did not do these things, with the result that their ultimate descendants— members of the present generation—generally have all of these behavioral tendencies" (Funder, 2001, p. 209). The genes for those behaviors that facilitate survival were "passed on through the generations because they were adaptive, enhancing survival or reproductive success, and eventually, they spread widely and became standard equipment" (Goode, 2000, p. D9).

Thus, we are shaped as much, if not more, by biology than by learning. While not denying that social and cultural forces can influence our behavior through learning, evolutionary psychologists proclaim that we are predisposed at birth to certain ways of behaving as shaped by evolution.

Evolutionary psychology deals with four fundamental propositions:

1. All psychological mechanisms at some basic level originate from, and owe their existence to, evolutionary processes.
2. Darwin's theories of natural and sexual selection are the most important evolutionary processes responsible for creating evolved psychological mechanisms.

3. Evolved psychological mechanisms can be described as information-processing devices.
4. Evolved psychological mechanisms are functional; they function to solve recurrent adaptive problems that confronted our ancestors. (quoted from David Buss interview in Barker, 2006, pp. 69–70)

Evolutionary psychology is a broad field that makes use of research findings from other disciplines, including animal behavior, biology, genetics, neuropsychology, and evolutionary theory. It applies these findings to all areas of psychology. We noted in chapter 1 that psychology today is fragmented into varying approaches to its subject matter, and that there has been no single unifying theme to bring these factions together into a single psychology. Proponents of evolutionary psychology claim that their definition can unite this disparate field.

A founder of evolutionary psychology, David Buss, wrote that it "represents a true scientific revolution, a profound paradigm shift in the field of psychology" (2005, p. xxiv). In an interview the following year he called evolutionary psychology "one of the most important scientific revolutions we've ever had in the history of psychology" (quoted in Barker, 2006, p. 73).

Antecedent Influences on Evolutionary Psychology

Clearly, any movement that calls itself evolutionary psychology owes a debt to Charles Darwin, as well as to Herbert Spencer and his notion of survival of the fittest. The idea that only those with certain characteristics will survive and reproduce others with the same characteristics is the cornerstone of evolutionary psychology, as it was with Darwin and Spencer.

In 1890, 31 years after Darwin published his monumental work on evolution, William James used the term "evolutionary psychology" in his book, *The Principles of Psychology*. James predicted that one day psychology would be based upon evolutionary theory. He also proposed that much of human behavior is programmed at birth by genetic predispositions he called instincts. These instinctive behaviors could be modified by experience or learning but initially are formed independently of experience.

James believed that a wide range of behaviors were instinctive, including fears of specific objects such as snakes, strange animals, and heights, all of which have obvious survival value. Other instinctive behaviors James discussed were parenting skills, love, sociability, and pugnacity (the tendency to quarrel and fight). James argued that instinctive behaviors evolved through natural selection and were adaptations designed to cope with specific problems of survival and reproduction.

During the reign of behaviorism, from 1913 to about 1960, the notion that any behavior might be determined genetically was anathema. All behavior was learned, said the behaviorists, but even during their years of supremacy and effective domination of psychology, there were scattered reports of genetic influences and inherited tendencies taking precedence over conditioned responses.

For example, in chapter 11 we discussed the work of Skinner's students, the Brelands, who trained animals to perform for the IQ Zoo, television commercials, and state fairs. You will recall that some of their animals demonstrated a tendency toward instinctive drift. The animals sometimes substituted instinctive behaviors for those that had been reinforced with food, even when the instinctive behaviors interfered with obtaining food, a clear violation of the basic behavioristic principle that reinforcement rules all.

You are probably familiar with the monkey-mother love research of psychologist Harry Harlow (Harlow, 1971). Harlow raised baby monkeys with artificial mothers of two types. Both were constructed of wire mesh, but one was covered in soft, cuddly terry cloth while the other was hard, uncovered, and contained a nipple for dispensing milk. To Skinnerians it was obvious that reinforcement would be associated only with the hard mother that supplied the reward of milk. When the monkeys were frightened, however, they clung to the terry cloth mother, not the one that had always supplied reinforcement. It would seem that some other guiding force was at work, which could not be explained by operant conditioning and reinforcement.

Research conducted by Martin Seligman, the initiator of positive psychology (discussed in chapter 14), showed that it was easy to condition people to fear snakes, insects, dogs, heights, and tunnels. It was harder, however, to condition them to fear a more neutral or less threatening object such as a car or screwdriver (Seligman, 1971).

A fear of snakes has always been useful for survival in evolution, and so presumably we are born wired with this predisposing tendency. Fearing a neutral object, on the other hand, has had no survival value over the generations and so has not been passed on. Seligman called this phenomenon *biological preparedness*. This idea suggests that "phobias are indeed learned through classical conditioning but that certain fears that may have served some adaptive purpose in ancestral environments are more readily conditionable" (Siegert & Ward, 2002, p. 244).

The cognitive revolution was also a precursor of evolutionary psychology. The cognitive movement likened the human mind to a computer that could process whatever information it received. Part of the computer metaphor of the mind is the realization that the mind, like a computer, must be programmed to perform its multitude of tasks.

Thus evolutionary psychology both draws on the cognitive revolution and expands its importance as a necessary framework within which to understand human and animal nature. It focuses on the importance of consciousness as it has evolved over time, and it places a greater emphasis on the notion of the computer as a metaphor for all conscious processes. Two leading evolutionary psychologists wrote:

> The programs comprising the human mind were designed by natural selection to solve the adaptive problems regularly faced by our hunter-gatherer ancestors—problems such as finding a mate, cooperating with others, hunting, gathering, protecting children, navigating, avoiding predators, avoiding exploitation, and so on. The brain's evolved function is to extract information from the environment and use that information to generate behavior and regulate physiology. Hence, the brain is not just like a computer. It *is* a computer—that is, a physical system that was designed to process information. (Tooby & Cosmides, 2005, p. 5).

The Influence of Sociobiology

Another impetus for evolutionary psychology occurred in 1975 when Edward O. Wilson, a biologist, published a groundbreaking book entitled *Sociobiology: A New Synthesis* (Wilson, 1975). The book was both hailed and reviled. Two years later it was featured on the cover of *Time* magazine. That same year Wilson was awarded the National Medal of Science and had a pitcher of ice water poured over his head at the annual meeting of the American Association for the Advancement of Science, an organization not noted for physical violence.

Wilson's bold and simple thesis was an affront to many people because it challenged their cherished belief that everyone is created equal, and that environmental and social forces alone can foster or limit human development. Wilson angered people by appearing to argue that genetic influences may be more important than cultural ones. If all behavior is determined genetically, then there is no hope of changing it through child-rearing practices, education, or any other way. That was not Wilson's central point, however, though he did take a strong hereditarian position at a time when such a view was anathema. Wilson wrote:

> Human beings inherit a propensity to acquire behavior and social structures, a propensity that is shared by enough people to be called human nature. The defining traits include division of labor between the sexes, bonding between parents and children, heightened altruism toward closest kin, incest avoidance, other forms of ethical behavior, suspicion of strangers, tribalism, dominance orders within groups, male dominance overall, and territorial aggression over limiting resources. Although people have free will and the choice to turn in many directions, the channels of their psychological development are nevertheless—however much we might wish otherwise—cut more deeply by genes in certain directions than others. (Wilson, 1994, pp. 332–333)

As a result of the outcry over Wilson's book, the word *sociobiology* developed such a negative connotation that it was dropped from use. In 1989, when a group of American scientists decided to form a professional association to study the field Wilson began, they called it the Human Behavior and Evolution Society and tried not to use the word *sociobiology* at their meetings.

The field of study Wilson started became incorporated into the changing views of a number of American psychologists who called their work *evolutionary psychology*. Under that somewhat more acceptable name, the field has become immensely popular.

Current Status of Evolutionary Psychology

Evolutionary psychology deals with evolved psychological mechanisms that are wired or programmed into human cognition and behavior because they have been successful in solving specific problems of survival and reproduction in the organism's evolutionary history.

Despite the popularity of evolutionary psychology, it has generated considerable criticism, as every new movement does. As mentioned earlier, people who believe that humans are solely, or at least primarily, the products of learning oppose any discussion of biological determinants of behavior. If human nature is determined by genetic endowment alone, then there is no possibility of positive social and cultural forces changing behavior for the better, or for people to try to exercise free will.

The evolutionary psychologists' response to this criticism is to note, as Wilson did earlier, that they do not claim that all behavior is immutably determined by our genes. Human behavior is changeable; we remain free to choose. Social and cultural forces are influential and sometimes override or alter inherited programming to respond in certain ways.

Opponents argue that the breadth of the field "makes the theory difficult to test in any convincing way. The ability of evolutionary psychology to explain nearly everything is not an absolute virtue" (Funder, 2001, p. 210). Critics also question how it is possible to clearly identify a history of adaptation in a particular behavior, through hundreds of generations, to primitive peoples where the survival value of the behavior presumably originated.

Comment

We have seen throughout this book that all approaches to psychology, all attempts to define the field, have had critics and points of apparent vulnerability. As with cognitive psychology, it is too early in the development of evolutionary psychology to judge its ultimate value. It, too, is history in the making. One advocate of the evolutionary psychology movement summed up the current status of the field in these terms: "We now have a powerful principle that will eventually provide a foundation for a deeper and richer psychology. But we have a lot of work to do" (Nesse, quoted in Goode, 2000, p. D9).

And so the search for the truly definitive approach to psychology, for the ultimate school of thought that might characterize the field for more than a few decades, continues. Will evolutionary psychology or cognitive psychology become that final arbiter of what psychology ought to be and do? Based on what we have seen so far, probably not.

All we can say with certainty is that if the history of psychology as we have recounted it tells us anything, it is that when a movement becomes formalized into a school it gains momentum that can be stopped only by its success in overthrowing the established position. When that happens, the unobstructed arteries of the once vigorous youthful movement begin to harden. Flexibility turns to rigidity, revolutionary passion to protection of position, and eyes and minds begin to close to new ideas. In this way a new establishment is born. So it is in the progress of any science, an evolutionary building to higher levels of development. There is no completion, no finish, just a never-ending process of growth, as newer species evolve from older ones and attempt to adapt to an ever-changing environment.

Discussion Questions

1. Describe the accomplishments, failures, and ultimate fates of the major schools of thought in psychology.
2. What were the precursors of cognitive psychology?
3. How did the changing Zeitgeist in physics influence cognitive psychology?
4. What were the early signs of a cognitive revolution in psychology?
5. What personal factors motivated Miller and Neisser?
6. In what ways did cognitive psychology differ from behavioral psychology?
7. What does the term "ecological validity" mean?
8. Discuss the shift from clocks to computers as metaphors for the mind.
9. What practical need in World War II led to the development of the modern computer? What was ENIAC?
10. What did the most famous chess match of the twentieth century tell us about the ability of machines to think?
11. How are the Turing Test and the Chinese Room problem used to examine the proposition that computers can think?

12. Discuss three ways in which cognitive psychology differs from behaviorism.

13. Describe cognitive neuroscience and the techniques used to map the brain.

14. How does cognitive neuroscience relate to earlier attempts to explain brain functioning?

15. What is neuroprosthetics and how does it involve cognitive neuroscience?

16. What are the limitations to the use of introspection in cognitive psychology?

17. In what ways does the current version of the cognitive unconscious differ from the Freudian view of the unconscious?

18. Describe the current view of animal cognition.

19. In your opinion, are animals capable of cognitive activities, or are we attributing human functions to them that they do not really possess?

20. How does evidence favoring the existence of personality in animals support Darwin's notion of evolution and the field of evolutionary psychology?

21. What is the present status of cognitive psychology?

22. Describe the relationship between evolutionary psychology and cognitive psychology. Which one draws upon the other?

23. In your opinion, has psychology reached the stage of a unified paradigm that unites all the different approaches to psychology? Do you think evolutionary psychology is likely to be the final stage in the fractious and fragmented history of the field?

Suggested Readings

Baars, B. J. (1986). *The cognitive revolution in psychology.* New York: Guilford.
    Describes the transition from post-Watsonian behaviorism to cognitive psychology. Includes interviews with Miller, Neisser, and other cognitive psychologists.
Leavitt, D. (2006). *The man who knew too much: Alan Turing and the invention of the computer.* New York: Norton.
    A highly readable biography of this groundbreaking thinker and originator of the ideas that led to the invention of the computer. Recounts his tragic personal life at a time when homosexuality in England was considered indecent and illegal.

Miller, G. A. (1989). Autobiography. In G. Lindzey (Ed.), *A history of psychology in autobiography* (Vol. 8, pp. 391–418). Stanford, CA: Stanford University Press.
Includes Miller's recollections of the teachers who influenced his career in psychology.

Pinker, S. (2002). *The blank slate: The modern denial of human nature.* New York: Viking.
Illustrates the common evolutionary themes in human nature over disparate cultures and argues for acceptance of our genetic heritage. Also evaluates popular past conceptions of human nature such as the "blank slate," the "noble savage," and the "ghost in the machine."

Rychlak, J. F. (1997). *In defense of human consciousness.* Washington, DC: American Psychological Association.
See especially chapter 7 on computers and consciousness, with machines as the metaphor for human mental functions.

Siebert, C. (June 22, 2006). The animal self. *The New York Times Magazine*, pp. 48ff.
Reviews research on personality in animals and raises some provocative questions.

Skinner, B. F. (1987). Whatever happened to psychology as the science of behavior? *American Psychologist, 42,* 780–786.
Presents Skinner's view that humanistic psychology and cognitive psychology are obstacles in the way of psychology's acceptance of his program for the experimental analysis of behavior.

CHOOSING A MAJOR: IS PSYCHOLOGY FOR YOU?

CHAPTER GUIDE

If you're like most students, one of the most difficult decisions that you face is choosing a college major. How do you decide what to do with your life? Deciding on a major can be tough if you believe that your undergraduate major determines your career; fortunately, this isn't true. Choosing a major is not the same as choosing a lifelong career, yet this myth persists. For example, many people assume that students who major in the arts, humanities, or social sciences (e.g., psychology) either are not qualified for any type of job or are qualified only for careers in those specific areas. Actually, students who earn undergraduate degrees in sociology, history, psychology, and similar majors find jobs in business, research, human resources, teaching, the military, and a variety of other occupations. (See Chapter 7 for more information about careers with a bachelor's degree in psychology.) Your major will not limit you to only one career choice.

Within 10 years after graduation, most people are working in careers that are not directly connected to their undergraduate majors. In addition, new types of jobs are emerging each year, and most of us have no way of knowing what these jobs will be or what type of education will be needed in order to qualify for them. For example, 15 years ago, most people had never heard of a web designer (someone who creates web pages and designs Internet sites). It's likely that other careers will evolve over the coming years. Consequently, career counselors recommend that college students focus on developing general, transferable skills, such as writing, speaking, computer competence, problem solving, and team building, that employers want and that graduates will need in order to adjust to a rapidly changing world. Choose a major that reflects *your* interests and abilities and provides you with opportunities to develop and hone skills that are useful in a variety of careers. The exercises in this chapter will help you to learn more about yourself; assess your interests, skills, and abilities; and determine which major is right for you.

WRITING AND SELF-AWARENESS

The first step in choosing a major is understanding yourself. Reflective and personal writing are important tools to help you understand yourself. Consider keeping a journal, a record of self-reflective writing. Although journal writing often evokes images of an adolescent girl locked away in her bedroom secretively scribbling into a locked volume, "Dear Diary," this picture is far from the truth. A diary is a daily recording of events, but a journal is so much more. A journal is a collection of your creative activity and can take many forms: a notebook, a computer file, a personal digital assistant (PDA) file, or even a web log. It is a place where you can reflect on yourself and on your experiences, goals, dreams, and anxieties. Your journal is a private learning space, a place where you can make discoveries about yourself—and understanding yourself is critical to choosing a major that you'll love.

Why Write?

Believe it or not, I was skeptical about the power of self-reflective writing—until I tried it. Here are some benefits of journal writing, or the reasons for you to consider keeping a journal.

Self-Exploration   Journal writing offers a chance to explore your own thoughts. Sometimes we're not aware of our true thoughts and feelings until we capture them with the written word. Writing is a way of learning about yourself and the world around you. It forces you to focus your thoughts, providing an opportunity to identify your opinions and values. It also helps you to clarify your sense of identity and learn about yourself.

Therapy   After a long day or a difficult experience, your journal provides a place for reflection. It's a private opportunity to let out feelings of frustration, anger, or anxiety. Writing about your deepest thoughts and feelings, or even about everyday mundane matters, can help you to release pent-up stress, which is vital for your emotional and physical health. What's even better is that a journal will never say, "I told you so." Don't censor yourself in your journal; just get it all out onto the written page and you'll feel better. You'll find that you will be better able to concentrate after you've cleared your head by journal writing.

Get Organized   Writing is an organizational tool. A journal can be a place to gather your thoughts, brainstorm ideas, and plan. Don't set any expectations for your journal. It doesn't have to be filled with descriptions of monumental experiences. Journal entries don't have to be well written or scholarly. Don't let these myths rob you of the chance to benefit from journal writing. Perhaps the easiest way to begin keeping a journal is to use it as a place to record lists of immediate tasks to be accomplished as well as long-term plans. In this way, a journal can help to organize your daily life. With regular use, writing will become a habit and expand beyond everyday topics to include self-reflection, planning, and goal setting. You can write about your goals and document the steps needed to achieve them, as well as about your progress.

Solve Problems   Writing is an effective tool for problem solving because writing is thinking. The next time you find yourself confronted with a problem or a big decision, try writing about it. Explain the problem in words: What do you know about it? Discuss your feelings about the problem and analyze it. You may find that your writing leads you to brainstorm potential solutions. Then your writing might shift toward analyzing each solution. Expressing ideas in written form requires a different thought process than does thinking. We think in new ways when we write. This allows us to conceptualize problems differently and find solutions more quickly.

Enhance Communication   The more often you write, the more your writing will improve. Journal writing strengthens communication skills, both oral and written. It provides practice in identifying and expressing ideas, which is one of your major goals as a college student.

Unleash Your Creativity   Writing offers a creative outlet, a place to generate stories, essays, and poetry. If you're having a tough time thinking up ideas for class papers or essays, your journal is the place to turn. Through writing we become more creative. There are a variety of techniques and exercises that can help you to find your center of creativity and inspire new ways of thinking and expressing yourself. Check out the exercises in this chapter and throughout this book. Also, take note of the web resources at the end of this chapter for places where you can learn how to record your ideas.

Record Your Experience   A journal provides a record of your life. Days, weeks, and months pass all too quickly. Memory is fallible. A journal helps you to remember events, experiences, feelings, and intentions. It offers a place to record accomplishments, hopes, and dreams as well as to retain details that you would probably otherwise forget. From a therapeutic perspective, looking back over old journals allows an opportunity to reflect on patterns of experience, interaction, and emotion, providing insight into yourself and your perspective on life. How have you changed and grown? Review your journal for insights into yourself.

STARTING A JOURNAL

"OK, you've convinced me. How do I start?"

First, find a place to record your thoughts. Your journal can take many forms. Some students prefer to keep their journals as word processing files on a computer. Others write in bound composition books or simply keep folders of journal entries. You can keep your journal on your PDA or perhaps even create a web log or an online journal using web log software like that found on livejournal.com (http://www.livejournal.com), typepad.org (http://www .typepad.org), blogger.com (http://www.blogger.com), or a similar site. The cardinal rule of journal writing is to remember that your journal is for you. Don't let spelling, handwriting, and grammar be major concerns. Put your feelings and experiences down in writing any way that you can. No one else will review or grade it.

What Should You Write About?

There are no rules when it comes to journals. You can write about anything that comes to mind, such as poetry, story ideas, and reflections, as well as more everyday items such as lists of accomplishments and tasks to be completed. Even everyday frustrations can be topics for your writing. Take time to observe your life. If you're having difficulty, try writing about the trouble you're experiencing in starting a journal. Write down your thoughts as they come, even if you're writing that you don't know what to write. Try describing events that are happening to you or around you from a third-person perspective. For example, begin writing with the phrase, "It was a time when . . . ," and then describe the event in detail using as many of your senses as possible. What sounds, smells, sights, and feelings were present? Pretend that you're an outside observer and use pronouns such as *he* and *she*. This exercise can help you to put things into perspective; it is especially effective when writing about life changes (like the transition to college), relationships (like that argument with your boyfriend or girlfriend), and events that you have found upsetting (like finding out that you didn't do so well on that test). Throughout this book, you'll find plenty of topics and ideas to write about in your journal, which will help you learn more about yourself and make plans for your future.

When Should You Write?

The goal of keeping a journal is to catch your thoughts. The more often you write in your journal, the more you'll learn about yourself. Take your journal with you. If you have 15 minutes between classes, write in your journal. You might even write about what you've learned in your prior class and how it relates to your experience. Try writing at bedtime or right after waking up. It doesn't take much time. You'll be surprised at how much you can write in just a few minutes. The key is to avoid censoring yourself. Allow yourself to be thoughtful and write what's on your mind. Explore your thoughts about a specific topic or about life in general. Try to get into the habit of writing each day, even if it is just a short entry. Also, try to write some longer entries because they will give you an opportunity to develop your thoughts and discover insights about yourself.

Give journal writing a shot in whatever format works for you—whether it is a handwritten page, a computer file, a PDA file, or a web log. Writing will help you to explore who you are and who you hope to become. In your journal, the mundane can become profound. Take a chance and explore yourself through writing.

SELF-ASSESSMENT

Understanding yourself is critical to choosing a major that intrigues you. Journal writing is an important start, but selecting a major requires a more thorough self-assessment. It sounds technical, but self-assessment is the process by which you examine your skills, abilities, motivations, interests, values, experience, and accomplishments. In other words, it's how you learn about yourself. Through self-assessment you can build a firm foundation of knowledge about yourself and then use this knowledge to make sound decisions about your major. The exercises in this chapter will help you to better understand yourself, but remember that self-awareness will not be achieved instantaneously. It takes hard work, soul-searching, and time.

Assess Your Personality and Attitudinal Traits

Who are you? What personality characteristics best describe you? Understanding your unique personality will help you to choose a major that is right for you. After you graduate, knowledge about your personality traits will help you to find a position or career that meshes with these characteristics and is rewarding and fulfilling. Exercise 2.1 will help you obtain a better understanding of your personality, which is essential in choosing a major that you'll be happy with. Consider writing in your journal about what you learn about yourself after completing Exercise 2.1.

EXERCISE 2.1
Assessing Your Personality Traits

Check off the traits that describe you, including additional traits if needed. Take your time to think about each one and be honest with yourself. Then complete the questions below.

❑ Academic	❑ Broad-minded	❑ Courageous
❑ Active	❑ Businesslike	❑ Creative
❑ Accurate	❑ Calm	❑ Critical
❑ Adaptable	❑ Candid	❑ Curious
❑ Adept	❑ Capable	❑ Daring
❑ Adventurous	❑ Caring	❑ Decisive
❑ Affectionate	❑ Cautious	❑ Deliberate
❑ Aggressive	❑ Charitable	❑ Delicate
❑ Alert	❑ Cheerful	❑ Democratic
❑ Ambitious	❑ Clean	❑ Dependable
❑ Analytical	❑ Clear	❑ Detail-oriented
❑ Appreciative	❑ Competent	❑ Diligent
❑ Articulate	❑ Competitive	❑ Discreet
❑ Artistic	❑ Congenial	❑ Distinctive
❑ Assertive	❑ Conscientious	❑ Dominant
❑ Astute	❑ Conservative	❑ Dynamic
❑ Athletic	❑ Considerate	❑ Eager
❑ Attentive	❑ Consistent	❑ Easygoing
❑ Balanced	❑ Conventional	❑ Effective
❑ Brave	❑ Cooperative	❑ Efficient

❏ Eloquent
❏ Emotional
❏ Empathetic
❏ Extroverted
❏ Farsighted
❏ Feeling
❏ Firm
❏ Flexible
❏ Forceful
❏ Formal
❏ Frank
❏ Frugal
❏ Future-oriented
❏ Generous
❏ Gentle
❏ Good-natured
❏ Gregarious
❏ Hardy
❏ Helpful
❏ Honest
❏ Hopeful
❏ Humorous
❏ Idealistic
❏ Imaginative
❏ Impersonal
❏ Independent
❏ Individualistic
❏ Industrious
❏ Informal
❏ Initiator
❏ Innovative
❏ Intellectual
❏ Intelligent
❏ Introverted
❏ Intuitive
❏ Inventive
❏ Jovial
❏ Judicious
❏ Just
❏ Kind
❏ Liberal

❏ Likable
❏ Literary
❏ Logical
❏ Loyal
❏ Mature
❏ Methodical
❏ Meticulous
❏ Mistrustful
❏ Modest
❏ Motivated
❏ Nurturant
❏ Objective
❏ Observant
❏ Open-minded
❏ Opportunistic
❏ Optimistic
❏ Orderly
❏ Organized
❏ Original
❏ Outgoing
❏ Patient
❏ Peaceable
❏ Perceptive
❏ Persistent
❏ Practical
❏ Productive
❏ Progressive
❏ Protective
❏ Prudent
❏ Punctual
❏ Quick
❏ Quiet
❏ Rational
❏ Realistic
❏ Receptive
❏ Reflective
❏ Relaxed
❏ Reliable
❏ Reserved
❏ Resourceful
❏ Responsible

❏ Responsible
❏ Risk-taker
❏ Sedentary
❏ Self-confidentl
❏ Self-controlled
❏ Self-disciplined
❏ Self-starter
❏ Sensible
❏ Sensitive
❏ Serious
❏ Sincere
❏ Sociable
❏ Sophisticated
❏ Stable
❏ Strong
❏ Strong-minded
❏ Structured
❏ Subjective
❏ Successful
❏ Tactful
❏ Talented
❏ Tenacious
❏ Thorough
❏ Thoughtful
❏ Tolerant
❏ Trusting
❏ Trustworthy
❏ Truthful
❏ Understanding
❏ Unexcitable
❏ Uninhibited
❏ Uninhibited
❏ Uninhibited
❏ Vigorous
❏ Warml
❏ Wholesomel
❏ Wise

Examine the list of personality descriptors that you have checked off. Carefully consider each one. How well does each adjective describe you? Choose the three that are the most important.

1. Why do these words describe you? Provide examples from your experience that illustrate how each word describes you.
2. Clear your mind and think back to when you were a child. Do you remember talking to friends and family about what you wanted to be when you grew up? Write about your memories. Consider the careers listed above. Why did you select those occupations? How have your views changed, if at all?
3. Compare your personality traits as described in question 1 with your views about occupations as a child and your views now. In what ways are your personality characteristics similar to those needed for the occupations that you find interesting?

A more precise way to use what you know about yourself to choose a major is to identify your Holland personality style. Your personality determines the work environment that you'll find most appealing. Holland (1959) proposed that people's personalities and the matching work environments can be loosely categorized into six groups. Which of the following personality types best describes you? You may find that your personality is a combination of several types.

Realistic   Someone with a realistic personality type is athletically or mechanically inclined. He or she would probably prefer to work outdoors with tools, plants, or animals. Some of the traits that describe the realistic personality type include practical, candid, a nature lover, calm, reserved, restrained, independent, systematic, and persistent.

Investigative   The investigative type enjoys learning, observing, problem solving, and analyzing information. Traits that describe the investigative type include curious, logical, observant, precise, intellectual, cautious, introspective, reserved, unbiased, and independent.

Artistic   Imaginative and creative, the artistic personality type likes to work in unstructured situations that allow for creativity and innovation. Personality characteristics of the artistic type include intuitive, unconventional, moody, nonconforming, expressive, unique, pensive, spontaneous, compassionate, bold, direct, and idealistic.

Social   The social personality type enjoys helping and training others. Characteristics that describe the social type include friendly, cooperative, idealistic, perceptive, outgoing, understanding, supportive, generous, dependable, forgiving, patient, compassionate, and eloquent.

Enterprising   The enterprising personality type likes to work with people in persuasive, performance, or managerial situations to achieve goals that are organizational or economic in nature. Characteristics that describe the enterprising type include confident, assertive, determined, talkative, extroverted, energetic, animated, social, persuasive, fashionable, spontaneous, daring, accommodating, and optimistic.

Conventional   The conventional personality type is well organized, has clerical or numerical ability, and likes to work with data and carry out tasks in detail. The conventional type can be described as meticulous, numerically inclined, conscientious, precise, adept, conforming, orderly, practical, frugal, structured, courteous, acquiescent, and persistent.

After reading these descriptions, you will probably have a good idea of where your interests lie. Most people find that one or two of the personality types fit them well. For a more precise assessment, consider taking the Self-Directed Search (Holland, 1994). The Self-Directed Search is a self-report questionnaire that assesses your personality type according to Holland's theory. Check with the career development office at your university to learn more about it; there's even an online version, which you can take for a fee at http://www .self-directed-search.com. Understanding your personality type may make it easier to choose a major because some majors are better suited to particular personalities than are others. Table 2.1 lists college majors organized by Holland personality type. Remember that this is just a guide to careers. Not all possible careers are listed, and the categories are much more fluid than they appear.

TABLE
2.1   **HOLLAND PERSONALITY TYPES AND COLLEGE MAJORS**

Realistic	Investigative	Artistic
Aerospace Engineering	Animal Science	Advertising
Agriculture/Forestry	Anthropology	Art History
Animal Science	Astronomy	Art Education
Architecture	Biochemistry	Architecture
Biosystems Engineering	Biological Sciences	Classics
Civil Engineering	Chemistry	Communications
Criminal Justice	Computer Science	English
Electrical Engineering	Engineering	Foreign Language
Engineering	Forestry	Graphic Design
Environmental Studies	Geography	History

(continued)

TABLE 2.1   HOLLAND PERSONALITY TYPES AND COLLEGE MAJORS (CONTINUED)

Realistic	Investigative	Artistic
Exercise Science	Geology	Interior Design
Geology	Mathematics	Journalism
Health and Physical Education	Medical Technology	Music
Industrial Engineering	Medicine	Music Education
Mechanical Engineering	Nursing	Speech/Drama
Medical Technology	Nutrition	
Nuclear Engineering	Pharmacy	
Plant and Soil Sciences	Philosophy	
Radiological Technology	Physical Therapy	
Recreation and Tourism Management	Physics	
Sports Management	Psychology	
	Sociology	
	Statistics	

Social	Enterprising	Conventional
Audiology	Advertising	Accounting
Counseling	Agricultural Economics	Business
Criminal Justice	Broadcasting	Computer Science
Elementary Education	Communications	Economics
History	Economics	Finance
Human Development	Finance	Mathematics
Human Services	Industrial Relations	Statistics
Library Sciences	Insurance	
Occupational therapy	Journalism	
Nursing	Law	
Nutrition	Management	
Philosophy	Marketing	
Political Science	Political Science	
Recreation and Physical Education	Public Administration	
Psychology	Speech	
Religious Studies		
Sociology		
Social Work		
Special Education		
Urban planning		

Adapted from Lock, 1988; University of Tennessee, n.d.

Assess Your Skills and Abilities

In addition to understanding your personality, your choice of major should reflect your skills and abilities. What are your skills? What activities do you do best? If you're unsure, try writing an experiential diary to get a better grip on your abilities. An experiential diary lists all the jobs, leadership positions, and extracurricular activities that you've engaged in and then lists all the tasks constituting each of these activities and jobs (DeGalan & Lambert, 1995). Once you've created this master list, write down all the skills required to perform the tasks on your list. For example, if your task was answering the phone, it probably entailed the following skills: communication skills (the effective use of language), problem solving, and the ability to direct inquiries. Also, identify specific skills that you've learned, such as the ability to use a computer programming language or speak a foreign language. Even with an experiential diary, it is sometimes difficult to list and remember all your skills and abilities. Exercise 2.2 will help you to better understand your capabilities.

EXERCISE 2.2
Assess Your Skills

Check off all the skills that apply to you; then complete the activity that follows.

- ❑ Acting or performing
- ❑ Administering
- ❑ Advising
- ❑ Analyzing Data
- ❑ Applying
- ❑ Arranging social functions
- ❑ Budgeting
- ❑ Calculating
- ❑ Checking for accuracy
- ❑ Coaching
- ❑ Collecting money
- ❑ Communicating
- ❑ Compiling statistics
- ❑ Conceptualizing
- ❑ Controlling
- ❑ Coordinating events
- ❑ Counseling
- ❑ Creating new ideas
- ❑ Decision-making
- ❑ Designing
- ❑ Dispensing information

- ❑ Dramatizing ideas or problems
- ❑ Editing
- ❑ Entertaining people
- ❑ Evaluating
- ❑ Expressing feelings
- ❑ Finding information
- ❑ Fund-raising
- ❑ Generalizing
- ❑ Goal setting
- ❑ Handling complaints
- ❑ Identifying problems
- ❑ Illustrating
- ❑ Implementing
- ❑ Improving
- ❑ Initiating with strangers
- ❑ Innovating
- ❑ Interpreting
- ❑ Interviewing
- ❑ Investigating problems
- ❑ Judging
- ❑ Leading

❏ Listening to others
❏ Managing
❏ Measuring
❏ Mediating
❏ Motivating
❏ Navigating
❏ Negotiating
❏ Observing
❏ Organizing
❏ Painting
❏ Persuading
❏ Photography
❏ Planning
❏ Problem Solving
❏ Programming
❏ Promoting
❏ Proofreading
❏ Questioning
❏ Reading
❏ Reasoning

❏ Recording
❏ Record keeping
❏ Recruiting
❏ Researching
❏ Scheduling
❏ Selling
❏ Singing
❏ Sketching
❏ Speaking
❏ Supervising
❏ Synthesizing information
❏ Teaching or training
❏ Team building
❏ Thinking logically
❏ Tolerating ambiguity
❏ Translating
❏ Troubleshooting
❏ Visualizing
❏ Writing

1. Look back over the skills that you have checked. Can you think of examples of how each skill has developed or how you've used it to achieve a goal? Based on these considerations, choose the top three to five skills and explain your choices. These skills are your strengths.
2. Now look at all the skills that you have checked, including those you didn't choose as your final set as well as those that you would have chosen but for which you couldn't think of supporting examples. Do any of these skills need further development? Which of these skills do you prefer using? Why? Which skills are you interested in using in the future? Why? Which skills do you dislike? Why?
3. Are there any skills that you don't currently have but would like to develop? Explain.

Assess Your Interests

What interests you? The happiest and most successful students choose majors that they find engaging. Many students decide on a major before considering their interests and values. They take courses for a semester or two and then realize that they've chosen a major in which they have minimal interest. Identifying your interests early in your college career can save you from changing majors and wasting time. What appeals to you?

An effective way of assessing your interests is to write about your personal history. In your journal, on scrap paper, or on a word processor, write about all the times you can think of when you have encountered a problem (regardless of its size) and taken action to solve that problem. In other words, write about all your accomplishments. List as many as you can. Don't stop when it becomes difficult, but probe further. If you're stumped, try freewriting about your achievements (yes, another use for your journal). Freewriting entails writing whatever comes to mind without censoring or editing it. Keep the ideas flowing or even write about the difficulty you're experiencing in coming up with ideas. Eventually you'll produce a number of interesting items to reflect on. Remember, the accomplishments that you list don't have to be enormous. Accomplishments can be small, and they don't have to be recognized by other people. Write about the achievements that are personally relevant to you and that you are proud of.

Next examine your accomplishments carefully. Which have brought you the most satisfaction? Which do you value the most highly? Why? This exercise helps you to identify your strengths and is a fantastic self-esteem builder. By understanding which achievements you cherish, you'll have a better idea of your interests and values, which is essential in choosing a major or career.

Values

Although choosing a major does not tie you to a particular career, it is useful to consider what career you aspire to in order to select a major and seek the educational experiences that will prepare you for it. What do you want out of life? How do you define success? Would you rather live in a city or in a rural area? Is personal time and flexibility important to you? Would you like a family (and if so, large or small)? Is financial success important? Values concern the things that are important to you, that you see as desirable in life. Spend time thinking through your priorities. Journal writing can help you to understand and clarify your values.

Putting It All Together

Now that you're aware of your personality traits, skills, interests, and values, put them all together to get a comprehensive view of yourself. Look through the lists and descriptions of majors in your college handbook. Do any seem to fit your set of traits, skills, and interests? Some majors and careers will require many of the personal traits and skills that you possess, and others will not match your self-description (DeGalan & Lambert, 1995). In your journal, list all the majors that sound interesting and seem to fit. Examine the courses required for each. Study your college handbook and the department web site to find information about the programs and opportunities for majors after graduation.

Speak with recent graduates to learn about their majors and their career experiences. If you don't know any recent graduates, visit your school's career center. Most college career centers maintain databases of recent graduates; you can contact a few graduates with different majors to learn more about their work. Also, visit the career center to seek advice. Tell the career counselor what you've learned about yourself by completing the worksheets in this chapter, and he or she can help you narrow your choice of majors.

Don't forget to talk with professors to learn more about potential majors. Visit the office of a professor whose class you enjoy to learn more about his or her work and about the field in general. Ask questions about the undergraduate major and what kinds of jobs recent graduates have obtained. Checklist 2.1 will help you to keep track of all these tasks.

CHECKLIST 2.1
Steps in Choosing a Major

❑ Assess your personality and attitudinal traits
❑ Assess your skills and abilities
❑ Assess your values and life goals
❑ Research majors
❑ Explore courses
❑ Talk with other students and recent graduates
❑ Visit the career center
❑ Talk with professors
❑ Compare alternatives
❑ Reflect on your choice
❑ Remember that your major is not your career

Once you have narrowed down your choice of majors to two (or even three), compare them with regard to the following:

Your level of interest
The curriculum (What kinds of classes are you required to take?)
Your skills and abilities (Is the major too easy or too challenging for you?)
Professors (How many are there? What do they study? What are they like?)
Your motivation to study the subject.
The kinds of jobs that graduates hold (Is it likely that the major will prepare you for the kind of career you desire?)

In short, consider the pros and cons of each major.

Finally, once you have chosen a possible major, again reflect on your choice. Freewrite about the following questions to be sure that you've made the choice that is right for you.

- Do I enjoy this subject?
- Can I perform well in this subject?

- Do I tend to seek out other students and faculty in this department for discussions and other informal interactions?
- How will this major prepare me for graduate study or employment?

DECIDING ON PSYCHOLOGY

Is psychology right for you? Only you can answer this question. Psychology offers many opportunities. As a psychology major, you will develop and expand your knowledge of human behavior. You'll become increasingly able to discriminate relevant from trivial information. You'll learn how to find and pull together (or *synthesize,* in "professor-speak") information from a variety of sources. You'll learn about psychological theories, concepts, and terms that will help you to understand and influence the world around you. If you study and take college seriously, you'll develop advanced critical thinking, communication, and interpersonal skills, which are valuable in all careers regardless of whether they are directly related to psychology.

What does majoring in psychology entail? Table 2.2 presents courses that you can expect to take as a psychology major. Some psychology courses are required for majors at nearly all schools, whereas others are electives found at a handful of schools. Of course, the exact titles of courses, requirements, and prerequisites can vary by institution. Chapter 7 provides more information about

TABLE 2.2   COMMON PSYCHOLOGY COURSES

Abnormal Psychology	Educational Psychology	Psychology and Law
Adolescent Psychology	Experimental Psychology	Psychology of Adjustment
Adulthood and Aging	Family Psychology	Psychology of Creativity
Applied Psychology	Group Dynamics	Psychology of Gender
Behavior Modification	Health Psychology	Psychology of Learning
Careers in Psychology	History of Psychology	Psychology of Motivation
Child Psychology	Industrial Psychology	Psychology of Personality
Clinical Psychology	Introductory Psychology	Psychology of Women
Cognitive Psychology	Life-Span Development	Psychopharmacology
Cognitive Neuroscience	Organizational Psychology	Sensation and Perception
Consumer Psychology	Physiological Psychology	Social Psychology
Cross-Cultural Psychology	Psychological Statistics	Sports Psychology
Developmental Psychopathology	Psychological and Educational Testing	Research Methods

the skills and abilities that you'll develop as a psychology major, as well as employment opportunities for graduates with baccalaureate degrees in psychology.

Remember that this is your decision. In choosing your major, you are the only expert. No one else can do it for you, and no test provides all the answers. Although parents, friends, professors, and counselors might offer assistance and advice, ultimately this is your decision. Your major will not lock you into one career path—there are many roads, and a psychology major can be the first step toward a variety of careers.

SUGGESTED READINGS

Andrews, L. L. (1998). *How to choose a college major*. Chicago: NTC Publishing Group.

Johnston, S. M. (1998). *The career adventure: Your guide to personal assessment, career exploration, and decision making*. Upper Saddle River, NJ: Prentice Hall.

Kuther, T. L., & Morgan, R. D. (2004). *Careers in psychology: Opportunities in a changing world*. Belmont, CA: Wadsworth.

Reeves, D. L., & Bradbury, M. J. (1998). *Majors exploration: A search and find guide for college and career direction*. Upper Saddle River, NJ: Prentice Hall.

Lock, R. D. (2005). *Taking charge of your career direction—Career planning guide*, Book 1. Belmont, CA: Wadsworth.

WEB RESOURCES

The following web sites are hot-linked at *The Psychology Major's Handbook* web site at *http://info.wadsworth.com/kuther*

Career Assessment

http://www.quintcareers.com/career_assessment.html

This is an excellent and comprehensive site with articles, tools, and other resources for assessing your career interests.

Self-Directed Search

http://www.self-directed-search.com

Available for a fee, this self-report questionnaire assesses your personality type according to Holland's theory.

About Web Logs

http://weblogs.about.com/

As we discussed, your journal can take the form of a web log. This web site provides articles, tips, prompts, and resources for beginning and experienced web log writers.

Writing the Journey

http://www.writingthejourney.com/

Get the most out of your journal with these free articles designed to be a complete
journal-writing workshop.

Career Key

http://www.careerkey.org/english/

The Career Key is a free web site with assessments to help you with career choices, career
changes, career planning, job searches, and choosing a college major or training
program.

JOURNAL EXERCISES

My Questions

This exercise helps you to identify unanswered questions and gives you
prompts for future journal entries. Use your journal to formulate and record
questions that you wonder about. What questions do you have about your
schoolwork, personal life, and values, or about current events and items you've
read about in newspapers, magazines, or books? As a college student, what do
you need to know? Don't worry about the answers yet; just let your questions
flow. Later on, weeks, months, or even years from now, when you're looking
for something new to write about, look over your list. If any of the questions
strike you as compelling, begin formulating answers in your journal.

Journal Reflection

Once you've amassed several weeks' or months' worth of journal entries, you
might use your journal to reflect on how you're changing. Read over earlier
journal entries. How have you changed? Do you have different ideas about a
particular journal entry? Do you have new interpretations of events? Do you
disagree with an earlier entry? Try to track how you think and how your thinking is changing. Can you draw conclusions about yourself from what you've
written?

Life's Pleasures

What makes you happy? Record your favorite things and activities. What are
you grateful for? This isn't just a corny exercise. Writing about the good things
in your life is a form of celebration that makes you a happier person. Stop and
feel the moment. Find something beautiful in your immediate surroundings.

Record all your senses. What does it look like? Listen to it. Can you smell it? What does it feel like?

Why College?

Why did you decide to attend college? What did you hope to gain? What have you learned since beginning college? Do you still have the same reasons for attending?

1

Introduction to Psychology and Research Methods

THEME:

Psychology is science and a profession. Scientific observation is the most powerful way to answer questions about behavior.

Key Questions

What is psychology? What are its goals?

How did psychology emerge as a field of knowledge?

What are the major trends and specialties in psychology?

How do psychologists collect information?

How is an experiment performed?

What other research methods do psychologists use?

How does psychology differ from false explanations of behavior?

How dependable is psychological information in the popular media?

Preview

Why Study Psychology?

You are a universe, a collection of worlds within worlds. Your brain is possibly the most complicated device in existence. Through its action you are capable of art, music, science, war, philosophy, love, hatred, and charity. You are the most challenging riddle ever written, a mystery at times even to yourself. Your thoughts, emotions, and actions—your behavior and conscious experience—are the subject of this book.

Look around you: Newspapers, radio, magazines, television, and the Internet are brimming with psychological topics. Psychology is an ever-changing panorama of people and ideas. You really can't call yourself educated without knowing something about it. And, although we might envy those who have walked on the moon or explored the ocean's depths, the ultimate frontier still lies close to home. Psychology can help you better understand yourself and others. This book is a guided tour of human behavior. We hope you enjoy the adventure. What, really, could be more fascinating than a journey of self-discovery?

Psychology—Spotlight on Behavior

Psychology touches us in many ways. Psychology is about memory, stress, therapy, love, persuasion, hypnosis, perception, death, conformity, creativity, learning, personality, aging, intelligence, sexuality, emotion, happiness, and much more. Psychologists use scientific investigation to study, describe, understand, predict, and control human behavior.

Psychology is both a *science* and a *profession*. Some psychologists are scientists who do research to create new knowledge. Others are teachers who pass knowledge on to students. Still others apply psychology to solve problems in mental health, education, business, sports, law, and medicine (Halpern, 2003). Later we will return to the profession of psychology. For now, let's focus on

Psychologists are highly trained professionals. In addition to the psychological knowledge they possess, psychologists learn specialized skills in counseling and therapy, measurement and testing, research and experimentation, statistics, diagnosis, treatment, and many other areas.

how knowledge is created. Whether they work in a lab, a classroom, or a clinic, all psychologists rely on information from scientific research.

What Is Psychology?

The word *psychology* comes from the roots *psyche,* which means "mind," and *logos,* meaning "knowledge or study." However, when did you last see or touch a "mind"? Because the mind can't be studied directly, **psychology** is now defined as the scientific study of behavior and mental processes.

What does behavior refer to in the definition of psychology? Anything you do—eating, sleeping, talking, or sneezing—is a behavior. So are dreaming, gambling, watching television, learning Spanish, basket weaving, and reading this book. Naturally, we are interested in *overt behaviors* (observable actions and responses). But psychologists also study *covert behaviors*. These are hidden, internal events, such as thinking and remembering (Leary, 2004).

Seeking Empirical Evidence

At various times in the last 100 years, experts have stated that "Heavier-than-air flying machines are impossible," "Radio has no future," "X-rays are a hoax," and "Computers will never serve any practical purpose." Obviously, all of these ideas proved to be wrong.

Self-appointed "authorities" are also often wrong about human behavior. Because of this, psychologists have a special respect for *empirical evidence* (information gained from direct observation). We study behavior directly and collect data (observed facts) so that we can draw valid conclusions (Martin, 2004). Would you say it's true, for instance, that "You can't teach an old dog new tricks"? Why argue about it? As psychologists, we would simply get ten "new" dogs, ten "used" dogs, and ten "old" dogs and then try to teach them all a new trick to find out!

CRITICAL THINKING

Testing Common-Sense Beliefs

It may seem that psychological research confirms what we already know from everyday experience. Why waste time and money confirming the obvious? Actually, common-sense beliefs are often wrong. See if you can tell which of the following common-sense beliefs are true and which are false (Landau & Bavaria, 2003).

• The basis of the baby's love for his mother is the fact that his mother fills his physiological need for food. True or False?
• Most humans use only 10 percent of their potential brain power. True or False?
• Blind people have unusually sensitive organs of touch. True or False?
• The more motivated you are, the better you will do at solving a complex problem. True or False?
• The weight of evidence suggests that the major factor in forgetting is the decay of memory traces with time. True or False?
• Psychotherapy has its greatest success in the treatment of psychotic patients who have lost touch with reality. True or False?
• Personality tests reveal one's basic motives, including those you may not be aware of. True or False?

• To change people's behavior toward members of ethnic minority groups, we must first change their attitudes. True or False?
• "The study of the mind" is the best brief definition of psychology today. True or False?
• Boys and girls exhibit no behavioral differences until environmental influences begin to produce such differences. True or False?

It turns out that research has shown that *all* of these common-sense beliefs are false. Yet in a survey, *all* of the beliefs were accepted as true by a large number of college students (Landau & Bavaria, 2003). How did you do?

We can all benefit from being more reflective in evaluating common-sense beliefs. When you find yourself wondering about the truth of a particular belief, apply your critical thinking skills by asking whether the belief makes logical sense. Can it be explained by any of the concepts in this book? Can you imagine what sort of research might yield empirical evidence to get you closer to the truth? Critical Thinking boxes like this one will appear throughout this book to help you be more reflective and think critically about human behavior.

Basically, the empirical approach says, "Let's take a look" (Stanovich, 2004). Have you ever wondered if drivers become more hostile when it's blazing hot outside? Douglas Kenrick and Steven MacFarlane (1986) decided to find out. They parked a car at a green light in a one-lane intersection in Phoenix, Arizona, in temperatures ranging from 88°F to 116°F. Then they recorded the number of times other frazzled drivers (in cars without air-conditioning) honked at the stalled car and how long they honked. The results are shown in ● Figure 1.1. Notice that when it was very hot, drivers spent more time leaning on the horn (which may be why cars have horns instead of cannons).

Isn't the outcome of this study fairly predictable? In this instance, you may have guessed how drivers would react. You might even see this research as doing little more than confirming common-sense beliefs. However, the results of many studies are surprising or unexpected. Take a moment and read "Testing Common-Sense Beliefs" for more information. Even in the case of this research, it's possible that drivers become lethargic in hot weather, not more aggressive. Thus, the study tells us something interesting about frustration, discomfort, and aggression.

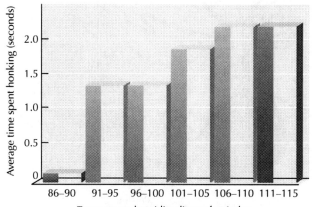

● **Figure 1.1** Results of an empirical study. The graph shows that horn honking by frustrated motorists becomes more likely as air temperature increases. This suggests that physical discomfort is associated with interpersonal hostility. Riots and assaults also increase during hot weather. Here we see a steady rise in aggression as temperatures go higher. However, research done by other psychologists has shown that hostile actions that require physical exertion, such as fist fights, may become *less* likely at very high temperatures. (Data from Kenrick & MacFarlane, 1986.)

Psychological Research

Many fields, such as history, law, art, and business, are interested in human behavior. How is psychology different? Psychology's great strength is that it uses **scientific observation** to answer questions

Psychology The scientific study of behavior and mental processes.

Scientific observation An empirical investigation that is structured so that it answers questions about the world.

about behavior (Stanovich, 2004). For instance, some parents believe that the music of Mozart increases babies' intelligence. Is this true? Many popular magazines and books say yes. Scientific testing says no.

Of course, some topics can't be studied because of ethical or practical concerns. More often, questions go unanswered for lack of a suitable **research method** (a systematic process for answering scientific questions). In the past, for example, we had to take the word of people who say they never dream. Then the EEG (electroencephalograph, or brain-wave machine) was invented. Certain EEG patterns, and the presence of eye movements, can reveal that a person is dreaming. People who "never dream," it turns out, dream frequently. If they are awakened during a dream they vividly remember it. Thus, the EEG helped make the study of dreaming more scientific.

Science and Critical Thinking

Because we all deal with human behavior every day, we tend to think that we already know what is true in psychology. For example, many people believe that punishment (a spanking) is a good way to reinforce learning in children. However, scientific studies have shown that spanking is a poor way to discipline young children. Such studies illustrate why critical thinking is important in psychology. **Critical thinking** is the ability to evaluate, compare, analyze, critique, and synthesize information. Critical thinkers analyze the evidence supporting their beliefs, they question assumptions, and they look

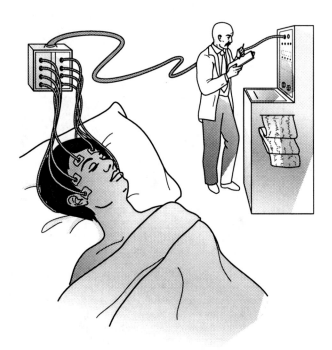

The scientific study of dreaming was made possible by use of the EEG, a device that records the tiny electrical signals generated by the brain as a person sleeps. The EEG converts these electrical signals into a written record of brain activity. Certain shifts in brain activity, coupled with the presence of rapid eye movements, are strongly related to dreaming. (See Chapter 7 for more information.)

for alternate conclusions. For example, with regard to spanking, a critical thinker would ask, "Does punishment work? If so, when? Under what conditions does it not work? What are its drawbacks? Are there better ways to guide learning?" (Halpern, 2000).

Thinking About Behavior

The core of critical thinking is a willingness to actively *evaluate* ideas. True knowledge comes from constantly revising and improving our understanding of the world. As Susan Blackmore (2001) said when her studies caused her to abandon some long-held beliefs, "Admitting you are wrong is always hard—even though it's a skill that every psychologist has to learn."

Critical thinking is built on four basic principles (Gill, 1991; Shore, 1990):

1. *Few "truths" transcend the need for empirical testing.* It is true that religious beliefs and personal values may be held without supporting evidence, but most other ideas can be evaluated by applying the rules of logic and evidence.
2. *Judging the quality of evidence is crucial.* Imagine that you are a juror in a courtroom, judging claims made by two battling lawyers. To decide correctly, you can't just weigh the amount of evidence. You must also critically evaluate the *quality* of the evidence. Then you can give greater weight to the most credible facts.
3. *Authority or claimed expertise does not automatically make an idea true.* Just because a teacher, guru, celebrity, or authority is convinced or sincere doesn't mean you should automatically believe him or her. Always ask, "What evidence convinced her or him? How good is it? Is there a better explanation?"
4. *Critical thinking requires an open mind.* Be prepared to consider daring departures and go wherever the evidence leads. However, don't become so "open-minded" that you are simply gullible. Critical thinkers strike a balance between open-mindedness and healthy skepticism. They are ready to change their views when new evidence arises (Bartz, 2002).

Research Specialties

What kinds of topics do psychologists study? Here's a sample of what various psychologists might say about their work:

> "In general, *developmental psychologists* study the course of human growth and development, from conception until death. I'm especially interested in how young children develop the ability to think, speak, perceive, and act."
>
> "I'm also interested in how people get to be the way they are. Like other *learning theorists,* I study how and why learning occurs in humans and animals. Right now I'm investigating how patterns of reward affect learning."
>
> "I'm a *personality theorist.* I study personality traits, motivation, and individual differences. I am especially interested in the personality profiles of highly creative college students."
>
> "As a *sensation and perception psychologist,* I investigate how we discern the world through our senses. I am studying how we recognize familiar faces."

The variety and complexity of human behavior make psychological investigation challenging. How would you explain the behaviors shown here?

"*Comparative psychologists* study and compare the behavior of different species, especially animals. Personally, I'm fascinated by the communication abilities of porpoises."

"*Biopsychologists* are interested in how behavior relates to biological processes, especially activities in the nervous system. I've been doing some exciting research on how the brain controls hunger."

"*Cognitive psychologists* are primarily interested in thinking. I want to know how reasoning, problem solving, memory, and other mental processes relate to human behavior."

"*Gender psychologists* study differences between females and males. I want to understand how gender differences are influenced by biology, child rearing, education, and stereotypes."

"*Social psychologists* explore human social behavior, such as attitudes, persuasion, riots, conformity, leadership, racism, and friendship. My own interest is interpersonal attraction. I analyze how friendships develop."

"*Cultural psychologists* study the ways in which culture affects human behavior. The language you speak, the foods you eat, how your parents disciplined you, what laws you obey, who you regard as 'family,' whether you eat with a spoon or your fingers—these and countless other details of behavior are strongly influenced by culture."

"*Evolutionary psychologists* are interested in how our behavior is guided by patterns that evolved during the long history of humankind. I am studying some interesting trends in male and female mating choices that don't seem to be merely learned or based on culture."

This small sample should give you an idea of the diversity of psychological research. It also hints at some of the kinds of information we will explore in this book.

Animals and Psychology

Research involving animals was mentioned in some of the preceding examples. Why is that? You may be surprised to learn that psychologists are interested in the behavior of *any* living creature—from flatworms to humans. Indeed, some comparative psychologists

Research method A systematic approach to answering scientific questions.

Critical thinking An ability to evaluate, compare, analyze, critique, and synthesize information.

Some of the most interesting research with animals has focused on attempts to teach primates to communicate with sign language. Such research has led to better methods for teaching language to aphasic children (children with serious language impairment). (See Chapter 10 for more information.)

spend their entire careers studying rats, cats, dogs, turtles, or chimpanzees.

Sometimes psychologists use **animal models** to discover principles that apply to humans. For instance, animal studies have helped us understand stress, learning, obesity, aging, sleep, and many other topics. Psychology also benefits animals. For example, caring for endangered species in zoos relies on behavioral studies. Overall, about 8 percent of all psychological research is done with animals (McCarty, 1998).

Psychology's Goals

What do psychologists hope to achieve? In general, the goals of psychology as a science are to *describe, understand, predict,* and *control* behavior. Beyond that, psychology's ultimate goal is to benefit humanity (O'Neill, 2005). What do psychology's goals mean in practice? Imagine that we would like to answer questions such as these: What happens when the right side of the brain is injured? Is there more than one type of memory? How do hyperactive children interact with their parents?

Description

Answering psychological questions requires a careful description of behavior. **Description,** or naming and classifying, is typically based on making a detailed record of behavioral observations.

But a description doesn't explain anything, does it? Right. Useful knowledge begins with accurate description, but descriptions fail to answer the important "why" questions. *Why* do more women attempt suicide, and *why* do more men complete it? *Why* are peo-

BRIDGES

Bystander apathy and conditions that influence whether people will help in an emergency are of great interest to social psychologists.

See Chapter 19, pages 653–654, for details.

ple more aggressive when they are uncomfortable? *Why* are bystanders often unwilling to help in an emergency?

Understanding

We have met psychology's second goal when we can explain an event. That is, **understanding** usually means we can state the causes of a behavior. Take our last "why" question as an example: Research on "bystander apathy" reveals that people often fail to help when *other* possible helpers are nearby. Why? Because a "diffusion of responsibility" occurs. Basically, no one feels personally obligated to pitch in. As a result, the more potential helpers there are, the less likely it is that anyone will help (Darley & Latané, 1968). Now we can explain a perplexing problem.

Prediction

Psychology's third goal, **prediction,** is the ability to forecast behavior accurately. Notice that our explanation of bystander apathy makes a prediction about the chances of getting help. If you've ever been stranded on a busy freeway with car trouble, you'll recognize the accuracy of this prediction: Having many potential helpers nearby is no guarantee that anyone will stop to help.

Control

Description, explanation, and prediction seem reasonable, but is control a valid goal? Control may seem like a threat to personal freedom. However, to a psychologist, **control** simply refers to altering conditions that affect behavior. If we suggest changes in a classroom that help children learn better, we have exerted control. If a clinical psychologist helps a person overcome a terrible fear of heights, control is involved. Control is also involved in designing airplanes to keep pilots from making fatal errors. Clearly, psychological control must be used wisely and humanely.

In summary, psychology's goals are a natural outgrowth of our desire to understand behavior. Basically, they boil down to asking the following questions:

- What is the nature of this behavior? (description)
- Why does it occur? (understanding and explanation)
- Can we forecast when it will occur? (prediction)
- What conditions affect it? (control)

KNOWLEDGE BUILDER

The Science of Psychology

REFLECT
At first, many students think that psychology is primarily about abnormal behavior and psychotherapy. Did you? How would you describe the field now?

LEARNING CHECK
To check your memory, see if you can answer these questions. If you miss any, skim over the preceding material before continuing to make sure you understand what you just read.

1. Psychology is the _____ study of _____
_____ and _____ processes.
2. The best psychological information is typically based on
   a. proven theories
   b. opinions of experts and authorities
   c. anthropomorphic measurements
   d. empirical evidence
3. In psychological research, animal _____ may be used to discover principles that apply to human behavior.
4. Which of the following questions relates most directly to the goal of *understanding* behavior?
   a. Do the scores of men and women differ on tests of thinking abilities?
   b. Why does a blow to the head cause memory loss?
   c. Will productivity in a business office increase if room temperature is raised or lowered?
   d. What percentage of college students suffer from test anxiety?

Match the following research areas with the topics they cover.

_____ 5. Developmental psychology
_____ 6. Learning
_____ 7. Personality
_____ 8. Sensation and perception
_____ 9. Biopsychology
_____ 10. Social psychology
_____ 11. Comparative psychology

A. Attitudes, groups, leadership
B. Conditioning, memory
C. The psychology of law
D. Brain and nervous system
E. Child psychology
F. Individual differences, motivation
G. Animal behavior
H. Processing sensory information

CRITICAL THINKING

12. All sciences are interested in controlling the phenomena they study. True or false?

Answers: 1. scientific, behavior, mental **2.** d **3.** models **4.** b **5.** E **6.** B **7.** F **8.** H **9.** D **10.** A **11.** C **12.** False. Astronomy and archaeology are examples of sciences that do not share psychology's fourth goal.

Scientific Research—How to Think Like a Psychologist

Suppose that your grandfather goes back to college. What do people say? "Ah . . . never too old to learn." And what do they say when he loses interest and quits? "Well, you can't teach an old dog new tricks." Let's examine another *common-sense statement*. It is often said that "absence makes the heart grow fonder." Those of us separated from friends and lovers can take comfort in this knowledge—until we remember, "Out of sight, out of mind"! Much of what passes for common sense is equally vague and inconsistent. Notice also that most of these B.S. statements work best after the fact. (B.S., of course, stands for *Before Science*.)

As we have noted, *scientific* observations must be *systematic* so that they reveal something about behavior (Stanovich, 2004). To use an earlier example, little would be gained if you drove around a city during the summer and made haphazard observations of aggressive horn honking.

Applying the scientific method to the study of behavior requires careful observation. Here, a psychologist videotapes a session in which a child's thinking abilities are being tested.

The Scientific Method

The **scientific method** is based on careful collection of evidence, accurate description and measurement, precise definition, controlled observation, and repeatable results (Leary, 2004). In its ideal form the scientific method has six elements:

1. Making observations
2. Defining a problem
3. Proposing a hypothesis
4. Gathering evidence/testing the hypothesis
5. Publishing results
6. Theory building

Let's take a closer look at some elements of the scientific method.

Hypothesis Testing

Yes, what does "proposing a hypothesis" mean? A **hypothesis** (hi-POTH-eh-sis) is a tentative explanation of an event or relationship. In common terms, a hypothesis is a *testable* hunch or educated guess about behavior. For example, you might hypothesize that "frustration encourages aggression." How could you test this hypothesis? First you would have to decide how you are going to frustrate people. (This part might be fun.) Then you will need to find a way to measure whether or not they become more aggressive. (Not so much fun if you plan to be nearby.) Your observations would then provide evidence to confirm or disconfirm the hypothesis.

Operational Definitions

Because we cannot see or touch frustration, it must be defined operationally. An **operational definition** states the exact procedures used to represent a concept. Operational definitions allow abstract ideas to be tested in real-world terms (see ● Figure 1.4). For example, you might define frustration as "interrupting an adult before he or she can finish a puzzle and win a $100 prize." Aggression might be defined as "the number of times a frustrated individual insults the person who prevented work on the puzzle."

Clever Hans

Several steps of the scientific method can be illustrated with the story of Clever Hans, a famous "wonder horse" (Rosenthal, 1965). Clever Hans seemed to solve difficult math problems, which he answered by tapping his hoof. If you asked Hans, "What is 12 times 2, minus 18?" Hans would tap his hoof six times. This was so astonishing that a scientist decided to find out if Hans really could do arithmetic. Assume that you are the scientist and that you are just itching to discover how Hans *really* does his trick.

Can a Horse Add?

Your investigation of Hans's math skills would probably begin with careful *observation* of both the horse and his owner. Assume that these observations fail to reveal any obvious cheating. Then the *problem* becomes more clearly *defined*: What signals Hans to start and stop tapping his hoof? Your first *hypothesis* might be that the owner is giving Hans a signal. Your proposed *test* would be to make the owner leave the room. Then someone else could ask Hans questions. Your test would either confirm or deny the owner's role. This *evidence* would

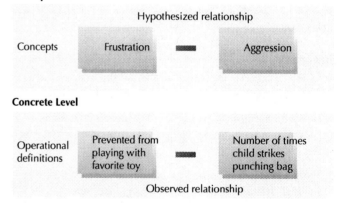

● **Figure 1.4** Operational definitions are used to link concepts with concrete observations. Do you think the examples given are reasonable operational definitions of frustration and aggression? Operational definitions vary in how well they represent concepts. For this reason, many different experiments may be necessary to draw clear conclusions about hypothesized relationships in psychology.

Scientific method Testing the truth of a proposition by careful measurement and controlled observation.

Hypothesis The predicted outcome of an experiment or an educated guess about the relationship between variables.

Operational definition Defining a scientific concept by stating the specific actions or procedures used to measure it. For example, "hunger" might be defined as "the number of hours of food deprivation."

support or eliminate the cheating hypothesis. By changing the conditions under which you observe Hans, you have *controlled* the situation to gain more information from your observations.

Incidentally, Hans could still answer when his owner was out of the room. But a brilliant series of controlled observations revealed Hans's secret. If Hans couldn't see the questioner, he couldn't answer. It seems that questioners always *lowered their heads* (to look at Hans's hoof) after asking a question. This was Hans's cue to start tapping. When Hans had tapped the correct number, a questioner would always *look up* to see if Hans was going to stop. This was Hans's cue to stop tapping!

Theories

What about theory formulation? Because Clever Hans's ability to do math was an isolated problem, no theorizing was involved. However, in actual research, a **theory** acts as a map of knowledge (Halpern, 2003). Good theories summarize observations, explain them, and guide further research (● Figure 1.5). Without theories of forgetting, personality, stress, mental illness, and the like, psychologists would drown in a sea of disconnected facts (Stanovich, 2004).

Publication

Scientific information must always be *publicly available.* The results of psychological studies are usually published in professional journals (see ■ Table 1.4). That way, anyone willing to make appropriate observations can see whether or not a claim is true (Leary, 2004).

Summary

Now let's summarize more realistically. All the basic elements of the scientific method are found in the example that follows.

Observation Suzanne, a psychologist, observes that some business managers seem to experience less work-related stress than others do.

Defining a Problem Suzanne's problem is to identify the ways in which high-stress and low-stress managers are different.

Observation Suzanne carefully questions managers about how much stress they experience. These additional observations suggest that low-stress managers believe they have more control over their work.

Proposing a Hypothesis Suzanne hypothesizes that having control over difficult tasks reduces stress.

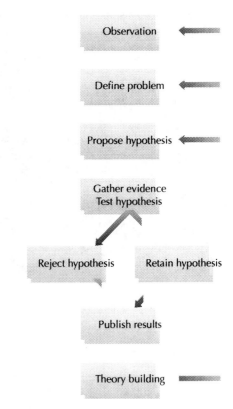

● **Figure 1.5** Psychologists use the logic of science to answer questions about behavior. Specific hypotheses can be tested in a variety of ways, including naturalistic observation, correlational studies, controlled experiments, clinical studies, and the survey method. Psychologists revise their theories to reflect the evidence they gather. New or revised theories then lead to new observations, problems, and hypotheses.

Gathering Evidence/Testing the Hypothesis Suzanne designs an experiment in which people must solve a series of very difficult problems. In one group, people solve the problems at a forced pace, dictated by Suzanne. In another group, they are allowed to set the pace themselves. While working, the second group reports lower stress levels than the first did. This suggests that Suzanne's hypothesis is correct.

Publishing Results In a scholarly article, Suzanne carefully describes the question she investigated, the methods she used, and the results of her experiment. The article is published in the *Journal of Clinical Psychology.*

Theory Building Drawing on the results of similar experiments, Suzanne and other psychologists create a theory to explain why having control over a task helps reduce stress.

BRIDGES

IQ tests serve as operational definitions of intelligence. Without such tests, it would be difficult to study intelligence.

See Chapter 11, pages 366–369.

BRIDGES

One of the major limitations of Freudian personality theory is that many of its concepts are not testable or falsifiable.

See Chapter 14, page 472.

TABLE 1.4

Outline of a Research Report

- **Abstract** Research reports begin with a very brief summary of the study and its findings. The abstract allows you to get an overview without reading the entire article.
- **Introduction** The introduction describes the question to be investigated. It also provides background information by reviewing prior studies on the same or related topics.
- **Method** This section tells how and why observations were made. It also describes the specific procedures used to gather data. That way, other researchers can repeat the study to see if they get the same results.
- **Results** The outcome of the investigation is presented. Data may be graphed, summarized in tables, or statistically analyzed.
- **Discussion** The results of the study are discussed in relation to the original question. Implications of the study are explored and further studies may be proposed.

Baron Hugo van Lawick/National Geographic Society

● **Figure 1.6** A special moment in Jane Goodall's naturalistic study of chimpanzees. A chimp uses a grass stem to extract a meal from a termite nest. Goodall's work also documented the importance of long-term emotional bonds between chimpanzee mothers and their offspring, as well as fascinating differences in the behavior and "personalities" of individual chimps (Goodall, 1990).

Research Methods

Psychologists gather evidence and test hypotheses in many ways: They observe behavior as it unfolds in natural settings (**naturalistic observation**); they make measurements to discover relationships between events (**correlational method**); they use the powerful technique of controlled experimentation (**experimental method**); they study psychological problems and therapies in clinical settings (**clinical method**); and they use questionnaires to poll large groups of people (**survey method**). Let's see how each of these is used to advance psychological knowledge.

Naturalistic Observation— Psychology Steps Out!

Psychologists sometimes actively observe behavior in a *natural setting* (the typical environment in which a person or animal lives). The work of Jane Goodall provides a good example. She and her staff have been observing chimpanzees in Tanzania since 1960. A quote from her book, *In the Shadow of Man*, captures the excitement of a scientific discovery:

> Quickly focusing my binoculars, I saw that it was a single chimpanzee, and just then he turned my direction. . . . He was squatting beside the red earth mound of a termite nest, and as I watched I saw him carefully push a long grass stem into a hole in the mound. After a moment he withdrew it and picked something from the end with his mouth. I was too far away to make out what he was eating, but it was obvious that he was actually using a grass stem as a tool. (● Figure 1.6) (Excerpt from *In the Shadow of Man* by Jane Goodall. Copyright © 1971 by Hugo and Jane Van Lawick-Goodall. Reprinted by permission of Houghton Mifflin Company. All rights reserved.)

Notice that naturalistic observation only provides *descriptions* of behavior. To *explain* observations we may need information from other research methods. Just the same, Goodall's discovery helped us realize that humans are not the only tool-making animals (Lavallee, 1999).

Chimpanzees in zoos use objects as tools. Doesn't that demonstrate the same thing? Not necessarily. Naturalistic observation allows us to study behavior that hasn't been tampered with by outside influences. Only by observing chimps in their natural environment can we tell if they use tools without human interference.

Limitations

Doesn't the presence of human observers affect the animals' behavior? Yes. The observer effect is a major problem. The **observer effect** refers to changes in a subject's behavior caused by an awareness of being observed. Naturalists must be very careful to keep their distance and avoid "making friends" with the animals they are watching. Likewise, if you are interested in schoolyard bullying,

Theory A system of ideas designed to interrelate concepts and facts in a way that summarizes existing data and predicts future observations.

Naturalistic observation Observing behavior as it unfolds in natural settings.

Correlational method Making measurements to discover relationships between events.

Experimental method Investigating behavior through controlled experimentation.

Clinical method Studying psychological problems and therapies in clinical settings.

Survey method Using questionnaires and surveys to poll large groups of people.

Observer effect Changes in a person's behavior brought about by an awareness of being observed.

you can't simply stroll onto a playground and start taking notes. As a stranger, your presence would probably change children's behavior. When possible, this problem can be minimized by concealing the observer. Another solution is to use hidden recorders. For example, a naturalistic study of playground aggression was done with video cameras and remote microphones (Pepler, Craig, & Roberts, 1998).

Observer bias is a related problem in which observers see what they expect to see or record only selected details. For instance, teachers in one study were told to watch normal elementary school children who had been labeled (for the study) as "learning disabled," "mentally retarded," "emotionally disturbed," or "normal." Sadly, teachers gave the children very different ratings, depending on the labels used (Foster & Ysseldyke, 1976). In some situations, observer bias can have serious consequences. For example, psychotherapists tend to get better results with the type of therapy they favor (Lambert, 1999).

The Anthropomorphic Error

A special trap that must be avoided while observing animals is the **anthropomorphic** (AN-thro-po-MORE-fik) **error.** This is the error of attributing human thoughts, feelings, or motives to animals—especially as a way of explaining their behavior (Blumberg & Wasserman, 1995).

Why is it risky to attribute motives or emotions to animals? The temptation to assume that an animal is "angry," "jealous," "bored," or "guilty" can be strong, but it can lead to false conclusions. If you have pets at home, you probably already know how difficult it is to avoid anthropomorphizing.

Recording Observations

Psychologists doing naturalistic studies make a special effort to minimize bias by keeping a formal log of data and observations, called an **observational record.** As suggested in the study of playground aggression, videotaping often provides the best record of all (Pepler & Craig, 1995).

Despite its problems, naturalistic observation can supply a wealth of information and raise many interesting questions. In most scientific research it is an excellent starting point.

Correlational Studies—In Search of the Perfect Relationship

Let's say a psychologist notes an association between the IQs of parents and their children, or between beauty and social popularity, or between anxiety and test performance, or even between crime and the weather. In each instance, two observations or events are **correlated** (linked together in an orderly way).

A **correlational study** finds the degree of relationship, or correlation, between two existing traits, behaviors, or events. First, two factors of interest are measured. Then a statistical technique is used to find their degree of correlation. (See the Statistics Appendix near the end of this book for more information.) For example, we could find the correlation between the number of hours slept at night and afternoon sleepiness. If the correlation is large, knowing how long a person sleeps at night would allow us to predict his or her degree of sleepiness in the afternoon. Likewise, afternoon sleepiness could be used to predict the duration of nighttime sleep.

Correlation Coefficients

How is the degree of correlation expressed? The strength and direction of a relationship can be expressed as a **coefficient of correlation.** This is simply a number falling somewhere between +1.00 and -1.00 (see the Appendix). If the number is zero or close to zero, the association between two measures is weak or nonexistent. For example, the correlation between shoe size and intelligence is zero. (Sorry, size 12 readers.) If the correlation is +1.00, a perfect positive relationship exists; if it is -1.00, a perfect negative relationship has been discovered.

Correlations in psychology are rarely perfect, but the closer the coefficient is to +1.00 or -1.00, the stronger the relationship. For example, identical twins tend to have almost identical IQs. In contrast, the IQs of parents and their children are only generally similar. The correlation between the IQs of parents and children is .35; between identical twins it's .86.

What do the terms "positive" and "negative" correlation mean? A **positive correlation** shows that increases in one measure are matched by increases in the other (or decreases correspond with decreases). For example, there is a positive correlation between high school grades and college grades; students who do better in high school tend to do better in college (and the reverse). In a **negative correlation,** increases in the first measure are associated with decreases in the second (● Figure 1.7). We might observe, for instance, that the higher the air temperature, the lower the activity level of animals in a zoo.

Would that show that air temperature causes changes in activity level? It might seem so, but we cannot be sure without performing an experiment.

Correlation and Causation

Correlational studies help us discover relationships and make predictions. However, correlation *does not demonstrate causation.* Just because two things *appear* to be related does not mean that **causation** (a cause-and-effect connection) exists (Halpern, 2003). The animals' activity might be affected by seasonal changes in weight, hormone levels, or even the feeding schedule at the zoo. Just because one thing to be related to another does not mean that a cause-and-effect connection exists.

BRIDGES

Correlations between the IQs of family members are used to estimate the degree to which intelligence is affected by heredity and environment.

See Chapter 11, pages 376–378.

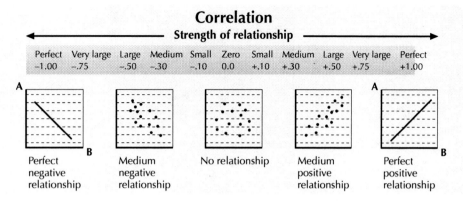

Correlation
Strength of relationship

Perfect	Very large	Large	Medium	Small	Zero	Small	Medium	Large	Very large	Perfect
−1.00	−.75	−.50	−.30	−.10	0.0	+.10	+.30	+.50	+.75	+1.00

Perfect negative relationship

Medium negative relationship

No relationship

Medium positive relationship

Perfect positive relationship

● **Figure 1.7** The correlation coefficient tells how strongly two measures are related. These graphs show a range of relationships between two measures, A and B. If a correlation is negative, increases in one measure are associated with decreases in the other. (As B gets larger, A gets smaller.) In a positive correlation, increases in one measure are associated with increases in the other. (As B gets larger, A gets larger.) The center-left graph ("medium negative relationship") might result from comparing anxiety level (B) with test scores (A): Higher anxiety is associated with lower scores. The center graph ("no relationship") would result from plotting a person's shoe size (B) and his or her IQ (A). The center-right graph ("medium positive relationship") could be a plot of grades in high school (B) and grades in college (A) for a group of students: Higher grades in high school are associated with higher grades in college.

Here is another example of mistaking correlation for causation: What if a psychologist discovers that the blood of patients with schizophrenia contains a certain chemical not found in the general population? Does this show that the chemical *causes* schizophrenia? It may seem so, but schizophrenia could cause the chemical to form. Or both schizophrenia and the chemical might be caused by some unknown third factor, such as the typical diet in mental hospitals.

Just because one thing *appears* to cause another does not *confirm* that it does. This fact can be seen clearly in the case of obviously noncausal relationships. For example, there is a correlation between the number of churches in American cities and the number of bars; the more churches, the more bars. Does this mean that drinking makes you religious? Does it mean that religion makes you thirsty? No one, of course, would leap to such conclusions about cause and effect. But in less obvious situations, it's tempting. (The real connection is that both the number of churches and the number of bars are related to the population size of cities.)

Relationships in Psychology

Do students who study more get better grades? To answer this question we could record how long a number of students study each week. Then we could match hours studied with grades earned. Suppose we find that low study times correspond to low grades. Likewise, high amounts of studying are associated with high grades. If this were the case, there would be a positive relationship between studying and grades. Similarly, we might discover that students who watch many hours of television tend to get lower grades than those who watch few hours. (This is the well-known TV zombie effect.) This time, a negative relationship would exist. That is, low viewing times go with high grades, and high viewing times go with low grades. Obviously, these examples are only hypothetical. However, when real patterns can be identified, they have great value. Relationships summarize large amounts of data and allow us to make accurate predictions.

Graphical Data

Drawing graphs of relationships can help clarify their nature. For instance, ● Figure 1.8 shows the results of a memory experiment. Before being tested, subjects learned from one to twenty word lists. The question was, "How well would they remember the last list?" The graph shows that when participants learned only one list, they remembered 80 percent of it. When they learned four lists, their scores on the last list dropped to 43 percent (blue arrows). When they memorized ten other lists, their recall fell even more, to 22 percent (red arrows). Overall, there was a negative relationship between the number of lists memorized and

Observer bias The tendency of an observer to distort observations or perceptions to match his or her expectations.

Anthropomorphic error The error of attributing human thoughts, feelings, or motives to animals, especially as a way of explaining their behavior.

Observational record A detailed summary of observed events or a videotape of observed behavior.

Correlation The existence of a consistent, systematic relationship between two events, measures, or variables.

Correlational study A nonexperimental study designed to measure the degree of relationship (if any) between two or more events, measures, or variables.

Coefficient of correlation A statistical index ranging from −1.00 to +1.00 that indicates the direction and degree of correlation.

Positive correlation A statistical relationship in which increases in one measure are matched by increases in the other (or decreases correspond with decreases).

Negative correlation A statistical relationship in which increases in one measure are matched by decreases in the other.

Causation The act of causing some effect.

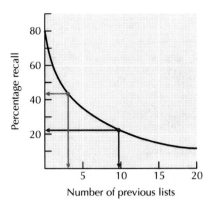

● **Figure 1.8** Effects of interference on memory. A graph of the approximate relationship between percentage recalled and number of different word lists memorized. Adapted from Underwood, 1957

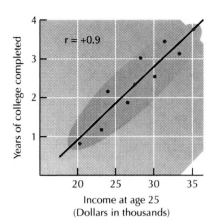

● **Figure 1.9** The relationship between years of college completed and personal income (hypothetical data).

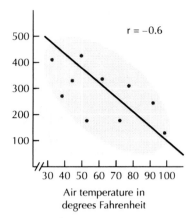

● **Figure 1.10** The relationship between air temperature and amount of coffee consumed (hypothetical data.)

recall of the last list. (The meaning of this finding is discussed in Chapter 9. For now, let's just say that you shouldn't memorize a telephone book before studying for a test.)

Some graphs reveal **linear** (straight-line) **relationships**. Others are **curvilinear** (kur-vih-LIN-ee-er) and consist of a curved line, like Figure 1.8. In either case, relationships need not be perfect to be useful. Suppose, for instance, that we randomly select 10 people. We then compare the years of college completed with each person's income at age 25. Results like those shown in ● Figure 1.9 would make it clear that there is a strong positive relationship between education and earnings. Remember that such correlations do not prove education increases earnings. Nevertheless, a pattern like this might be of great interest to a high school student thinking about whether to attend college.

The shaded area and the colored line in ● Figure 1.9 show that the relationship is approximately linear, but not perfect. (If it were perfect, all the dots would lie on the colored line.) The correlation coefficient (*r*) also shows that the relationship is strong and positive, but not perfect. (How often do you find a perfect relationship?) If the relationship *were* perfect, the coefficient would be 1.00.

For comparison, ● Figure 1.10 plots more hypothetical data. Assume that the manager of a college cafeteria has recorded the amount of coffee sold on 10 different days, as well as the air temperature on each day. Notice again that the relationship appears to be linear. However, this time it is negative. Also note how the shaded area and the correlation coefficient both indicate a weaker relationship. Even so, knowing the correlation between temperature and coffee drinking would help anyone planning how much "mud" to brew each morning.

On a higher plane, psychologists seek to identify relationships concerning memory, perception, stress, aging, therapy, and a host of similar topics. Much of this book is a summary of such relationships.

The best way to be confident that a cause-and-effect relationship exists is to perform a controlled experiment. You'll learn how in the next section.

KNOWLEDGE BUILDER

Research Methods, Naturalistic Observation, and Correlation

REFLECT
You probably hypothesize daily about why people act the way they do. Do you seek to verify your hypotheses? Usually we closely observe others to determine whether our "educated guesses" about them are correct. But casual observation can be misleading. To really test a hypothesis, systematic observation and formal research methods are necessary.

If you were going to do some informal naturalistic observation in your psychology classroom, what behavior would you observe and record?

See if you can identify at least one positive relationship and one negative relationship that involves human behavior.

LEARNING CHECK
1. Most of psychology can rightfully be called common sense because psychologists prefer naturalistic observation to controlled observation. T or F?
2. A psychologist does a study to see if having control over difficult tasks reduces stress. In the study he will be testing an
   a. experimental hypothesis   c. empirical definition
   b. operational definition   d. anthropomorphic theory
3. Two major problems in naturalistic observation are the effects of the observer and observer bias. T or F?
4. The _____ fallacy involves attributing human feelings and motives to animals.
5. Correlation typically does not demonstrate causation. T or F?
6. Which correlation coefficient represents the strongest relationship?
   a. −0.86   b. +0.66   c. +0.10   d. +0.09

CRITICAL THINKING
7. Can you think of some additional "common-sense" statements that contradict each other?

8. Adults who often ate Frosted Flakes cereal as children now have half the cancer rate seen in adults who never ate Frosted Flakes. What do you think explains this strange correlation?

The Psychology Experiment— Where Cause Meets Effect

Psychologists want to be able explain *why* we act the way we do. Sometimes this can be achieved with naturalistic observation or correlations. However, usually we must do an experiment to discover the *causes* of behavior. Experiments bring cause-and-effect relationships into sharp focus, allowing us to answer the important "why" questions in psychology.

The most powerful research tool is an **experiment** (a formal trial undertaken to confirm or disconfirm a hypothesis). Psychologists carefully control conditions in experiments to identify cause-and-effect relationships. To perform an experiment you would do the following:

1. Directly vary a condition you think might affect behavior.
2. Create two or more groups of subjects. These groups should be alike in all ways *except* the condition you are varying.
3. Record whether varying the condition has any effect on behavior.

Assume that you want to find out if hunger affects memory. First, you would form two groups of people. Then you could give the members of one group a memory test while they are hungry. The second group would take the same test after eating a meal. By comparing average memory scores for the two groups, you could tell if hunger affects memory.

As you can see, the simplest psychological experiment is based on two groups of **subjects** (animals or people whose behavior is investigated). One group is called the *experimental group;* the other becomes the *control group.* The control group and the experimental group are treated exactly alike except for the condition you intentionally vary. This condition is called the *independent variable.*

Variables and Groups

A **variable** is any condition that can change and that might affect the outcome of the experiment. Identifying causes and effects in an experiment involves three types of variables:

1. **Independent variables** are conditions altered or varied by the experimenter, who sets their size, amount, or value.

Independent variables are suspected *causes* for differences in behavior.
2. **Dependent variables** measure the results of the experiment. That is, they reveal the *effects* that independent variables have on *behavior.* Such effects are often revealed by measures of performance, such as test scores.
3. **Extraneous variables** are conditions that a researcher wishes to prevent from affecting the outcome of the experiment.

We can apply these terms to our hunger/memory experiment in this way: Hunger is the independent variable—we want to know if hunger affects memory. Memory (defined by scores on the memory test) is the dependent variable—we want to know if the ability to memorize depends on how hungry a person is. All other conditions that could affect memory scores are extraneous. Examples are the number of hours slept the night before the test, intelligence, or difficulty of the questions.

As you can see, an **experimental group** consists of subjects exposed to the independent variable (hunger in the preceding example). Members of the **control group** are exposed to all conditions except the independent variable.

Let's examine another simple experiment. Suppose you notice that you seem to study better while listening to music. This suggests the hypothesis that music improves learning. We could test this idea by forming an experimental group that studies with music. A control group would study without music. Then we could compare their scores on a test.

Is a control group really needed? Can't people just study with music on to see if they do better? Without a control group it would be impossible

---

Linear relationship A relationship that forms a straight line when graphed.

Curvilinear relationship A relationship that forms a curved line when graphed.

Experiment A formal trial undertaken to confirm or disconfirm a fact or principle.

Experimental subjects Humans or animals whose behavior is investigated in an experiment.

Variable Any condition that changes or can be made to change; a measure, event, or state that may vary.

Independent variable In an experiment, the condition being investigated as a possible cause of some change in behavior. The values that this variable takes are chosen by the experimenter.

Dependent variable In an experiment, the condition (usually a behavior) that is affected by the independent variable.

Extraneous variables Conditions or factors excluded from influencing the outcome of an experiment.

Experimental group In a controlled experiment, the group of subjects exposed to the independent variable or experimental condition.

Control group In a controlled experiment, the group of subjects exposed to all experimental conditions or variables *except* the independent variable.

CONTROL GROUP   OUT OF CONTROL GROUP

to tell if music had any effect on learning. The control group provides a *point of reference* for comparison with scores of the experimental group. If the average test score of the experimental group is higher than the average of the control group, we can conclude that music improves learning. If there is no difference, it's obvious that the independent variable had no effect on learning.

In this experiment, the amount learned (indicated by scores on the test) is the *dependent variable*. We are asking, Does the independent variable *affect* the dependent variable? (Does music affect or influence learning?)

Experimental Control

How do we know that the people in one group aren't more intelligent than those in the other group? It's true that personal differences might affect the experiment. However, they can be controlled by randomly assigning people to groups. **Random assignment** means that a subject has an equal chance of being in either the experimental group or the control group. Randomization evenly balances personal differences in the two groups. In our musical experiment, this could be done by simply flipping a coin for each subject: heads, the subject is in the experimental group; tails, it's the control group. This would result in few differences in the number of people in each group who are geniuses or dunces, hungry, hung over, tall, music lovers, or whatever.

Other *extraneous,* or outside, variables—such as the amount of study time, the sex of subjects, the temperature in the room, the time of day, the amount of light, and so forth—must also be prevented from affecting the outcome of an experiment. But how? Usually this is done by making all conditions (except the independent variable) *exactly* alike for both groups. When all conditions are the same for both groups—*except* the presence or absence of music—then a difference in the amount learned *must* be caused by the music (● Figure 1.11).

Cause and Effect

Now let's summarize. In an experiment two or more groups of subjects are treated differently with respect to the independent variable. In all other ways they are treated the same. That is, extraneous variables are equalized for all groups. The effect of the independent variable (or variables) on some behavior (the dependent

variable) is then measured. In a carefully controlled experiment, the independent variable is the only possible *cause* for any *effect* noted in the dependent variable. This allows clear cause-and-effect connections to be identified (● Figure 1.12).

Evaluating Results

How can we tell if the independent variable really made a difference? The problem is handled statistically. Reports in psychology journals almost always include the statement, "Results were **statistically significant.**" What this means is that the obtained results would occur very rarely by chance alone. To be statistically significant, a difference must be large enough so that it would occur by chance in less than 5 experiments out of 100. (See the Statistics Appendix for more information.) Of course, findings also become more convincing when they can be *replicated* (repeated) by other researchers.

Meta-Analysis

As you might guess, numerous studies are done on important topics in psychology. Although each study adds to our understanding, the results of various studies don't always agree. Let's say we are interested in whether males or females tend to be greater risk takers. A computer search would reveal that more than 100 studies have investigated various types of risk-taking (for example, smoking, fast driving, or unprotected sex).

Is there a way to combine the results of the studies? Yes, a statistical technique called **meta-analysis** can be used to combine the results of many studies as if they were all part of one big study (Rosenthal & DiMatteo, 2001). In other words, a meta-analysis is a study of the results of other studies. In recent years, meta-analysis has been used

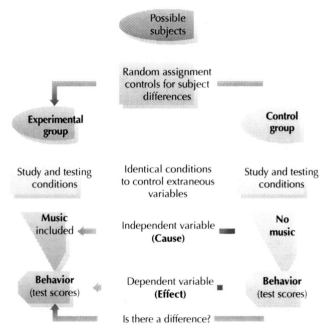

● **Figure 1.11** Elements of a simple psychological experiment to assess the effects of music during study on test scores.

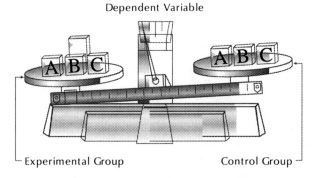

Dependent Variable

Experimental Group   Control Group

▢ Extraneous Variables

▢ Independent Variable

● **Figure 1.12** Experimental control is achieved by balancing extraneous variables for the experimental group and the control group. For example, the average age (A), education (B), and intelligence (C) of group members could be made the same for both groups. Then we could apply the independent variable to the experimental group. If their behavior (the dependent variable) changes (in comparison with the control group), the change must be caused by the independent variable.

to summarize and synthesize mountains of psychological research. This allows us to see the big picture and draw conclusions that might be missed in a single, small-scale study. Oh, and about that risk-taking question: A meta-analysis showed that males do tend to take more risks than females (Byrnes, Miller, & Schafer, 1999). (The most frequent last words uttered by deceased young males is rumored to be, "Hey, watch this!")

Placebo Effects—Sugar Pills and Saltwater

Let's do an experiment to see if the drug amphetamine (a stimulant) affects learning: Before studying, members of our experimental group take an amphetamine pill. Control group members get nothing. Later, we assess how much each subject learned. Does this experiment seem valid? Actually, it is seriously flawed.

Why? The experimental group took the drug and the control group didn't. Differences in the amount they learned must have been caused by the drug, right? No, because the drug wasn't the only difference between the groups. People in the experimental group swallowed a pill, and control subjects did not. Without using a placebo (plah-SEE-bo), it is impossible to tell if the drug affects learning. It could be that those who swallowed a pill *expected* to do better. This alone might have affected their performance, even if the pill didn't.

What is a placebo? Why would it make a difference? A **placebo** is a fake pill or injection. Inert substances such as sugar pills and saline (saltwater) injections are common placebos. Thus, if a placebo has any effect, it must be based on suggestion, rather than chemistry (Moerman, 2002).

The **placebo effect** (changes in behavior caused by belief that one has taken a drug) can be powerful. For instance, a saline injection is 70 percent as effective as morphine in reducing pain. That's why doctors sometimes prescribe placebos. Placebos have been shown to affect pain, anxiety, depression, alertness, tension, sexual arousal, cravings for alcohol, and many other processes (Kirsch & Lynn, 1999).

How could an inert substance have any effect? Placebos alter our expectations about our own emotional and physical reactions. Because we associate taking medicine with feeling better, we expect placebos to make us feel better, too (Stewart-Williams, 2004). After a person takes a placebo, there is a reduction in brain activity linked with pain, so the effect is not imaginary (Wager et al., 2004).

Controlling Placebo Effects

To control for placebo effects, we could use a **single-blind experiment.** In this case, subjects do not know if they are receiving a real drug or a placebo. All subjects get a pill or injection. People in the experimental group get a real drug, and those in the control group get a placebo. Because subjects are *blind* as to whether they received the drug, their expectations are the same. Any difference in their behavior must be caused by the drug.

Keeping subjects "blind" is not necessarily enough, however. In a **double-blind experiment** neither subjects nor experimenters know who received a drug and who took a placebo. This keeps researchers from unconsciously influencing subjects. Typically, someone else prepares the pills or injections so that experimenters don't know until after testing who got what. Double-blind testing has shown that about 50 percent of the effectiveness of antidepressant drugs, such as the "wonder drug"

Random assignment The use of chance (for example, flipping a coin) to assign subjects to experimental and control groups.

Statistical significance Experimental results that would rarely occur by chance alone.

Meta-analysis A statistical technique for combining the results of many studies on the same subject.

Placebo An inactive substance given in the place of a drug in psychological research or by physicians who wish to treat a complaint by suggestion.

Placebo effect Changes in behavior due to expectations that a drug (or other treatment) will have some effect.

Single-blind experiment An arrangement in which subjects remain unaware of whether they are in the experimental group or the control group.

Double-blind experiment An arrangement in which both subjects and experimenters are unaware of whether subjects are in the experimental group or the control group.

FOCUS ON RESEARCH   Abducted by Space Aliens?

In upcoming chapters you will find other "Focus on Research" boxes like this one. These boxes will help you reflect on the role of research methods in psychology.

Because the placebo effect is based, in part, on suggestion, it is tempting to conclude that placebos have no value. You might even think it is wrong for doctors to deliberately use placebos to "fool" their patients (Moerman, 2002). But some research methods suggest otherwise. For example, in one study patients recovering from surgery were given morphine. Some patients knew they were getting the morphine because they watched a doctor give them an injection. Patients in another group received the same dose of morphine, but they didn't know they were getting it. (The drug was given through an infusion machine to which the patients

were already connected.) Thus, the experimental group received a visible medical treatment and the control group got a concealed medical treatment (Benedetti, Maggi, & Lopiano, 2003).

What were the results? Patients who knew they were getting morphine experienced more pain relief than patients who didn't know they'd been given a painkiller. One way to interpret this result is that a placebo effect is *always* present when medicines are administered. This suggests that doctors should administer medicine as openly as possible. That way, patients benefit from the medicine *and* the placebo effect. In other words, medicine works best when doctors help people *make sense* of their medical condition, to maximize healing (Moerman, 2002).

Prozac, is due to the placebo effect (Kirsch & Sapirstein, 1998). Much of the popularity of herbal health remedies is also based on the placebo effect (Seidman, 2001). (See "Investigating the Placebo Effect" for more information about how psychologists study placebos.)

The placebo effect is a major factor in medical treatments. Would you also expect the placebo effect to occur in psychotherapy? (It does, which complicates studies on the effectiveness of new psychotherapies.)

Sometimes researchers themselves affect experiments by influencing the behavior of their subjects. Let's see how this occurs.

The Experimenter Effect

How could a researcher influence subjects? The **experimenter effect** (changes in behavior caused by the unintended influence of an experimenter) is a common problem. In essence, experimenters run the risk of finding what they expect to find. This occurs because humans are very sensitive to hints about what is expected of them (Rosenthal, 1994).

The experimenter effect even applies outside the laboratory. Psychologist Robert Rosenthal (1973) reports an example of how expectations influence people: At the U.S. Air Force Academy Preparatory School, 100 airmen were randomly assigned to five different math classes. Their teachers did not know about this random placement. Instead, each teacher was told that his or her students had unusually high or low ability. Students in the classes labeled "high ability" improved much more in math scores than those in "low-ability" classes. Yet, initially, all of the classes had students of equal ability.

Apparently, the teachers subtly communicated their expectations to students. Most likely, they did this through tone of voice, body language, and by giving encouragement or criticism. Their "hints," in turn, created a self-fulfilling prophecy that affected the students. A *self-fulfilling prophecy* is a prediction that prompts people to act in ways that make the prediction come true. For instance, many teachers underestimate the abilities of ethnic minority children, which hurts the students' chances for success (Weinstein, Gregory, & Strambler, 2004). In short, people sometimes become what we prophesy for them. It is wise to remember that others tend to live *up* or *down* to our expectations for them (Madon, Jussim, & Eccles, 1997; Madon et al., 2001).

KNOWLEDGE BUILDER

The Psychology Experiment

REFLECT

In a sense, we all conduct little experiments to detect cause-and-effect connections. If you are interested in gardening, for example, you might try adding plant food to one bed of flowers but not another. The question then becomes, "Does the use of plant food (the independent variable) affect the size of the flowers (the dependent variable)?" By comparing unfed plants (the control group) with those receiving plant food (the experimental group) you could find out if plant food is worth using. Can you think of at least one informal experiment you've run in the last month? What were the variables? What was the outcome?

LEARNING CHECK

1. To understand cause and effect, a simple psychological experiment is based on creating two groups: the _____ _____ group and the _____ _____ group.
2. There are three types of variables to consider in an experiment: _____ variables (which are manipulated by the experimenter); _____ variables (which measure the outcome of the experiment); and _____ variables (factors to be excluded in a particular experiment).
3. A researcher performs an experiment to learn if room temperature affects the amount of aggression displayed by college students under crowded conditions in a simulated prison environment. In this experiment, the independent variable is which of the following?
   a. room temperature   c. crowding
   b. the amount of aggression d. the simulated prison environment
4. A procedure used to control both the placebo effect and the experimenter effect in drug experiments is the
   a. correlation method   c. double-blind technique
   b. extraneous prophecy   d. random assignment of subjects

CRITICAL THINKING

5. There is a loophole in the statement, "I've been taking vitamin C tablets, and I haven't had a cold all year. Vitamin C is great!" What is the loophole?
6. How would you determine if sugary breakfasts affect children's activity levels and their ability to learn in school?
7. People who believe strongly in astrology have personality characteristics that actually match, to a degree, those predicted by their astrological signs. Can you explain why this occurs?

Answers: 1. experimental, control 2. independent, dependent, extraneous 3. a 4. c 5. The statement implies that vitamin C prevented colds. However, not getting a cold just could be a coincidence. A controlled experiment with a group given vitamin C and a control group not taking vitamin C would be needed to learn if vitamin C actually has any effect on susceptibility to colds. 6. An actual experiment on this question used a double-blind design in which children were given a breakfast drink containing either 50 grams of sucrose (sugar), a placebo (aspartame), or only a very small amount of sucrose. Observed changes in activity levels and in scores on a learning task did not support the view that sugar causes major changes in children's behavior (Rosen et al., 1988). 7. Belief in astrology can create a self-fulfilling prophecy in which people alter their behaviors and self-concepts to match their astrological signs (van Rooij, 1994).

The Clinical Method— Data by the Case

It can be difficult or impossible to use the experimental method to study mental disorders, such as depression or psychosis. Many experiments are impractical, unethical, or impossible to do. In such instances, a **case study** (an in-depth focus on a single subject) may be the best source of information. Clinical psychologists rely heavily on case studies, especially as a way to investigate rare or unusual problems.

Case studies may sometimes be thought of as **natural clinical tests** (accidents or other natural events that provide psychological data). Gunshot wounds, brain tumors, accidental poisonings, and similar disasters have provided much information about the human brain. One remarkable case from the history of psychology is reported by Dr. J. M. Harlow (1868). Phineas Gage, a young foreman on a work crew, had a 13-pound steel rod blown through the front of his brain by a dynamite explosion (● Figure 1.13). Amazingly, he survived the accident. Within 2 months Gage could walk, talk, and move normally, but the injury forever changed his personality. Instead of the honest and dependable worker he had been before, Gage became a surly, foul-mouthed liar. Dr. Harlow carefully recorded all details of what was perhaps the first in-depth case study of an accidental frontal lobotomy (the destruction of front brain matter).

When a Los Angeles carpenter named Michael Melnick suffered a similar injury, he recovered completely, with no lasting ill effects. Melnick's very different reaction to a similar injury shows why psychologists prefer controlled experiments and often use lab animals for studies of the brain. Case studies lack formal control groups, which limits the conclusions that can be drawn. Nonetheless, case studies are especially valuable for studying rare events, such as unusual mental disorders, childhood "geniuses," or "rampage" school shootings (Harding, Fox, & Mehta, 2002). Also, case studies of psychotherapy have provided many useful ideas about how to treat emotional problems (Hersen, 2002).

Case studies can provide special opportunities to answer interesting questions. For instance, a classic case study in psychology concerns four identical quadruplets, known as the Genain sisters. In addition to having identical genes, all four women became schizophrenic before age 25 (Rosenthal & Quinn, 1977). The Genains, who are now in their late sixties, have been in and out of mental hospitals all their lives. The fact that they share identical genes suggests that mental disorders are influenced by heredity. The fact that some of the sisters are more disturbed than others suggests that environmental conditions also affect mental illness.

Experimenter effect Changes in subjects' behavior caused by the unintended influence of an experimenter's actions.

Case study An in-depth focus on all aspects of a single person.

Natural clinical test An accident or other natural event that allows the gathering of data on a psychological phenomenon of interest.

Indeed, Myra, the least ill of the four, was the only sister who was able to avoid her father, an alcoholic who terrorized, spied on, and sexually molested the girls. (See Chapter 13 for more information about the causes of schizophrenia.)

The Genain sisters have been studied for 40 years. The chances of four identical quads all becoming schizophrenic are about one in 1.5 billion. Thus, cases like theirs provide insights that can't be obtained by any other means (Edwards, 1998; Mirsky et al., 2000).

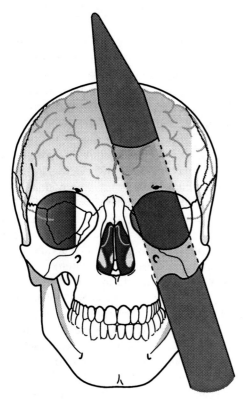

● **Figure 1.13** Some of the earliest information on the effects of damage to frontal areas of the brain came from a case study of the accidental injury of Phineas Gage.

Survey Method—Here, Have a Sample

Sometimes psychologists would like to ask everyone in the world a few well-chosen questions: "Do you drink alcoholic beverages? How often per week?" "What form of discipline did your parents use when you were a child?" "What is the most creative thing you've done?" The answers to such questions can reveal much about people's behavior, but because it is impossible to question everyone, doing a survey is often more practical.

In the **survey method,** public polling techniques are used to answer psychological questions (Tourangeau, 2004). Typically, people in a representative sample are asked a series of carefully worded questions. A **representative sample** is a small group that accurately reflects a larger population. A good sample must include the same proportion of men, women, young, old, professionals, blue-collar workers, Republicans, Democrats, whites, African Americans, Latinos, Asians, and so on as found in the population as a whole. In contrast, a **biased sample** does not accurately reflect characteristics of the whole population.

Pretesting of survey questions can usually remove those that are bad, confusing, or easily misunderstood. Also, new computerized surveys can ask a different series of questions, depending on the answers to the first few items. This helps avoid asking unnecessary questions and it brings a person's responses into sharper focus (Krosnick, 1999).

A **population** is an entire group of animals or people belonging to a particular category (for example, all college students or all married women). Ultimately, we are interested in entire populations, but by selecting a smaller sample we can draw conclusions about the larger group without polling each and every person. Representative samples are often obtained by *randomly* selecting who will be included (● Figure 1.14). (Notice that this is similar to randomly assigning subjects to groups in an experiment.)

In recent years, 93 percent of human subjects in psychology experiments have been recruited from introductory psychology courses (Sieber & Saks, 1989). The majority of these subjects have

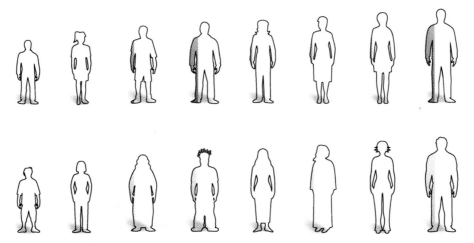

● **Figure 1.14** If you were conducting a survey in which a person's height might be an important variable, the upper, nonrandom sample would be very unrepresentative. The lower sample, selected using a table of random numbers, better represents the group as a whole.

HUMAN DIVERSITY

Is There a Gender Bias in Psychological Research?

As you read through this book you may find yourself wondering whether or not a particular concept, theory, or research finding applies equally well to women and men, to members of various races or ethnic groups, or to people of different ages or sexual orientations. "Human Diversity" boxes like this one will help you be more reflective about our multicultural, multifaceted society. Here, let's begin with a basic question: Is there is a gender bias in the research process itself?

Many doctors continue to recommend that adults take an aspirin a day to help prevent a heart attack. Both men and women are given this advice. The problem? Not a single woman was included in the sample on which the advice is based. Although females make up more than half the population, they continue to be neglected in psychological and medical research (Hyde, 2004).

This oversight is just one form of **gender bias in research.** This term refers to the tendency for females to be underrepresented as research subjects and female topics to be ignored by many investigators. Consequently, the investigators assumed that conclusions based on men also apply to women. But without directly studying women it is impossible to know how often this assumption is wrong. A related problem occurs when researchers combine results from men and women. Doing so can hide important male–female differences. An additional problem is that unequal numbers of men and women may volunteer for some kinds of research. For example, in studies of sexuality, more male

college students volunteer to participate than females (Wiederman, 1999). What a surprise!

Another form of gender bias in research occurs when women are underrepresented among the researchers themselves. In one example, Laurence Kohlberg (1969) proposed a theory about how we develop moral values. His studies suggested that women were morally "immature" because they were not as concerned with justice as men were. However, few women were involved in doing the studies and the researchers merely *assumed* that theories based on men also apply to women. In response, Carol Gilligan (1982) provided evidence that women were more likely to make moral choices based on caring, rather than justice. From this point of view, it was men who were morally immature. Today, we recognize that both justice and caring perspectives may be essential to adult wisdom (see Chapter 4 for more details).

Similar biases exist concerning the race, ethnicity, age, and sexual orientation of researchers and participants in psychological research (Denmark, Rabinowitz, & Sechzer, 2005; Guthrie, 2004). Far too many conclusions are created by and/or based on small groups of people who do not represent the rich tapestry of humanity. However, the solution to such problems is straightforward: We need to encourage a wider array of people to become researchers and, when possible, researchers need to include a wider array of people in their studies. In recognition of human diversity, many researchers are doing just that (Reid, 2002).

---

been white members of the middle class and most of the researchers themselves have been white males (Guthrie, 2004). None of this automatically invalidates the results of psychology experiments. However, it may place some limitations on their meanings. (See "Is There a Gender Bias in Psychological Research?") The distinguished psychologist Edward Tolman once noted that much of psychology is based on two sets of subjects: rats and college sophomores. Tolman urged scientists to remember that rats are certainly not people and that college sophomores may not be!

Internet Surveys

Recently, psychologists have started doing surveys and experiments on the Internet. Web-based research has the advantage of low cost and it can reach very large groups of people. Internet studies have provided interesting information about topics such as anger, decision making, racial prejudice, what disgusts people, religion, sexual attitudes, and much more. Biased samples can limit web-based research, but psychologists are finding ways to gather valid information with it (Birnbaum, 2004; Gosling et al., 2004).

Social Desirability

Even well-designed surveys may be limited by another problem. If a psychologist were to ask you detailed questions about your sexual history and current sexual behavior, how accurate would your replies be? Would you exaggerate? Would you be embarrassed? Replies to survey questions are not always accurate or

Survey method The use of public polling techniques to answer psychological questions.

Representative sample A small, randomly selected part of a larger population that accurately reflects characteristics of the whole population.

Biased sample A subpart of a larger population that does not accurately reflect characteristics of the whole population.

Population An entire group of animals or people belonging to a particular category (for example, all college students or all married women).

Gender bias (in research) A tendency for females and female issues to be underrepresented in research, psychological or otherwise.

truthful. Many people show a distinct *courtesy bias* (a tendency to give "polite" or socially desirable answers). For example, answers to questions concerning sex, drinking or drug use, income, and church attendance tend to be less than truthful. Likewise, the week after an election more people will say they voted than actually did (Krosnick, 1999).

Summary

Despite their limitations, surveys frequently produce valuable information. For instance, the survey method was used to find out how often sexual harassment occurs and to raise public awareness about the problem (Janus & Janus, 1993). To sum up, the survey method can be a powerful research tool. Like other methods, it has limitations, but new techniques and strategies are providing valuable information about our behavior (Tourangeau, 2004).

Is so much emphasis on science really necessary in psychology? In a word, yes. As we have seen, science is a powerful way of asking questions about the world and getting trustworthy answers. (■ Table 1.5 summarizes many of the important ideas we have covered.)

Critical Thinking Revisited— Evaluating Claims and Evidence

Even if you never do any research of you own, you can benefit from the efforts of others. Many beliefs about human behavior can be evaluated by applying critical thinking to published evidence. For example, here's a typical scene: An anxious mother watches her son eat a candy bar and says, "Watch, it's like lighting a fuse on a skyrocket. He'll be bouncing off the walls in a few minutes." Is she right? Will a "sugar buzz" make her son "hyper"? How would you evaluate the claim that sugar adversely affects behavior? Here are some basic steps.

1. *State the claim clearly. What are its implications?* It's important to spell out what you would expect to see if the claim is true.
2. *Gather evidence.* Look for evidence both for and against the claim. Evidence may come from many sources, such as casual observations, opinions of authorities, published studies, or direct scientific observation.
3. *Evaluate the evidence.* Is the evidence consistent with the claim? If the information is conflicting, what conclusion does the strongest evidence support? (In general, scientific observations provide the highest-quality evidence.)
4. *Draw a conclusion.* If you have carefully evaluated the arguments and evidence bearing on a claim, you should have little trouble drawing a valid conclusion.

A Case Study of Critical Thinking

To see how the preceding steps apply, let's return to the question about sugar. What we want to know is this: Does eating excessive amounts of sugar adversely affect children's behavior? What are the implications of this claim? If it is true, children who eat sugar should display measurable changes in behavior.

Anecdotal Evidence

What evidence is there to support the claim? It should be easy to find parents who will attest that their children become high-strung after eating sugar. However, parents are not likely to be objective observers. Beliefs about "sugar highs" are common and could easily color parents' views.

Casual Observation

Perhaps it would help to observe children directly. Let's say you decide to watch children at a birthday party, where you know they will eat a lot of sugary foods. As predicted by the claim, children at the party become loud and boisterous after eating cake, ice cream,

TABLE 1.5

Comparison of Psychological Research Methods

	ADVANTAGES	DISADVANTAGES
Naturalistic Observation	Behavior is observed in a natural setting; much information is obtained, and hypotheses and questions for additional research are formed	Little or no control is possible; observed behavior may be altered by the presence of the observer; observations may be biased; causes cannot be conclusively identified
Correlational Method	Demonstrates the existence of relationships; allows prediction; can be used in lab, clinic, or natural setting	Little or no control is possible; relationships may be coincidental; cause-and-effect relationships cannot be confirmed
Experimental Method	Clear cause-and-effect relationships can be identified; powerful controlled observations can be staged; no need to wait for natural event	May be somewhat artificial; some natural behavior not easily studied in laboratory (field experiments may avoid these objections)
Clinical Method	Takes advantage of "natural clinical trials" and allows investigation of rare or unusual problems or events	Little or no control is possible; does not provide a control group for comparison, subjective interpretation is often necessary, a single case may be misleading or unrepresentative
Survey Method	Allows information about large numbers of people to be gathered; can address questions not answered by other approaches	Obtaining a representative sample is critical and can be difficult to do; answers may be inaccurate; people may not do what they say or say what they do

and candy. How persuasive is this evidence? Actually, it is seriously flawed. Birthday parties expose children to bright lights, loud noises, and unfamiliar situations. Any of these conditions, and others as well, could easily explain the children's "hyper" activity.

Authority

For nearly 50 years many doctors, teachers, nutritionists, and other "experts" have emphatically stated that sugar causes childhood misbehavior. Should you believe them? Unfortunately, most of these "expert" opinions are based on anecdotes and casual observations that are little better than those we have already reviewed.

Formal Evidence

The truth is, parents, casual observers, and many authorities have been wrong. Dr. Mark Wolraich and his colleagues reviewed 23 scientific studies on sugar and children. In each study, children consumed known amounts of sugar and were then observed or tested. The clear-cut conclusion in all of the studies was that sugar does not affect aggression, mood, motor skills, or cognitive skills (Wolraich, Wilson, & White, 1995).

Studies like those we just reviewed tend to be convincing because they are based on systematic, controlled observation. To evaluate psychological questions, you will often have to rely on similar published evidence. But don't just accept the study's conclusions. It is important to review the evidence yourself and decide if it is convincing. Our next topic illustrates the pitfalls of failing to scientifically test ideas.

Pseudo-Psychologies—Palms, Planets, and Personality

For an interesting contrast, let's see how some false beliefs compare with real psychology. A **pseudo-psychology** (SUE-doe-psychology) is any unfounded system that resembles psychology. (*Pseudo* means "false.") Pseudo-psychologies change little over time because their followers avoid evidence that contradicts their beliefs (Kelly & Saklofske, 1994). Scientists, in contrast, actively look for contradictions as a way to advance knowledge. They

Would you hire this man? Here's a sample of your author's handwriting. What do you think it reveals? Your interpretations are likely to be as accurate (or inaccurate) as those of a graphologist.

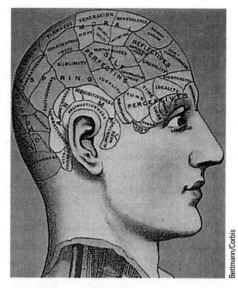

Phrenology was an attempt to assess personality characteristics by examining various areas of the skull. Phrenologists used charts such as the one shown here as guides. Like other pseudo-psychologists, phrenologists made no attempt to empirically verify their concepts.

skeptically evaluate and critique their own theories (Woodward & Goodstein, 1996).

Unlike the real thing, pseudo-psychologies are not based on scientific testing. For instance, *palmistry* is a false system that claims lines on the hand reveal personality and predict the future. Despite the overwhelming evidence against this, palmists can still be found separating the gullible from their money in many cities. A similar false system is *phrenology*, which claims that personality traits are revealed by the shape of the skull. Phrenology was popularized in the nineteenth century by Franz Gall, a German anatomy teacher. Modern research has long since shown that bumps on the head have nothing to do with talents or abilities. In fact, the phrenologists were so far off that they listed the part of the brain that controls hearing as a center for "combativeness"!

At first glance, a pseudo-psychology called *graphology* might seem more reasonable. Graphologists claim that personality traits are revealed by handwriting. Based on such claims, some companies use graphologists to select job candidates. This is troubling because graphologists score close to zero on tests of accuracy in rating personality (Ben-Shakhar et al., 1986). In fact, graphologists do no better than untrained college students in rating personality and job performance (Neter & Ben-Shakhar, 1989; Rafaeli & Klimoski, 1983). Even a graphological society recently concluded that handwriting analysis should not be used to select people for jobs (Simner & Goffin, 2003). (By the way, graphology's failure at revealing personality should be separated from its value for detecting forgeries.)

Pseudo-psychology Any false and unscientific system of beliefs and practices that is offered as an explanation of behavior.

Graphology might seem harmless enough. However, this false system has been used to determine who is hired, given bank credit, or selected for juries. In these and similar situations, pseudo-psychologies do, in fact, harm people (Barker, 1993).

If pseudo-psychologies have no scientific basis, how do they survive and why are they popular? There are several reasons, all of which can be demonstrated by a critique of astrology. Astrology is probably the most popular pseudo-psychology. Astrology holds that the positions of the stars and planets at the time of one's birth determine personality traits and affect behavior. Like other pseudo-psychologies, astrology has repeatedly been shown to have no scientific validity (Kelly, 1998, 1999; Stewart, 1996). The objections to astrology are numerous and devastating:

1. The zodiac has shifted in the sky by one full constellation since astrology was first set up. However, most astrologers simply ignore this shift. (In other words, if astrology calls you a Scorpio you are really a Libra, and so forth.)
2. There is no connection between the "compatibility" of couples' astrological signs and their marriage and divorce rates.
3. Studies have found no connection between astrological signs and leadership, physical characteristics, career choices, or personality traits.
4. Astrologers have failed to explain why the moment of birth should be more important than the moment of conception.
5. A study of more than 3,000 predictions by famous astrologers found that only a small percentage were fulfilled. These "successful" predictions tended to be vague ("There will be a tragedy somewhere in the east in the spring") or easily guessed from current events.
6. If astrologers are asked to match people with their horoscopes, they do no better than would be expected by chance (Kelly, 1999).
7. A few astrologers have tried to test astrology. Their results have been just as negative as those obtained by critics (Kelly, 1998, 1999; Martens & Trachet, 1998; Stewart, 1996).

In short, astrology doesn't work.

Then why does astrology often seem to work? The following discussion tells why.

Uncritical Acceptance

If you have ever had your astrological chart done, you may have been impressed with its apparent accuracy. However, such perceptions are typically based on **uncritical acceptance** (the tendency to believe positive or flattering descriptions of yourself). Many astrological charts are made up of mostly flattering traits. Naturally, when your personality is described in *desirable* terms, it is hard to deny that the description has the "ring of truth." How much acceptance would astrology receive if a birth sign read like this:

> Virgo: You are the logical type and hate disorder. Your nitpicking is unbearable to your friends. You are cold, unemotional, and usually fall asleep while making love. Virgos make good doorstops.

Positive Instances

Even when an astrological description contains a mixture of good and bad traits it may seem accurate. To find out why, read the following personality description.

Your Personality Profile

You have a strong need for other people to like you and for them to admire you. You have a tendency to be critical of yourself. You have a great deal of unused energy which you have not turned to your advantage. While you have some personality weaknesses, you are generally able to compensate for them. Your sexual adjustment has presented some problems for you. Disciplined and controlled on the outside, you tend to be worrisome and insecure inside. At times you have serious doubts as to whether you have made the right decision or done the right thing. You prefer a certain amount of change and variety and become dissatisfied when hemmed in by restrictions and limitations. You pride yourself on being an independent thinker and do not accept other opinions without satisfactory proof. You have found it unwise to be too frank in revealing yourself to others. At times you are extroverted, affable, sociable, while at other times you are introverted, wary, and reserved. Some of your aspirations tend to be pretty unrealistic.*

Does this describe your personality? A psychologist read this summary individually to college students who had taken a personality test. Only 5 students out of 79 thought that the description was inaccurate. Another study found that people rated this "personality profile" as more accurate than their actual horoscopes (French et al., 1991).

Reread the description and you will see that it contains both sides of several personality dimensions ("At times you are extroverted . . . while at other times you are introverted"). Its apparent accuracy is an illusion based on the **fallacy of positive instances**, in which we remember or notice things that confirm our expectations and forget the rest. The pseudo-psychologies thrive on this effect. For example, you can always find "Leo characteristics" in a Leo. If you looked, however, you could also find "Gemini characteristics," "Scorpio characteristics," or whatever.

The fallacy of positive instances is used by various "psychic mediums" who pretend to communicate with the deceased friends and relatives of audience members. An analysis of their performances shows that the number of "hits" (correct statements) made by these fakes tends to be very low. Nevertheless, many viewers are impressed because of the natural tendency to remember apparent hits and ignore misses. Also, embarrassing misses are edited out before the shows appear on television (Nickell, 2001).

The Barnum Effect

Pseudo-psychologies also take advantage of the **Barnum effect**, which is a tendency to consider personal descriptions accurate if they are stated in general terms. P. T. Barnum, the famed circus

---

*Reprinted with permission of author and publisher from R. E. Ulrich, T. J. Stachnik, and N. R. Stainton, "Student acceptance of generalized personality interpretations," *Psychological Reports*, 13, 1963, 831–834.

Non Sequitur

Non Sequitur, © 1993. Reprinted by permission of Universal Press Syndicate.

showman, had a formula for success: "Always have a little something for everybody." Like the all-purpose personality profile, palm readings, fortunes, horoscopes, and other products of pseudo-psychology are stated in such general terms that they can hardly miss. There is always "a little something for everybody." To observe the Barnum effect, read *all 12* of the daily horoscopes found in newspapers for several days. You will find that predictions for other signs fit events as well as those for your own sign do.

Pseudo-psychologies may seem like no more than a nuisance, but they can do harm. For instance, people seeking treatment for psychological disorders may become the victims of self-appointed "experts" who offer ineffective, pseudo-scientific "therapies" (Kalal, 1999). Valid psychological principles are based on observation and evidence, not fads, opinions, or wishful thinking.

Summary: Science and Critical Thinking

Most of us would be skeptical when buying a used car. But all too often we may be tempted to "buy" outrageous claims about topics such as the occult, the Bermuda Triangle, UFOs, herbal "cures," Tarot cards, healing crystals, "miraculous" therapies, and so forth. To put the principles of science and critical thinking into action, here are some questions to ask over and over again as you evaluate new information (Bartz, 1990):

1. What claims are being made?
2. What test (if any) of these claims has been made?
3. Who did the test? How good is the evidence?
4. What was the nature and quality of the tests? Are they credible? Can they be repeated?
5. How reliable and trustworthy were the investigators? Do they have conflicts of interest? Do their findings appear to be objective? Has any other independent researcher duplicated the findings?
6. Finally, how much credibility can the claim be given? High, medium, low, provisional?

A Look Ahead

To help you get the most out of psychology, each chapter of this text includes a "Psychology in Action" section like the one that follows. There you will find ideas you can actually use, now or in the future. To complete our discussion, let's take a critical look at information reported in the popular press. You should find this an interesting way to conclude our first tour of psychology and its methods.

KNOWLEDGE BUILDER

Cases Studies, the Survey Method, and Critical Thinking

REFLECT

If you were going to do a case study of a celebrity or other public feature, who would you choose? What aspect of the person's behavior would you investigate?

Have you ever known someone who suffered a brain injury or disease? How did his or her behavior change? Was the change clear-cut enough to serve as a natural clinical test?

If you could ask only three questions in a psychological survey, what would they be? What population would you be interested in studying? How would you obtain a valid sample? Is it likely that any of your questions would be affected by a courtesy bias?

It is nearly impossible to get through a day without encountering people who believe in pseudo-psychologies or who make unscientific or unfounded statements. How stringently do you evaluate your own beliefs and the claims made by others?

LEARNING CHECK

1. Case studies can often be thought of as natural tests and are frequently used by clinical psychologists. T or F?
2. For the survey method to be valid, a representative sample of people must be polled. T or F?
3. The phenomenon of multiple personality would most likely be investigated by use of
   a. a representative sample
   b. a correlational experiment
   c. the double-blind procedure
   d. case studies
4. A problem with the survey method is that answers to questions may not always be _____ or _____.
5. People who abuse certain "designer drugs" develop neurological symptoms similar to Parkinson's disease. Studying damage to the brains of these people would provide a _____ _____ test of theories about the causes of Parkinson's.

Uncritical acceptance The tendency to believe generally positive or flattering descriptions of oneself.

Fallacy of positive instances The tendency to remember or notice information that fits one's expectations while forgetting discrepancies.

Barnum effect The tendency to consider a personal description accurate if it is stated in very general terms.

6. The fallacy of positive instances refers to graphology's accepted value for the detection of forgeries. T or F?
7. Personality descriptions provided by pseudo-psychologies are stated in general terms, which provide "a little something for everybody." This fact is the basis of the
   a. palmist's fallacy
   b. uncritical acceptance pattern
   c. fallacy of positive instances
   d. Barnum effect

CRITICAL THINKING

8. A psychologist conducting a survey at a shopping mall (The Gallery of Wretched Excess) flips a coin before stopping passersby. If the coin shows heads, he interviews the person; if it shows tails, he skips that person. Has the psychologist obtained a random sample?

9. Each New Year's Day, phony "psychics" make predictions about events that will occur during the coming year. The vast majority of these predictions are wrong, but the practice continues each year. Can you explain why?

Answers: 1. T 2. T 3. d 4. d 5. accurate, truthful 5. natural clinical 6. F 7. d 8. The psychologist's coin flips *might* produce a reasonably good sample of people *at the mall*. The real problem is that people who go to the mall may be mostly from one part of town, from upper income groups, or from some other nonrepresentative group. The psychologist's sample is likely to be seriously flawed. 9. Because of the fallacy of positive instances, people only remember predictions that seemed to come true and forget all of the errors. Incidentally, "predictions" that appear to be accurate are usually easily deduced from current events or are stated in very general terms to take advantage of the Barnum effect.

PSYCHOLOGY IN ACTION

Psychology in the News—Separating Fact from Fiction

Psychology is a popular topic in magazines and newspapers. Unfortunately, much of what you will read is based on wishful thinking rather than science. Here are some suggestions for separating high-quality information from misleading fiction.

Suggestion 1: Be skeptical. Reports in the popular press tend to be made uncritically and with a definite bias toward reporting "astonishing" findings. Remember, saying, "That's incredible" means, "That's not believable"—which is often true.

Example 1: Some years ago, news articles described an amazing new "sixth sense" called "dermo-optical perception." A few gifted people, the articles claimed, could use their fingertips to identify colors and read print while blindfolded.

In reality, such "abilities" are based on what stage magicians call a "nose peek." It is impossible to prepare a blindfold (without damaging the eyes) that does not leave a tiny space on each side of the nose. Were the people who claimed to have "X-ray eyes" taking nose peeks? Apparently they were, because "dermo-optical abilities" disappeared as soon as the opportunity to peek was controlled.

Example 2: The *National Enquirer* once reported that "Top University Researchers Reveal . . . 8 million Americans may have been abducted by UFOs." However, one of the researchers cited in the article actually concluded, "The public can rest assured that there is no evidence that millions of Americans are being abducted." In other words, the *Enquirer* story completely *reversed* the real findings. You'll find similar misinformation and sensationalism throughout the popular media. Be on guard.

Example 3: The Internet is awash with rumors, hoaxes, half-truths, and urban legends. One recent classic was a story about the health department in Oregon seeking a Klingon interpreter for mental health patients who only speak in the fictional language used on the *Star Trek* TV series.

This tale started when a newspaper reported that Klingon was on a list of languages that some psychiatric patients claimed they could speak. The article specifically noted that "in reality, no patient has yet tried to communicate in Klingon." Nevertheless, as the story spread around the web, the idea that Oregon was looking for someone fluent in Klingon had become a "fact" (O'Neill, 2003).

Suggestion 2: Consider the source of information. It should come as no surprise that information used to sell a product often reflects a desire for profit rather than the objective truth. Here is a typical advertising claim: "Government tests prove that no pain reliever is stronger or more effective than Brand X aspirin." A statement like this usually means that there was *no difference* between the products tested. No other pain reliever was stronger or more effective—but none was weaker either.

Keep the source in mind when reading the claims of makers of home biofeedback machines, sleep-learning devices, subliminal tapes, and the like. Remember that psychological services may be merchandised as well. Be wary of expensive courses that promise instant mental health and happiness, increased efficiency, memory, ESP or psychic ability, control of the unconscious mind, an end to smoking, and so on. Usually they are promoted with a few testimonials and many unsupported claims (Lilienfeld, 2005).

Psychic claims should be viewed with special caution. Stage mentalists make a living by deceiving the public. Understandably, they are highly interested in promoting belief in their nonexistent powers. Psychic phenomena, when (and if) they do occur, are quite unpredictable. It would be impossible for a mentalist to do three shows a night, six nights a week, without consistently using deception. The same is true of the so-called psychic advisors promoted in TV commercials. These charlatans make use of the Barnum effect to create an illusion that they know private information about the people who call them (Nickell, 2001).

Suggestion 3: Ask yourself if there was a control group. The key importance of a control group in any experiment is often overlooked by the unsophisticated—an error to which you are no longer susceptible. The popular press is full of reports of "experiments" performed without control groups: "Talking to Plants Speeds Growth"; "Special Diet Controls Hyperactivity in Children"; "Food Shows Less Spoilage in Pyramid Chamber"; "Graduates of Firewalking Seminar Risk Their Soles."

Consider the last example for a moment. In recent years, expensive commercial courses have been promoted to teach people to walk barefoot on hot coals. (Why anyone would want to do this is itself an interesting question.) Firewalkers supposedly protect their feet with a technique called "neurolinguistic programming." Many people have paid good money to learn the technique, and most do manage a quick walk on the coals. But is the technique necessary? And is anything remarkable happening? We need a comparison group.

Fortunately, physicist Bernard Leikind has provided one. Leikind showed with volunteers that anyone (with reasonably callused feet) can walk over a bed of coals without being burned. The reason is that the coals, which are light, fluffy carbon, transmit little heat when touched. The principle involved is similar to briefly putting your hand in a hot oven. If you touch a pan, you will be burned because metal transfers heat efficiently. But if your hand stays in the heated air you'll be fine because air transmits little heat (Mitchell, 1987). Mystery solved.

Suggestion 4: Look for errors in distinguishing between correlation and causation. As you now know, it is dangerous to presume that one thing *caused* another just because they are correlated. In spite of this, you will see many claims based on questionable correlations. Here's an example of mistaking correlation for causation: Jeanne Dixon, an astrologer, once answered a group of prominent scientists—who had declared that there is no scientific foundation for astrology—by saying, "They would do well to check the records at their local police stations, where they will learn that the rate of violent crime rises and falls with lunar cycles." Dixon, of course, believes that the moon affects human behavior.

If it is true that violent crime is more frequent at certain times of the month, doesn't that prove her point? Far from it. Increased crime could be due to darker nights, the fact that many people expect others to act crazier, or any number of similar factors. More important, direct studies of the alleged "lunar effect" have shown that it doesn't occur (Simon, 1998; Wilkinson et al., 1997). Moonstruck criminals, along with "moon madness," are a fiction (Raison, Klein, & Steckler, 1999).

Suggestion 5: Be sure to distinguish between observation and inference. If you see a person *crying*, is it correct to assume that she or he is *sad*? Although it seems reasonable to make this assumption, it is actually quite risky. We can observe objectively that the person is crying, but to *infer* sadness may be in error. It could be that the individual has just peeled 5 pounds of onions. Or maybe he or she just won a million-dollar lottery or is trying contact lenses for the first time.

Psychologists, politicians, physicians, scientists, and other experts often go far beyond the available facts in their claims. This does not mean that their inferences, opinions, and interpretations have no value; the opinion of an expert on the causes of mental illness, criminal behavior, learning problems, or whatever can be revealing. But be careful to distinguish between fact and opinion.

Suggestion 6: Beware of oversimplifications, especially those motivated by monetary gain. Courses or programs that offer a "new personality in three sessions," "six steps to love and fulfillment in marriage," or newly discovered "secrets of unlocking the

Firewalking is based on simple physics, not on any form of supernatural psychological control. The temperature of the coals may be as high as 1,200°F. However, coals are like the air in a hot oven: They are very inefficient at transferring heat during brief contact.

powers of the mind" should be immediately suspect.

An excellent example of oversimplification is provided by a brochure entitled, "Dr. Joyce Brothers Asks: How Do You Rate as a 'Superwoman'?" Dr. Brothers, a "media" psychologist who has no private practice and is not known for research, wrote the brochure as a consultant for the Aerosol Packaging Council of the Chemical Specialties Manufacturers Association. A typical suggestion in this brochure tells how to enhance a marriage: "Sweep him off to a weekend hideaway. Tip: When he's not looking spray a touch of your favorite *aerosol* cologne mist on the bed sheets and pillows" (italics added). Sure, Joyce.

Suggestion 7: Remember, "for example" is not proof. After reading this chapter you should be sensitive to the danger of selecting single examples. If you read, "Law student passes state bar exam using sleep-learning device," don't rush out to buy one. Systematic research has shown that these devices are of little or no value (Druckman & Bjork, 1994; Wood et al., 1992). A corollary to this suggestion is to ask, "Are the reported observations important or widely applicable?"

Examples, anecdotes, single cases, and testimonials are all potentially deceptive. Unfortunately, *individual cases* tell nothing about what is true *in general* (Stanovich, 2004). For instance, studies of large groups of people show that smoking increases the

likelihood of lung cancer. It doesn't matter if you know a lifelong heavy smoker who is 94 years old. The general finding is the one to remember.

Summary We are all bombarded daily with such a mass of new information that it is difficult to absorb it. The available knowledge, even in a limited area like psychology, biology, medicine, or contemporary rock music, is so vast that no single person can completely know and comprehend it. With this situation in mind, it becomes increasingly important that you become a critical, selective, and informed consumer of information.

KNOWLEDGE BUILDER
Psychology in the Media

REFLECT
Do you tend to assume that a statement must be true if it is in print, on television, or made by an authority? How actively do you evaluate and question claims found in the media? Could you be a more critical consumer of information? *Should* you be a more critical consumer of information?

LEARNING CHECK
1. Newspaper accounts of dermo-optical perception have generally reported only the results of carefully designed psychological experiments. T or F?
2. Stage mentalists and psychics often use deception in their acts. T or F?
3. Blaming the lunar cycle for variations in the rate of violent crime is an example of mistaking correlation for causation. T or F?

4. To investigate possible links between drinking milk and delinquent behavior, it would be desirable to create an experimental group that consumes large amounts of milk and a control group that drinks none. T or F?

CRITICAL THINKING
5. Mystics have shown that fresh eggs can be balanced on their large ends during the vernal equinox when the sun is directly over the equator, day and night are equal in length, and the world is in perfect balance. What is wrong with their observation?

Answers: 1. F 2. T 3. T 4. T 5. The mystics have neglected to ask if eggs can be balanced at other times. They can. The lack of a control group gives the illusion that something amazing is happening, but the equinox has nothing to do with egg balancing (Halpern, 2003).